EDEXCEL
AS/A LEVEL
HISTORY

*Active*Book included

Paper 1&2 Student Book:
Communist states in the 20ᵗʰ century

Steve Phillips | Ben Gregory | Nigel Bushnell | Rob Owen |
Series editor: Rosemary Rees

ALWAYS LEARNING

PEARSON

Published by Pearson Education Limited, 80 Strand, London, WC2R 0RL.

www.pearsonschoolsandfecolleges.co.uk

Copies of official specifications for all Edexcel qualifications may be found on the website: www.edexcel.com

Text © Pearson Education Limited 2015

Designed by Elizabeth Arnoux for Pearson

Typeset and illustrated by Phoenix Photosetting, Chatham, Kent

Produced by Out of House Publishing

Original illustrations © Pearson Education Limited 2015

Cover design by Malena Wilson-Max for Pearson

Cover photo/illustration © akg-images Ltd: VISIOARS

The rights of Nigel Bushnell, Ben Gregory, Rob Owen and Steve Phillips to be identified as authors of this work have been asserted by them in accordance with the Copyright, Designs and Patents Act 1988.

First published 2015

20 19

10 9 8 7 6

British Library Cataloguing in Publication Data

A catalogue record for this book is available from the British Library

ISBN 978 1 447 985273

Printed in Slovakia by Neografia

Websites

Pearson Education Limited is not responsible for the content of any external internet sites. It is essential for tutors to preview each website before using it in class so as to ensure that the URL is still accurate, relevant and appropriate. We suggest that tutors bookmark useful websites and consider enabling students to access them through the school/college intranet.

A note from the publisher

In order to ensure that this resource offers high-quality support for the associated Pearson qualification, it has been through a review process by the awarding body. This process confirms that; this resource fully covers the teaching and learning content of the specification or part of a specification at which it is aimed. It also confirms that it demonstrates an appropriate balance between the development of subject skills, knowledge and understanding, in addition to preparation for assessment.

Endorsement does not cover any guidance on assessment activities or processes (e.g. practice questions or advice on how to answer assessment questions), included in the resource nor does it prescribe any particular approach to the teaching or delivery of a related course.

While the publishers have made every attempt to ensure that advice on the qualification and its assessment is accurate, the official specification and associated assessment guidance materials are the only authoritative source of information and should always be referred to for definitive guidance.

Pearson examiners have not contributed to any sections in this resource relevant to examination papers for which they have responsibility.

Examiners will not use endorsed resources as a source of material for any assessment set by Pearson.

Endorsement of a resource does not mean that the resource is required to achieve this Pearson qualification, nor does it mean that it is the only suitable material available to support the qualification, and any resource lists produced by the awarding body shall include this and other appropriate resources.

Contents

The results were not in the Bolsheviks' favour. They gained 175 seats in the Assembly with over nine million votes, but the SRs emerged as the largest single party with 410 seats and 21 million votes. To use the Assembly as a national parliament would clearly pose a threat to continued Bolshevik rule. Lenin therefore dissolved the Assembly after only one meeting and condemned it as an instrument of the bourgeoisie. In place of the Assembly, Lenin used the All-Russian Congress of Soviets as an instrument of popular support. It was, of course, a body where the Bolsheviks had more influence. Not only had Lenin ignored the calls for a socialist coalition, but he had also ensured that there was to be no real forum for opposition.

The destruction of other political parties

- The removal of the vote from 'bourgeois classes', such as employers and priests, stripped the opposition parties of a possible reservoir of support.

- The Mensheviks and SRs found it difficult to publish their newspapers due to restrictions imposed by the Bolsheviks.

- The left-wing SRs, who had been given a role within the Bolshevik government in 1917 and 1918, lost all influence when they walked out of the government in March 1918 in protest at the Bolshevik decision to pull out of the First World War.

- In March 1918, the Bolshevik Party renamed itself the Communist Party and, by 1921, all other parties were effectively banned.

- In April 1921, Lenin declared: 'The place for the Mensheviks and the SRs is in prison.' During the first three months of 1921, 5,000 Mensheviks were arrested. There were further waves of arrests of SR and Menshevik supporters later in 1921 and 1922, but by this stage they had ceased to exist as organised parties.

EXTEND YOUR KNOWLEDGE

The Socialist Revolutionaries (SRs)

A group committed to democratic socialism who believed in the right of groups to govern themselves, for example, peasant organisations. They gained support from sections of the peasantry and often stirred up peasant discontent. They were one of several groups who continued the Russian revolutionary tradition of populism, targeting their ideas at the peasantry, by far the largest social group in Russia at the time. The Socialist Revolutionaries won the elections to the Constituent Assembly but were weakened by divisions into right- and left-wing groupings. SRs were implicated in an assassination attempt on Lenin on 30 August 1918 by Fanya Kaplan. This led to a wave of arrests of SR members.

The Mensheviks

A communist group, more moderate than the Bolsheviks. They had split from the Bolsheviks in 1903 over differences of policy. The Mensheviks were prepared to work with the bourgeoisie in order to bring about gradual reform. They had a larger membership than the Bolsheviks in 1917, but they had been weakened by their co-operation with the Provisional Government. They demanded a role in the new Bolshevik government in the form of a coalition, which Lenin refused. Their opposition to Bolshevik rule was weakened by divisions among their leadership. Rival factions led by Fyodor Dan and Yuli Martov did not reunite until May 1918. By September 1920, Martov had left Russia for Germany. Dan was arrested in 1921 and sent into exile.

The Treaty of Brest-Litovsk, 1918

The initial opposition to the Bolsheviks came largely from the other socialist groups. This was because the conservatives had been so shocked by the events of October 1917 that the implications of the Revolution took some time to sink in. The demoralised conservatives were to find a cause of renewed outrage when Lenin put a quick end to Russian involvement in the First World War. Peace was concluded through the Treaty of Brest-Litovsk (1918). The treaty took Russia out of the war at a great cost. Russia lost control over the Baltic States of Lithuania, Estonia and Latvia, Finland, Ukraine and parts of the Caucasus region. It was a national humiliation for the conservatives, especially for military officers who had served in the Tsar's army: a humiliation that could not be tolerated. The only way to restore Russia's pride, and with it the reputation of the armed forces, was to overthrow the Bolshevik regime and reject the Treaty.

The Treaty also provided a necessary spur to those who wished to fight against the Bolsheviks, known as the **Whites**, because it offered the promise of foreign help. The Allied powers of Britain, France, the USA and Japan were anxious to keep Russia in the First World War and were willing to provide arms, money and troops to those who would ensure Russia rejoined the fight.

> **KEY TERM**
>
> **Whites**
> Those opposed to the Bolsheviks during the civil war of 1918–20. The Whites were largely conservative groups within Russia who did not want the old social order changed. The leaders of the Whites were generals and military leaders from the Tsar's armed forces.

So why did Lenin sign the Treaty of Brest-Litovsk if it increased opposition and the likelihood of civil war? He was aware that a key factor in bringing about the collapse of the Tsarist regime and the Provisional Government was the pressure of fighting the First World War. It sapped the energy and resources of the government, with little chance of military success. Lenin realised that if his new government was to consolidate its hold over Russia and deal with its internal enemies, it needed to pull out of the war to concentrate on the job at hand.

The Russian civil war, 1918–21

Given the ideology espoused by the Bolsheviks it was perhaps no surprise that they faced severe opposition from the more conservative elements within Russia. Yet the groups that supported the so-called Whites against the forces of the Bolshevik **Reds** encompassed rather more than just the conservatives.

> **KEY TERM**
>
> **Reds**
> The Bolsheviks and their supporters. The Bolshevik forces were known as the Red Army. Bolshevik support was made up of the industrial workers and many peasants who saw the Bolsheviks as the best guarantors of their gains from the Revolution.

This 'White' opposition included a range of political groups. There were those who wished to see the return of the Tsar; liberals, including supporters of the Provisional Government; military leaders unhappy with Russia pulling out of the First World War; national minorities seeking independence from Russia; and members of the Menshevik and SR parties who had been denied an involvement in the government. The Czech Legion, part of the Austro-Hungarian Army stranded in Russia as prisoners of war, rebelled against the Reds. The Whites also received aid from the Allies in the First World War.

Although initial opposition from the conservatives in Russia was limited, the Bolsheviks were attacked by the forces of General Krasnov at Pulkovo Heights near Petrograd immediately after the October Revolution. The Reds won this first encounter, but it was merely the prelude to the civil war. After the signing of the Treaty of Brest-Litovsk, opposition to the Bolsheviks mounted, resulting in a series of military campaigns. It was not until the end of 1920 that the Bolsheviks had defeated the Whites and secured communist rule over the country.

How did the Bolsheviks win the civil war?

At the beginning of the civil war, the situation looked bleak for the Bolsheviks. The area directly under Bolshevik control was limited to a central core based on Moscow, stretching to Petrograd in the north-west. They were surrounded on all sides by White forces. Nonetheless, it was the Bolsheviks who emerged victorious. This victory was largely achieved due to the better organisation of the Reds, in military, economic and political terms.

In contrast, the Whites were an amalgam of different groups united only by their desire to get rid of the Bolsheviks. These divisions were reflected in the military strategy of the Whites. Co-operation was limited and was not helped by the long front on which the Whites fought. The Whites did receive help from Russia's former Allies in the First World War but, through corruption and inefficiency, they failed to put this to good effect.

By the end of 1920, all of the White strongholds had been defeated and Bolshevik rule had been extended across the country. The Bolsheviks' military strategy had been more coherent than that of the Whites and a lot of the credit for this must go to the invaluable work of Leon Trotsky. Trotsky, who became Commissar for War in early 1918, turned the Red Army into an effective fighting machine. The army was formed from the Red Guard units and pro-Bolshevik elements of the old Tsarist armed forces. Conscription was introduced to swell the number of soldiers to over five million by the end of the war. The Bolsheviks had also been able to extend government direction over the economy to ensure resources were organised and deployed effectively through the imposition of policies known as War Communism. Large-scale nationalisation of industry ensured adequate supplies for the Red Army (if not for civilians) and food supplies were requisitioned from the peasants. This latter policy was deeply unpopular with the peasants, but it did provide enough food to keep the Red Army going. In this respect, the experience of the civil war had encouraged the Bolsheviks to adopt a highly authoritarian and centrally controlled system. Nevertheless, it was not just better organisation that resulted in the Bolshevik victory. There was also a degree of active support for what the Bolsheviks stood for, especially from the workers who saw the Bolsheviks as the best guarantors of their gains from the Revolution. The peasants did not like all aspects of Bolshevik rule, but the Land Decree of 1917 had guaranteed a distribution of land in their favour. Thus, the Bolsheviks did not neglect the political dimension of the war. Their victory dealt a serious blow to any realistic chance of enemies within Russia threatening the new Bolshevik government.

The key results of the civil war

Russia's civil war, together with the devastation and division caused by the First World War, had a long-term impact on Russia and the Bolshevik state that had been established in its wake.

- The Bolshevik state had become highly centralised due to the demands of the civil war. Fighting a war required quick decision-making and direction of resources by the government. Power was now firmly in the hands of the government (*Sovnarkom*) and party leadership (politburo) based in Moscow.

- The civil war had resulted in the Bolsheviks making extensive use of terror against their political opponents. This set the tone for the development of the Party after the civil war.

- The supporters of the Bolsheviks had been through a formative experience that must have affected them deeply. This experience seemed to reinforce militaristic values in the population. Those who fought in the war were a generation who did not buckle under pressure and who did not think twice about using force and terror.

These results were to be highly influential in moulding the system of government established by the Bolsheviks.

The Tenth Party Congress, 1921

By the time the Bolsheviks held their Tenth Party Congress in March 1921, the civil war was all but won and attention could be focused on dealing with divisions within the Bolshevik Party. The civil war had seen a huge growth in Party membership, from 300,000 at the end of 1917 to over 730,000 by 1921. This posed a threat to Party stability. To ensure conformity within the Party, a firm line was taken against dissent.

The ban on the formation of factions within the Party was put forward by Lenin at the Congress of 1921. This measure, known as 'On Party Unity', was an attempt to impose the view of the leadership on the Party. The penalty for those breaking this rule was expulsion from the Party. Despite victory in the civil war, this political tightening of the power of the Party leadership came at a time of continuing Bolshevik anxiety over their hold over Russia. In 1921, the Bolsheviks had faced the **Kronstadt Mutiny**, a revolt by sailors previously loyal to the Bolsheviks, and a major peasant uprising known as the **Tambov Rising**. Clearly the Bolsheviks could not take their position for granted.

SOURCE

Lenin addressing a session of the 10th Congress of the Russian Communist Party in 1921. It was a Congress where Lenin's powers of persuasion were needed to push through difficult policies.

ACTIVITY
KNOWLEDGE CHECK

The consolidation of Bolshevik power
1 Make a list of the methods used by the Bolsheviks to deal with other political groups between 1917 and 1921.

2 Which of these methods do you think was the most important? Explain your answer.

3 Explain how the civil war influenced the nature of Bolshevik government established by 1921.

The nature of government under Lenin

The apparatus of government

The machinery of government administration had fallen into chaos before the Bolsheviks came to power. Lenin needed to put in place a state administration that better suited his own revolutionary purposes. Governing a country the size of Russia would require a clear line of authority whereby decisions could be made and imposed on the country effectively and quickly.

Organisations that genuinely represented the proletariat, such as the soviets, **trade unions** and **factory committees**, were brought under Bolshevik control and then sidelined. A system was devised based on representative bodies that in theory stemmed from the All-Russian Congress of Soviets and was headed by the *Sovnarkom*.

The purges widen

As the 1930s progressed, Stalin used further purges to strengthen his hold over organisations that posed a threat to the Party's dominance:

- **Purges in the Red Army** in 1937 and 1938 saw an extensive purge of personnel. Three out of the five marshals were purged, 14 out of 16 army commanders and 35,000 officers were either shot or imprisoned. The navy lost every one of its admirals during the purge. The armed forces had been critical of the demoralising impact of collectivisation on the peasantry who made up the bulk of the soldiers. For Stalin, these criticisms were of concern due to the growth in the army's importance alongside the increase in defence resources in the 1930s. The power of the army leaders had to be cut down to size and their loyalty enforced.

- **The purge of the secret police**. With the purges, the amount of work generated for the secret police also grew, as did their influence. To ensure that the secret police posed no threat to Stalin, the purgers were themselves purged. In 1936, Yagoda, the head of the NKVD, was replaced by Nikolai Yezhov, known as the 'bloody dwarf'. Yezhov oversaw the most excessive phase of the purges including purging over 3,000 of his own personnel in his first six months as head of the secret police. Yet the 'Yezhovschina', as it became known, was to come to an end when he himself was dismissed in 1938. His arrest in early 1939 was partly due to Stalin's need for a scapegoat for the excesses of the purges, which were coming to an end.

Although the higher levels of the Party suffered the most, there were sweeping purges at local level too. Stalin went to the trouble of reading lists of those to be arrested, adding names on occasions or adding the comment that more victims were needed. A quota system was used, whereby each Party branch had its own target to meet. Nonetheless, the sheer scale of the purges suggests that there were factors at work other than Stalin himself. Denunciations of Communist officials were partly driven by a sense of justice, sometimes personal hatred. These tensions led to the purge of large numbers of Party members. In this situation, Stalin and the leadership sometimes found it difficult to assert their authority.

The purges played a significant role in the process by which Stalin removed his political opponents, and indeed anyone who could be considered a threat to his power. Stalin's agents caught up with Trotsky in 1940, when he was assassinated with an ice pick in Mexico.

Stalin had imposed a firm grip on the Party through fear and intimidation. To Trotsky it marked Stalin's betrayal of the Revolution; that a dictatorship of Stalin had replaced a dictatorship of the proletariat. However, Stalin could argue that the use of terror actually prevented a conservative reaction and kept the revolutionary spirit alive. The purges safeguarded not only the power of Stalin but also the position of the Communist Party. The Communists had always been a minority party and, as such, needed to employ terror to retain power when undertaking unpopular policies. What is striking is that the Great Terror was launched at a time when the Party's position appeared relatively secure. This would seem to indicate that Stalin was working to his own agenda, trying to secure his own personal position rather than that of the Party. In this sense, Stalin's use of terror differed from that of Lenin's. What Stalin did owe to the work of Lenin was the attitude of many Party members that had developed during the civil war – that terror was an acceptable method of dealing with opponents both within and outside the Party.

ACTIVITY
KNOWLEDGE CHECK

Stalin's use of terror
1 What were the similarities and differences between Lenin's system of government and that of Stalin?
2 Who relied most on the use of terror: Lenin or Stalin?

AS Level Exam-Style Question Section A

How far did Stalin's use of terror during the 1930s differ from that of Lenin's? (20 marks)

Tip
Do not forget to make direct comparisons between Stalin's and Lenin's use of terror. Think about the ways in which they were similar and different.

THINKING HISTORICALLY   Causation (3c&d)

Causation and intention

1 Work on your own or with a partner to identify as many causes of the Great Purge of the 1930s as you can. Write each cause on a separate card or piece of paper.

2 Divide your cards into those that represent:

   a) the actions or intentions of people

   b) the beliefs held by people at the time

   c) the contextual factors or events (that is, political, social or economic events)

   d) states of affairs (long- or short-term situations that have developed in particular ways).

3 Focus on the intentions and actions of the key people in the run-up to the Great Purge. For each person, draw on your knowledge to fill in the table below, identifying:

   a) their intentions

   b) the actions they took to achieve these

   c) the consequences of their actions (both intended and unintended)

   d) the extent to which their intentions were achieved.

Key figure	Intentions in 1930s	Actions taken	Consequences	How far intention achieved
Josef Stalin	To secure power as leader of the Soviet Union. To remove opposition to his policies. To strengthen the Soviet Union against foreign attack.	Used murder of Kirov to accuse Left of the Party of plotting with Trotsky to undermine the Soviet Union. Arrests of opponents in the Party and armed forces.	Removal of political opponents in the Politburo. (intended) Stalin's economic policies implemented without opposition. (intended) Triggered a snowball effect of purges at local level. (unintended)	Short term – Stalin emerged as an unchallenged dictator. Support for his policies was achieved through fear. However, the purges removed some of the Soviet Union's most able army officers and resulted in disruption of the economy. Led to distancing of foreign powers from the USSR at a time when the threat of Nazi Germany was growing. (unintended) Long term – The USSR was strong enough to defeat Nazi Germany in the Second World War, but lasting fear of terror prevented new initiatives being put forward after the war and led to long-term stagnation.
Leonid Nikolayev				
Genrikh Yagoda (Head of the Secret Police)				
Nicolai Yezhov				
Local Party officials				

4 Discuss the following questions with a partner:

   a) Did any one party intend for the Great Purge to become so widespread in the 1930s?

   b) How important are people's intentions in explaining the scale of the Great Purge?

Stalin's power over party and state

There is no doubt that Stalin had considerable control over the Communist Party and the Soviet Union, building on the foundations of power laid by Lenin. Trotsky's accusation that Stalin's Soviet Union was a personal dictatorship is supported by evidence regarding the level of control Stalin exerted.

Stalin's control over the Communist Party

In 1924, the Politburo was made up of the following members: Bukharin, Zinoviev, Kamenev, Rykov, Tomsky, Trotsky and Stalin. By the end of 1930 Stalin was the only surviving member from this group, the others had been removed during the disputes over economic policy in the late 1920s. In their place were cronies of Stalin, such as Molotov, Voroshilov, Kalinin and Lazar Kaganovich. Thus, Stalin was able to ensure the Politburo was in agreement with his own policies. The use of terror against previous opponents sent clear messages to members of the Politburo about the likely consequences of opposing Stalin's wishes.

The key consequence of Stalin's methods was the failure of political institutions within the Soviet Union to gain any real power. All Party and State institutions remained mechanisms for rubber-stamping official policies decided by the leadership, and the leadership meant Stalin.

The way the government and Party functioned reflected Stalin's growing control:

- As the 1930s went on, these institutions, including the Politburo, met less frequently as Stalin increased his control over them. In the 1920s, the Politburo had met weekly, but by the mid-1930s meetings were held only about nine times a year.

- Power became focused in subgroups set up outside the Politburo, over which Stalin could exercise firmer control.

- Stalin attended important meetings, where he would use the intimidating tactic of walking around the room while others spoke. There was a real fear that saying something disagreeable to Stalin would result in execution. This was the fate of Pavel Rychagov, commander of the Soviet air force, when he complained about the quality of Soviet aircraft.

Lenin could be forceful, but Stalin's style of intimidation was unique.

SOURCE

5 Stalin (third from right) arriving at the Seventeenth Party Congress, 1934. Molotov is on his right, Kalanin and Yezhov to his left.

- **The forcible requisitioning of food** from the peasants in order to feed the army and the towns. Around 150,000 Bolshevik volunteers were used to seize grain. The government attempted to use Committees of the Village Poor to spy on any peasants who might be hoarding food. The result was a rise in tension in the countryside and serious outbreaks of violence, often directed at the requisitioning teams. Malnutrition and starvation became commonplace.

- The introduction of **rationing** to ensure that, despite food shortages, the workers in the cities were fed. Those industrial workers whose work was crucial to the war effort received preferential treatment.

War Communism ensured that the Red Army got the resources it needed to fight and win the civil war, but it left the economy in a state of collapse. By 1921, industrial production was only one-fifth of the figure for 1913. Disease and starvation were common and a wave of serious unrest swept across the countryside.

ACTIVITY
KNOWLEDGE CHECK

War Communism

1 What do all the different elements of War Communism share? (Think of the motives behind the measures as a whole.) Make a list.

2 Choose three of the individual measures and explain how they each relate to the overall themes identified in your answer to Question 1.

3 Explain what is meant by the following descriptions of War Communism. For each one use specific measures of War Communism to highlight these key features.

   a. Necessary but unpopular.

   b. 'A siege economy with a communist ideology. A partly organised chaos.' (Nove, 1992)

   c. Agriculture and the countryside were sacrificed on behalf of industry and the cities.

Why was the NEP introduced in 1921?

The Bolsheviks hoped that, through War Communism, communist ideology could be converted into meaningful policy, or at least give them the pretence of doing so. By 1921, these hopes and pretensions were well and truly over. The reality of the social and economic situation, coupled with a worrying deterioration in the political position of the Bolsheviks, led the government to abandon War Communism and replace it with the New Economic Policy (NEP). War Communism may have delivered the resources needed to win the civil war, but it was at a huge cost in terms of its impact on the economy and on the popularity of the Bolsheviks. The ending of the civil war produced a new situation that required a different response from the government.

- **Economic considerations**
  By the end of the war, industry had ground to a virtual standstill. Production of heavy industry had fallen to 20 percent of its 1913 level and, in some sectors, production had stopped altogether. Food production had also fallen, to only 48 percent of the 1913 figure, and the breakdown in the transport and distribution systems had resulted in widespread famine (see Source 2). Weakened by a lack of food, many Russians succumbed to diseases such as typhus and smallpox and over 20 million died from famine and disease in the 1920s. In addition to this, army soldiers had to be resettled into civilian life. It was clear that War Communism was not delivering the goods, nor would it be able to cope with the post-war situation.

- **The unpopularity of War Communism**
  Several of the key features of War Communism were loathed by the Russian population. The system of rationing was disliked, as the size of the rations was dependent on the social classification a person was given. Members of the Red Army and industrial proletariat received the most; members of the bourgeoisie received very little and, in some cases, none at all. The use of managers and the return to hierarchical systems within the factories caused resentment among the industrial workers, leading to violence on occasions. Many workers felt that their opportunity for self-regulation was being undermined by the increasing dictates of the state.

Mir

An organisation made up of village elders that controlled the peasants and their agricultural work. After the Revolution of February 1917, the peasants were able to gain genuine control over the working of the *mir* and used this for their own benefit. The Bolsheviks soon came to dislike the *mir* as it provided an obstacle to their own control over the countryside and their aim of introducing collective farms. Under War Communism, the Bolsheviks drew up plans for the removal of the *mir*.

- **The Tambov Rising**

  In the countryside, resentment of War Communism was greatest in relation to the forcible requisitioning of food and the plans to get rid of the *mir* (village commune), which had become a genuinely peasant organisation since the Revolution. Peasant resentment against the government came to a head in a series of uprisings in 1920–21. There were risings in the important grain areas of the Volga basin, North Caucasus and Western Siberia. The most serious was the Tambov Rising in central Russia, where peasants reacted violently to requisitioning teams arriving in the area to seize grain. The revolt was only put down after 50,000 Red Army troops were sent into the area. The seriousness of these risings put pressure on the government to change its policy.

- **The Kronstadt Mutiny**

  This revolt by sailors at the naval base outside Petrograd increased pressure on the government. The mutiny alarmed the Bolsheviks because it was by a group that had previously been a mainstay of the Revolution and they could not be easily dismissed as 'counter-revolutionaries'. The mutiny was over the increase in the power of the Party and its officials at the expense of the workers. Its slogan was 'Soviets without Bolsheviks'. The mutiny was suppressed by Red Army troops, but the revolt was a shock to the Bolshevik leadership and was a key factor in Lenin's decision to change his economic policy. To Lenin, the Kronstadt Mutiny had 'lit up reality like a flash of lightning'.

It was clear to most in the Bolshevik Party that the situation that had developed under War Communism could not be sustained. The result was a series of measures, known as the NEP, that saw a move away from the tight state control of War Communism towards a more mixed economy, where a private sector could emerge in addition to that controlled directly by the state.

SOURCE

The observations of two doctors working in the Ufa region, an area badly affected by famine, in 1920. From *Endurance and Endeavour*, written by J. N. Westwood in 1981.

Sometimes desperate mothers and fathers feed their children human meat as a last resort. Sometimes a father, seeing no other way, cuts the throat of a neighbour's child and brings it to his children as 'mutton'. Sometimes parents at night seize part of a body from the cemetery and feed it to their children.

A Tartar killed a 13 year old girl, a relative, who had come to visit him, by hitting her over the head with a log. He not only ate her, but also cut off from her several pounds of fat, which he sold at the market.

What were the key features of the NEP?

The NEP was a series of measures, introduced in 1921, which moved away from the tight state control of the economy introduced under War Communism.

In agriculture:

- There was to be an end to requisitioning. It was to be replaced by a system of taxation, which allowed the peasants to sell any remaining food at market for a profit.

- The Bolsheviks also announced that there would be no forced programme of collectivisation. Without collective farms, the *mir* would stay as the means of peasants self-regulating their farming activities.

These measures were clearly a compromise with the peasantry, but the Bolsheviks knew that, without increased food production, the economy would never be able to revive.

In industry:

- The NEP returned small-scale industry to private hands, although the state kept control of heavy industry, transport and the banks. This allowed Lenin to claim that the party still held 'the commanding heights of the economy'.

- In state-owned factories, piecework and bonuses were used to try to raise production. To some Bolsheviks these were the techniques of the capitalist.

- The reintroduction of a currency for paying wages in 1921 was also viewed with suspicion by many communists as the re-emergence of capitalism.

- The legalisation of private trading seemed the logical way of stopping a growing black market, a factor that had already led to some local authorities allowing private trade.

- With the growth of small-scale business and private traders, the Soviet Union saw the development of the so-called '**Nepmen**', people who gained under the NEP.

Nepmen

A term of abuse used by Bolsheviks to describe those private business people and traders who profited from the NEP.

From a communist standpoint, the NEP, with its acceptance of private industry and private trade, was a retreat back to capitalism. The left-wing Bolsheviks were particularly hostile to this watering down of policy but, to Lenin, the Bolsheviks were in desperate economic circumstances and, without making compromises, the Revolution would not be secure. The NEP was seen by Lenin and his supporters as a short-term remedy. The economy would have to be restored before moving to socialism, as Lenin stated: 'One step backwards, two steps forward'.

The introduction of the NEP coincided with the arrest of many Mensheviks, and all political parties other than the Bolsheviks were outlawed. Economic compromise clearly did not extend to political relaxation, a factor which persuaded many on the left of the Bolshevik Party that the NEP could be tolerated in the short term.

ACTIVITY
KNOWLEDGE CHECK

The NEP

1 Explain how the NEP could be seen as a retreat backwards towards capitalism.

2 Mensheviks believed that Russia was not ready for socialism. In what sense did the Bolsheviks' retreat under the NEP prove that the Mensheviks were right all along?

3 How far would you agree with the view of the left-wing Bolsheviks that the NEP marked a betrayal of the Revolution?

State control of industry and agriculture

The NEP resulted in a mixed economy whereby private ownership coexisted alongside state control, yet the debate over the extent of state control in the Soviet economy, far from ending, intensified during the 1920s. The Bolsheviks considered the NEP to be a temporary measure before moving on to a socialist system with greater state intervention. The issue now arose as to when the NEP should be brought to an end.

SOURCE

3 A thriving street market during the period of the NEP. The stalls are being operated by private traders allowed under the policy.

As the rural population starved, the government seized food for export to gain foreign exchange. Widespread famine occurred in 1932–33, particularly affecting the Ukraine, Kazakhstan and the Caucasus region. Peasants started to move into the towns in search of food, until the government introduced a passport system to prevent peasants leaving the collectives. They became effectively tied to the collective in a system that began to partly resemble serfdom, from which the peasants had supposedly been liberated in 1861. Unable to move from the collective, some peasants resorted to eating their own children in order to survive. The government officially denied any existence of famine, dismissing rumours as a few 'local difficulties'. This claim was supported by foreign visitors to the USSR, such as the British socialists Sidney and Beatrice Webb, but they had been escorted to model collectives well away from the famine areas. Recent research carried out on newly available Soviet data puts the number of famine-related deaths at four million in 1933 alone.

SOURCE

8

Agricultural production during collectivisation (compiled by A. Nove in 1992 from Soviet sources).

	1930	1931	1932	1933
Cattle (millions)	52.5	47.9	40.7	38.4
Pigs (millions)	13.6	14.4	11.6	12.1
Sheep and goats (millions)	108.8	77.7	52.1	50.2
Grain harvest (million tons)	83.5	69.5	69.6	68.4
State procurements (million tons)	22.1	22.8	18.5	22.6

SOURCE
9

Victims of the famine during the 1930s.

A slow recovery in agriculture began after a relatively good harvest in 1933, but grain production rose very sluggishly. Good weather helped the 1937 harvest, and the fall in demand for animal fodder meant more grain could be used for human consumption. The decline in livestock that had accompanied collectivisation resulted in a lack of haulage power. The slow pace at which newly produced tractors got to collectives made this situation worse. In the absence of horses and tractors, humans resorted to pulling ploughs themselves. Recovery was hampered by continual government interference and hare-brained schemes, one of which involved growing crops of a plant that allegedly produced rubber.

Inadequate planning resulted in Party officials in Moscow giving orders to collectives, which took little account of conditions on the ground. Poor planning meant that the push to collectivise was not co-ordinated with the manufacture of tractors or other agricultural machinery, leaving the collectives without the tools to prosper.

The total cost, in terms of human lives, is difficult to quantify exactly but represents a human tragedy of epic proportions. Stalin had achieved his aim of 'liquidating' the kulaks as a class. This class had been estimated to be about 15 million in 1928. Historians' estimates of the number of deaths range from five to ten million. In 1986, historian Robert Conquest argued that collectivisation, with its resulting famine, was Stalin's deliberate policy of genocide against the Ukrainian people, sometimes referred to as the **holodomor**. An analysis of the grain harvest in 1932 indicates that it was Ukraine, the chief grain-growing region of the country, that bore the brunt of the food shortage. Ukrainian nationalism had been a worry to the Soviet government in the civil war of the 1920s. The case of the Kazakhs illustrates another human cost. This nomadic group were forced into collectives against their will. The change in their way of life had devastating consequences. Their sheep flocks were virtually wiped out, and a typhus epidemic reduced the Kazakh population by 40 percent. It was hardly surprising that some peasants cheered the invading German forces in 1941.

KEY TERM

Holodomor
Literally meaning murder by starvation. It is applied to Stalin's actions against Ukraine during the process of enforced collectivisation.

Given the devastating impact on economic performance and the immensely damaging social impact of collectivisation, the question of whether Stalin's prime aim was political can be raised. Where collectivisation did succeed was in imposing Party control over a reluctant rural population. In 1930 the *mir* was abolished and replaced by the *kolkhoz* administration, headed by a chairman who was a Party member and usually from the town. Party control was extended by the use of teenagers, members of the Communist youth organisation, who used wooden watchtowers to spy on the peasants in the fields to ensure they did not steal food to feed their own families. Control had been secured, but it deepened the divide between town and countryside. Agriculture and rural communities had been sacrificed for the needs of industry and the towns.

ACTIVITY
KNOWLEDGE CHECK

Collectivisation
1 Give three reasons for collectivisation.
2 List the effects of collectivisation. Which category would each of these effects come under: economic, social or political?

SOURCE
10 Tractors leaving the factory after production, 1929.

SOURCE
11 From N. Khrushchev, *Khrushchev Remembers*, published in 1971. Khrushchev was a member of the Politburo under Stalin.

During a trip from Kiev to Moscow in 1939, my chauffeur told me that the tyres which were being issued for our cars were wearing out much too quickly. In fact, they were blowing out at the sides while they were still almost brand new. When I got to Moscow, I told Stalin that this manufacturing defect was costing a lot of time and money: Stalin never liked to hear anyone criticise something that was Soviet-made. He listened to my complaint with obvious displeasure. Then he angrily instructed me to liquidate this situation and to find the culprits...

When I reported to Stalin, I stressed that we were producing poor-quality tyres because, in our desire to economise, we had violated the production procedure recommended by the firm from which the equipment was purchased... The tyre workers may have surpassed their quota, but they have overdone it. Our workers should have paid more attention to quality when applying the tyre cording. All the shock-workers on the honour board at the factory were, in actual fact, ruining what they produced.

EXTRACT
1 An assessment by the historian A. Nove, from *An Economic History of the USSR 1917–1991*, published in 1992.

Whatever the validity of certain official claims, it remains true beyond question that the second Five-year Plan period was one of impressive achievement, as is clear from the commodity statistics...

Both in volume and in degree of sophistication the advances recorded in these years did help to transform the whole balance of industry and to diminish very substantially the USSR's dependence on foreign countries for its capital goods.

THINKING HISTORICALLY — Evidence (3b)

It depends on the question

When considering the usefulness of a piece of evidence, people often think about authenticity in the case of artefacts, reliability in the case of witness statements, or methodology and structure in the case of secondary accounts. A better historical approach to the usefulness of a piece of evidence would be to think about the statements that we can make about the past based on it. Different statements can be made with different degrees of certainty, depending on the evidence.

Work in small groups and answer the following.

1 Look at Source 10.

   a) Write three statements that you can reasonably make about the First Five-Year Plan based solely on Source 10.

   b) Which of the statements can be made with the greatest degree of certainty? Why is this? Which statement can be made with the smallest degree of certainty?

   c) What else might you need to increase your confidence in your statements?

2 Source 10 shows an artefact (the tractor) and Source 11 is a witness statement. Which is more useful to the historian studying Soviet tractor production in the 1930s under the Five-Year Plans?

3 Look at Extract 1.

How would the historian have gone about constructing this piece? What kinds of evidence would they have needed?

Recovery from war after 1945

The impact of the Second World War on the Soviet economy

The German invasion of the USSR, which began on 22 June 1941, put an enormous strain on the resources of the country. The centralisation of the economy, which was an integral feature of the Stalinist system, proved to be effective in mobilising the resources of the Soviet Union for war. It was a mammoth task. At the local level, Defence Committees were set up to co-ordinate war production. Factories were quickly converted to the production of war materials. In Moscow, a children's bicycle factory was converted for the manufacture of flame-throwers. Whole factories were evacuated to safer areas of the USSR in the east, away from the invading Germans.

Despite the initial collapse in industrial output, which occurred in the immediate aftermath of the invasion, Soviet industrial production rose impressively, if unevenly, after 1941. Between 1943 and 1945, over 73,000 tanks and 94,000 aircraft were produced. The economy did find some products beyond its capability; tinned meat, including Spam, was imported from Britain under the Lend-Lease scheme, whereby supplies were provided with payment deferred. As the economy produced large amounts of military hardware, the production of consumer goods was virtually non-existent. By the end of the war, the damage in Nazi-occupied areas had reduced overall production: steel production had fallen to 12 million tonnes in 1945 compared with 18 million tonnes produced in 1940; oil production was less than two-thirds and wool production less than half of that produced in 1940.

In agriculture, the situation was also desperate. With the most able-bodied men from the collectives conscripted into the armed forces, and farm machinery and draft animals requisitioned by the Red Army, the impact of the war on food production was devastating. Grain output fell from 95 million tonnes in 1940 to 30 million tonnes in 1942, and the number of cattle halved. In these circumstances, the government lifted restrictions on the cultivation of private plots to provide an incentive for peasants to keep up production.

By the end of the war, much of the western part of the USSR was devastated; 25 million people were homeless and over 1,700 towns and 70,000 villages were classified as 'destroyed'. Reconstruction would be an enormous undertaking.

The Fourth Five-Year Plan (1946–50): economic reconstruction

The priority of the government was to bring about economic reconversion and reconstruction as quickly as possible. Many factories that had been converted to the production of wartime goods needed to be converted back to civilian production. Large industrial plants needed to be rebuilt. In order to achieve these aims, rigid state control was reinforced over the war-shattered economy. This process was made more difficult because of the ending of Lend-Lease.

One advantage that the USSR could now exploit was its control over Eastern Europe. Much of the region had fallen into the hands of the Red Army after the defeat of Nazi Germany. Large amounts of machinery were taken from East Germany as reparations, although once transported to the USSR it was often left to rust as workers were unable to reassemble them. Trade agreements were signed with the new Soviet-dominated governments of Eastern Europe, which were so one-sided to the advantage of the USSR that they amounted to little more than economic exploitation. In general, however, economic reconstruction was to be based largely on the efforts of the Soviet people using Soviet resources.

The Fourth Five-Year Plan (1946–50) aimed, through a programme of reconstruction, to restore the economy to pre-war levels, a massive undertaking in so short a time. The results were impressive. Industrial production recovered quickly, helped largely by the use of over two million slave labourers from the Gulag. Strong central planning by the government was an important factor in achieving such quick results. The government was able to redirect wartime labour for the purposes of reconstruction. Retraining programmes were effective at ensuring workers had the basic skills needed for the jobs now in demand. Penalties for slackers remained harsh. The focus was placed on heavy industry (as before the war), with the production of armaments receiving special attention. The metal industry and heavy engineering were especially successful. The Plan was overfulfilled, but problems persisted and consumer industries remained neglected. Moreover, the economy had returned to the priorities of the 1930s, a feature reinforced by a failure to adopt new technology, such as developments in plastics and chemicals.

- **Lack of investment**
  Investment in agriculture increased during the Khrushchev and Brezhnev years but it was not enough to address the chronic underfunding it had received under Stalin. Storage facilities, rural transport and reliable machinery were in very short supply throughout the Soviet period.

- **Outdated technology**
  Soviet successes had been in areas that were becoming outdated. Soviet production of steel, cement, oil and pig iron exceeded that of the USA by the end of the 1970s, but these were vital elements of an industrial power that were giving way to the requirements of a post-industrial society based on microchips and computers. By the 1980s, the USSR was struggling to keep up to date with the technological advances made in the West. Brezhnev's policy of coupling industries with scientific research institutions in the 1970s helped, but it could not solve the increasing use of outdated methods. In recognition of this, the Soviet government signed deals with the West in order to gain access to new technologies. Agreements were made with Fiat and Renault to import car-making technology into the USSR, but the impact rarely extended beyond the plant in which it were used. By 1980, most Soviet technology was old and physically worn out.

- **The dominance of the military-industrial complex**
  This soaked up at least 18 percent of Soviet resources and employed 30 million people out of a working population of 150 million. Brezhnev's foreign policy involved increasing intervention in the developing world and this made expenditure on arms and defence necessary. These resources could have been switched, at least in part, to consumer industry and agriculture.

The causes of economic decline pre-dated Brezhnev's time in office but had become obvious to all during his rule. The command economy had performed well when the focus was on improving output of a limited number of products. It was far less effective when continued growth depended on gains in quality and efficiency. The system had become increasingly complex and overburdened. Despite being overworked, central planners preferred to hold onto a system that gave them power and influence. As the guarantor of the power and privileges of the Party, Brezhnev was the leader they both wanted and deserved. By the early 1980s ill-health rendered Brezhnev and his successors, Andropov and Chernenko, incapable of initiating meaningful reform. The failure to grapple successfully with the economy was an important factor in the impending crisis that led to the collapse of the Soviet Union.

ACTIVITY
KNOWLEDGE CHECK

Soviet economic policy, 1964–85

1 a) Make a list of the economic reforms undertaken during the period 1964–85.

   b) Rate each reform according to its effectiveness.

2 List the differences and similarities between Khrushchev's economic policy and that of the Brezhnev years.

3 Assess the degree of change that had occurred between 1964 and 1985. What words would you use to describe the nature of this change?

Conclusions

From the seizure of power in 1917, the Communist regime had taken measures to extend its control over the economy. The extent of this control varied during the years 1917–21, from providing state direction to the more extensive control adopted during the civil war. The unpopularity of War Communism resulted in a subsequent step back towards a mixed economy of private and state ownership under the NEP in 1921, but the political pressures for pushing towards a command economy remained. Stalin's Five-Year Plans from 1928 brought the economy under state control and this brought enormous benefits in modernising the Soviet Union's economy and was able to meet the demands of the Second World War and post-war reconstruction. Yet, it also established an economic system that contained more negative features: it was a command economy that displayed alarming rigidity, a lack of focus on consumer goods, prioritised industry at the expense of agriculture and lacked enterprise and initiative. The reforms attempted during the period 1953 to 1985 were designed to address these problems. The fact that these reforms were to have only limited success showed that the economic system established under Stalin was too entrenched to allow more fundamental change without challenging the political power of the Party. This was the central dilemma of the Soviet economy.

ACTIVITY
SUMMARY

Economic policy, 1917–85

Look at the list of Soviet leaders:

Lenin; Stalin; Khrushchev; Brezhnev; Andropov

1 Rank these leaders in terms of the success of their economic policies.

2 For each leader identify the factors that (a) promoted and (b) hindered economic change.

3 Discuss the following statement: 'The performance of the Soviet economy between 1917 and 1985 shows the failure of a command economy.' How far would you agree with this view? Explain your answer.

AS Level Exam-Style Question Section A

Was the failure of Khrushchev's agricultural policies the main reason for economic problems in the USSR in 1964–82? (20 marks)

Tip

Think about the economic problems caused by Khrushchev's failures in agricultural policy (rather than just stating what his policies were). Focus on discussing whether you think this failure was the 'main reason' for economic problems. For example, were the economic problems of the USSR the result of failures to restructure industry as well as agriculture? Were these two areas of policy linked?

A Level Exam-Style Question Section A

How far was Soviet economic decline in the period 1964–85 a result of a failure of leadership? (20 marks)

Tip

This question requires careful explanation of how the Soviet leadership failed to address the issue of economic performance and requires you to assess the importance of this factor. Try to link factors rather than list them. Was it the leadership that failed or the system they headed?

ACTIVITY
WRITING

The Soviet economy in the 1980s

Use the words in the list below to complete these sentences so that they best describe the weaknesses of the Soviet economy in the early 1980s.

> discouraged; diminishing; non-productive; exacerbated; military-industrial complex; productivity; inertia; stemmed

By the 1980s, the Soviet economy was showing signs of serious weakness. Many of these .... from the fact that it was essentially a command economy. Control was exercised from Moscow by bureaucrats that were protective of their own power and influence. Any reforms attempted were seen as a threat and were ....

This produced a growing sense of ....

Despite increased investment and improvements in production, living standards remained low as more resources were used with .... returns.

Problems were .... by the diversion of considerable resources to the .... These resources were .... and starved other sectors of the economy of materials, technology and labour that could have been used in the promotion of consumer goods, which would have had a more beneficial impact on ....

THINKING HISTORICALLY Change (4b&c)

The bird's-eye view

The development	Medium-term consequences	Long-term consequences
The introduction of the NEP, 1921	The Soviet economy was stimulated by the reintroduction of elements of private enterprise	The NEP was replaced by the First Five-Year Plan in 1928, which brought an end to the private enterprise encouraged by the NEP. After the death of Stalin in 1953, the NEP was sometimes viewed as a model of how a mixed economy could be used to promote initiative and growth. In the 1980s, Gorbachev was keen on applying some of the features of the NEP to improve Soviet economic performance. Russian politicians still use it to highlight the relative role of private and state ownership in the economy.

Imagine you are looking at the whole of History using a zoomed-out interactive map like Google Maps. You have a general view of the sweep of developments and their consequences, but you cannot see much detail. If you zoom in to the time of the introduction of the NEP, you can see the event in detail but will know nothing of its consequences in the medium or long term. If you zoom out to look at the medium- or long-term consequences, you will know about them in detail but will know very little about the events that cause them, for example, the Tambov Rising and the Kronstadt Mutiny.

Look at the table above and answer the following.

1 What were the immediate consequences of the NEP?

2 In what ways are the medium-term consequences different to the long-term consequences?

Work in groups of three.

Each student takes the role of the teacher for one of the above (the development, medium-term consequences or long-term consequences) and gives a short presentation to the other two. They may comment and ask questions. After each presentation, the other two group members write a 100-word paragraph showing how the presentation links to their own.

Answer the following individually:

1 What happens to the detail when you zoom out to look at the whole sweep of history?

2 What are the advantages and disadvantages of zooming in to look at a specific time in detail?

3 How could you use the map in order to get a good understanding of history as a whole?

 WIDER READING

Most general surveys of the Soviet Union provide coverage of economic policy. More detailed accounts include:

Barnett, V. 'The Soviet Economy – an Experiment that was Bound to Fail?', *History Review* (2005).

Davies, R. W. *Soviet Economic Development from Lenin to Khrushchev*, Cambridge (1998)

Holland, A. *Russia and its Rulers 1855-1964*, Hodder Education (2010)

Kenez, P. *A History of the Soviet Union from the Beginning to the End*, second edition, Cambridge University Press (2006)

Laver, J. *The Modernisation of Russia 1856-1985*, Heinemann Advanced History, Heinemann (2002)

Nove, A. *An Economic History of the USSR 1917-1991*, Penguin (1992)

Oxley, P. *Russia 1855-1991: From Tsars to Commissars*, Oxford University Press (2001)

Suny, R. *The Soviet Experiment*, Oxford (1998)

Thompson, W. *The Soviet Union under Brezhnev*, Pearson (2003)

Yezhov delighted in undertaking the torture of suspects himself and once attended a Politburo meeting with the cuffs of his shirt covered in fresh blood from torturing 'enemies of the Revolution'. Yet by 1938, Stalin seems to have become concerned that the heavy use of terror was demoralising the population at a time when war with Germany was looming. Yezhov, whose health began to suffer from his frenetic work rate and excessive drinking, was dismissed in 1938. Stalin accused him of being responsible for the excesses of the purges. There is no doubt that there was some truth in this accusation, but it suited Stalin to use Yezhov as a scapegoat as he wished to reduce the level of terror.

The role of Beria

The man appointed as the new head of the secret police was Lavrenti Beria, an energetic man of impressive organisational skills and unsavoury characteristics (see Extract 1). These qualities had brought him to the notice of Stalin even though Stalin was irritated by his excessive flattery. Beria had undermined Yezhov by briefing Stalin with criticisms of Yezhov's work in order to secure his removal and therefore his job.

EXTRACT 1

An account of Beria's behaviour from the historian Rupert Butler, *Stalin's Instruments of Terror* (2006).

From the very start of his career, Beria had been heartily disliked by all. He was balding, short, and fleshy, with sensual lips and snake-like eyes glistening behind his professional pince-nez [eye glasses], and his sexual proclivities were both perverted and insatiable. His habit was to prowl the streets in his official limousine on the lookout for a young woman. When a suitable one was spotted, the driver was ordered to stop, seize her and throw her in the back of the car. She was then driven off to a quiet spot, where Beria raped her. Who dared complain?

Beria's appointment was viewed with some relief by the general population. Beria was presented as an uncle-like figure who would reform the excessive behaviour of the secret police. There was some truth in this perception. Beria felt that indiscriminate arrests were inefficient and a waste of manpower. A more productive method was needed. Beria reintroduced more conventional methods of police procedure and public trials were only held where solid evidence was available. Surveillance continued, but it only led to arrests when evidence was found. The arm of the Soviet secret police had a long reach. One of Beria's achievements was to oversee the murder of Trotsky, killed by a Stalinist agent in Mexico in 1940.

The focus on productivity also extended to the Gulag. Beria wanted to make the Gulag a profitable part of the Soviet economy. In 1939, food rations for inmates were improved, not due to humanitarian concerns but to get maximum work out of prisoners. Beria was instrumental in using the technical skills of inmates for specialist tasks. As a result, 1,000 scientists were put to work on various projects that – according to Beria's subsequent boasts – created many new pieces of military hardware. Although this claim was dubious, among the scientists were Andrei Tupolev, the aviation engineer, and Sergei Korolev, who played an essential part in the development of the Soviet space programme.

Early releases from the camps were cancelled so that prisoners' expertise could continue to be used. These measures resulted in a growth in Gulag economic activity from 2 billion roubles in 1937 to 4.5 billion roubles in 1940. Under Beria, the Gulag reached its biggest expanse. By the early 1950s, it was a major contributor to the Soviet economy. Over one-third of the country's gold and much of its timber and coal was produced through the Gulag.

Changes to the role of the secret police during the Second World War

The approach of the Second World War led to a strengthening of the powers of the secret police.

- In 1941 they were given some powers of supervision of the Red Army with responsibility for monitoring disloyalty and dealing with any desertions.

- The NKVD was given control over the process of deportations of those national minorities whose loyalty to the Soviet state was considered suspect. This included the Crimean Tartars, Volga Germans and Chechens. Their forcible removal to designated areas was particularly harsh. The process was conducted by three-person *Troikas* who were given powers outside the normal process of law.

- By 1943, the Red Army had started to overrun areas previously captured by the Germans. In these areas Beria set up Special Departments to root out traitors, deserters and cowards. Anyone suspected of co-operating with the Germans was either shot or deported to the Gulag. One department, called **SMERSH**, dealt with suspected spies and it was probably involved in the murder of more than 4,000 Polish officers at Katyn in 1943.

- Even Soviet troops who had escaped German capture were considered suspect. Order 270 treated all Soviet troops who had surrendered to the Germans during the initial invasion as traitors. Returning prisoners of war were automatically held in detention camps run by the secret police: some were used to clear minefields by simply walking through areas where mines had been laid by the enemy.

KEY TERM

SMERSH
A branch of the secret police whose task was to root out hostile elements in the Red Army. SMERSH was an acronym based on the phrase 'death to spies'. It was created in 1943. It later became a branch of the KGB whose main job was to arrange assassinations of opponents and dissidents. The organisation featured in several of Ian Fleming's James Bond novels.

Post-war rivalry

Stalin's last years saw a growing rivalry between members of the Politburo as Stalin's health began to fail. Beria saw the chance to use his role as head of the secret police to launch a fresh wave of purges to gain Stalin's favour. The target was the Leningrad branch of the Party. In 1949, over 2,000 members were imprisoned or exiled. Beria had gained considerable influence by undertaking Stalin's wishes. But Stalin was still the one with the power.

Stalin's next purges may well have been deliberate warnings to Beria. The Mingrelian Affair of 1951 involved a purge of the Party in Georgia. The purge seemed to be targeted at people who were of Mingrelian ethnicity, a group to which Beria belonged. In 1953, there is evidence that Stalin was planning another major purge before he died. In January a group of doctors were arrested, accused of trying to assassinate Stalin. The 'Doctors' Plot' was also notable in that most of the accused were Jewish. This may have been the prelude to a campaign of terror against Soviet Jews, but it was more likely to have been the first step towards the elimination of Beria and possibly other figures in the leadership. Certainly, statements that accused the secret police of a lack of vigilance must have concerned its head, Beria. Before the purge could take place, Stalin died.

Beria's power and influence at the time of Stalin's death was substantial. He controlled the secret police, the network of Soviet spies around the world, the Gulag system and its associated links to industry. Beria's enormous power was the reason why his Politburo colleagues moved so quickly to remove him from his position in June 1953. The lead was taken by Khrushchev, whom Beria had fatally underestimated as a 'moon-faced idiot'.

The impact of the removal of Beria on the use of terror

With Beria removed from power, the Politburo moved quickly to limit the independence of the secret police. It was brought firmly under Party control, answerable to a new organisation, the Soviet Security and Intelligence Service, otherwise known as the **KGB**. Khrushchev dismantled the Gulag system and forced labour never again played a part in the Soviet economy. Even the Lubyanka building ceased to be a prison. The last person to be held there was Gary Powers, the US pilot whose U-2 spy plane was shot down over the USSR in 1960.

KEY TERM

KGB
The Committee for State Security. It was established in 1954 and was the organisation that controlled the secret police. It had been set up after the death of Stalin to ensure that the secret police were brought back under Party control. Its main tasks were to deal with internal security, intelligence gathering both at home and abroad, and espionage. It also provided the bodyguard for Politburo members. It was run like a branch of the army, with military ranks. Yuri Andropov was head of the KGB from 1967 until he became General Secretary in 1982. Under his leadership, the KGB gained a reputation for its professionalism and effectiveness. It was no longer perceived as a group of thugs as had Stalin's secret police in the 1930s.

Responsibility for the apparatus of terror

It was a common saying of Gulag inmates that if only Stalin knew about their situation he would put an end to it. This view that Stalin had no role in the development of terror and the Gulag was naive in the extreme. Stalin did not create the Gulag system – it was already in existence under Lenin – but its growth was a consequence of the actions he pursued from 1928. The application of terror was something that Stalin took a particular interest in.

Evidence of Stalin's responsibility includes the following.

- Stalin personally signed many death warrants and often added comments on the lists of those arrested, asking his henchmen to add more names or adding names of his own choosing.

- Stalin gave the NKVD quotas to meet, just like the targets of the Five-Year Plans. If the quotas were not met, the local NKVD officers were expected to add their own names to the lists.

- The use of terror accompanied Stalin's policies and was an essential part of them. The rapid process of collectivisation required the kulaks and those peasants who opposed the policy to be swept away. The unrealistic demands of the Five-Year Plans put enormous pressure on officials to explain a failure to meet targets. It was often essential, for their own personal survival, for managers to label people as saboteurs or shirkers.

- Historians such as Ivan Chukhin have suggested that the huge expansion of terror in the 1930s was the result of the demand for slave labour to ensure that the targets of the Five-Year Plans were met. Forced labour played a key part in Stalin's desire to build prestige projects. It was perhaps no coincidence that some of the Soviet Union's top geologists were arrested on the eve of a camp being set up to exploit oil reserves in the Komi Republic.

- Stalin set the parameters for the purges. The death of Kirov, whether Stalin was directly responsible or not, was used to start the Great Purge of the Party, and the dismissal of Yezhov in 1938 was the signal that the purges were to be slowed down. The death of Stalin resulted in the dismantling of the Gulag system and a reduction in the use of terror.

- Many aspects of the terror reflect Stalin's paranoid personality. The assassination of Kirov in 1934 may well have exacerbated his paranoia. The Doctors' Plot of 1953 seems to have stemmed from Stalin's anti-Semitic views, coupled with suspicions that the Kremlin doctors were trying to kill him.

With so much evidence pointing to Stalin's responsibility for the use of terror, it raises the question of whether Yagoda, Yezhov and Beria were merely functionaries carrying out Stalin's orders or whether they had a role in influencing the development of terror.

- Yagoda, Yezhov and Beria all became powerful leaders of the secret police as a consequence of their willingness to follow Stalin's wishes. All three men had sadistic tendencies and had little, if any, moral conscience about using torture or terror. They owed their positions to Stalin and he dismissed Yagoda and Yezhov. Beria did not survive long after the death of Stalin.

- None of the three had much impact on the targets of the terror. These were decided by Stalin and stemmed from the requirements of his policies and personality. Yet all three took the opportunity to add to the death lists the names of those who stood in their way. Yagoda used his influence to enhance his career within the NKVD, Yezhov advanced his career by undermining Yagoda, and Beria in turn did the same to Yezhov.

- Where the leaders of the NKVD did have influence was in the implementation of terror and the operation of the Gulag. Under Yagoda, the Gulag expanded greatly but struggled to cope with the vast increase in inmates resulting from collectivisation.

Under Yezhov, the process of terror was speeded up, partly in response to the sheer scale of the task. Excessive use of terror was partly driven by the sadistic and frenetic personality of Yezhov himself. The result was that terror became all-pervasive in Soviet society. Beria oversaw a change in the Gulag to a greater emphasis on productivity, which made the system less cruel if no more humane.

Stalin enjoyed making others out to be his 'bad men'; he once introduced Beria to the US President Roosevelt as 'our Himmler', a reference to Hitler's head of the SS. It was a joke that embarrassed the US president. Where power really lay is perhaps best summed up by historian Anne Applebaum (2003) who stated: 'Stalin selected the victims – and his subordinates leaped at the opportunity to obey him.'

ACTIVITY
KNOWLEDGE CHECK

The use of the secret police under Stalin

1 Who were the main targets of terror during the period 1929 to 1953?

2 How did the methods of terror change during the period 1929 to 1953?

3 Who do you think should bear the most responsibility for the use of terror: Stalin, Yagoda, Yezhov or Beria? Justify your decision.

EXTEND YOUR KNOWLEDGE

Was the use of terror necessary?

Terror was a dominant feature of Stalin's economic transformation of the Soviet Union in the 1930s. The British economist and historian, Alex Nove, caused controversy in 1962 when he suggested that terror was a necessary part of this transformation. His views were put forward in his article 'Was Stalinism Necessary?' While not condoning the use of terror, he saw terror as a product of the time and circumstances within which Stalin had to operate. If a minority group like the Bolsheviks wanted to bring about rapid change, then terror was the only way this could be achieved. Persuasion through concessions and propaganda might have worked, but their use would have made the process of change much slower and, with the growing likelihood of invasion from Germany, this was not an option. Thus, terror was an integral part of Stalin's policies of industrialisation.

More recent studies have developed the economic aspect of the use of terror. James Harris (1997) has argued that the use of terror and the expansion of the Gulag after 1928 were consequences of the pressure exerted by the government on local Party officials and managers to meet targets for economic performance. Forced labour was used as one way of trying to ensure production increased at a time when there were labour shortages. Stalin's own recognition of the role of slave labour in boosting production is highlighted by his diversion of workers to pet projects such as the White Sea Canal. Stalin supported the methods used by Naftaly Frenkel, who applied 'rational' methods to exploit slave labour involving the distribution of food based on a prisoner's capacity to work and the elimination of 'useless extras'. Terror was also used to ensure scientists, technicians and engineers were arrested and sent to camps where their skills were needed. The economic function of the Gulag became particularly pronounced during Beria's period as head of the secret police.

However, it would be misleading to take this interpretation too far. The secret police often declared amnesties for political prisoners, often to relieve overcrowding in the camps. Even as late as 1937, there were some political prisoners who were forbidden to work. Stalin may have wanted prisoners to be put to economic use, but this does not seem to have been the prime reason for arrests. Among the prisoners were many women, children and elderly people who were of limited use for the heavy manual work of most camps. The Gulag was a chaotic and inefficient organisation that struggled with the demands placed upon it, with camp commanders unprepared for each new wave of arrests.

After Stalin's death, the pace and extent of change was much reduced. Khrushchev did not need, nor had he the desire, to use terror to control the Soviet people. The Party's hold on power was now secure and it could rely on the other methods of control that it had at its disposal, such as propaganda and welfare provision.

- **Music** also suffered from a pressure to toe the line. In 1935, Stalin walked out of a performance of Shostakovich's opera *Lady Macbeth of Mstensk* (a politically correct story of adultery) due to discordant notes. The real reason was Stalin's shock at the bedroom scene, where trombones were used to underline what was happening. In popular music, the government favoured military songs more than jazz. Government concern over the perceived decadent associations of jazz led to the banning of the saxophone in the 1940s. As in literature, it was better to stick to well-worn themes than experiment if you wished to carry on working.

- **Architecture** Socialist Realism promoted the style known as 'Stalinist baroque', better known as 'wedding cake' architecture, which made use of classical lines. Many public buildings were built in this style, the best example being Moscow University, which was rebuilt after 1945. The Moscow metro system was another fine example of Stalinist baroque, with stations decorated with chandeliers and elaborate murals, showing the endeavours of the workers.

- **Film** The achievements of the Revolution were conveyed through films, such as Eisenstein's *October* (1927), which presented the heroic version of the storming of the Winter Palace in 1917. This served the interests of the government in presenting the Revolution as a mass movement. Unfortunately, due to Eisenstein's excessive use of extras and live ammunition, more people died in the making of the film than in the actual events themselves. During the Second World War, the cinema was used to promote patriotism in defence of both Mother Russia and socialism: the film *Alexander Nevsky* was one of the most popular.

The focus of Socialist Realism on accessible art and popular culture provided a useful tool for government propaganda. Socialist Realism, rooted in 'the people', resulted in formalised but accessible styles in art and writing. It is easy to criticise Socialist Realism for being so out of touch with reality, but the work of social historians such as R. Stites has drawn attention to the range of purposes the arts and culture could have. Socialist Realism presented images that some committed Party members were willing to believe and others were prepared to use to inspire them to work harder. Other sections of the population, while not believing them, may have found the images to be a satisfying method of escapism. It was rather more than art for art's sake. This range of functions gave the government many opportunities to use the arts and popular culture to mobilise support at a range of levels for the regime.

ACTIVITY
KNOWLEDGE CHECK

Prolekult, avant-garde and Socialist Realism, 1917–53

Look at the examples of art shown in Sources 1 and 7. Explain how the Soviet government would have viewed each of these works when they were made.

Nonconformity from the 1950s

Culture during Stalin's last years

The last years of Stalin's leadership saw some changes of emphasis in cultural policy. Immediately after the Second World War there were signs that the government was prepared to allow artists and writers greater freedom. Both Boris Pasternak and Anna Akhmatova were allowed to give public readings of their unorthodox poetry in Moscow in 1946 to enthusiastic applause. The signs of greater freedom were quickly dispelled as elements of Western culture were condemned in a campaign referred to as the Zhdanovschina. Zhdanov was the Party boss in Leningrad and he had a particular interest in culture. In 1946, a campaign was launched to remove all aspects of 'bourgeois' culture from the West. It was heavily influenced by xenophobic attitudes that had been enhanced by the development of the Cold War. The classical composer, Dmitri Shostakovich, was subjected to the humiliation of being called into Zhdanov's office to have suitable tunes tapped out to him on a piano by Zhdanov himself. Zhdanov told Shostakovich that there was little point in composing music you could not hum. Shostakovich thereafter restricted himself to writing film scores.

The impact of de-Stalinisation on culture

Those artists and writers who wished to express themselves freely were to receive greater hope from Khrushchev's policy of de-Stalinisation after 1957. Not all of these hopes were fulfilled. In line with the criticism of Stalin and his 'errors', Khrushchev allowed works to be published that had been previously banned.

- Works by Isaac Babel, a writer who had been shot during the purges, were published.

- Younger poets, such as Yevgeny Yevtushenko and Andrei Voznesenski, were allowed to publish collections of more experimental poetry, and jazz music made a reappearance.

- Khrushchev's personal intervention led to the publication of the previously banned book by Solzhenitsyn, *One Day in the Life of Ivan Denisovich*, which recounted the appalling experiences of life in the Gulag. Further novels by Solzhenitsyn followed that attacked aspects of Stalin's terror and fitted in with the new political emphasis of de-Stalinisation. Where works did not fall so easily into the political context, however, writers could still come up against restrictions.

Other voices spoke out against the official culture. Sholokhov went as far as to openly describe official Soviet culture as 'grey trash'. Writers began to explore new themes such as spiritual concerns, the bleakness of rural life and the problems of adultery, divorce and alcohol abuse. This 'literature of conscience' did not focus on the idealised life portrayed by Socialist Realism. Even 'low-brow' literature was used to criticise the Soviet system. Science-fiction novels often contained messages that acted as critiques of society.

By the late 1950s, nonconformity was starting to have an important impact on youth culture in the USSR. Tired with the repetitive and unexciting themes of official cultural output, Soviet youth became influenced by music tastes from the West. Urban groups developed that listened to the pop and rock'n'roll music emerging in the West, the records having been smuggled into the country. These groups, wearing Western fashions of tight suits and short skirts, were labelled *stilyagi* by the authorities, who described them as rude and ignorant freaks. From 1955, this music was broadcast into the USSR by the radio station Voice of America.

One notable development in popular music was that of the guitar-poet. Its leading figure was Alexander Galich, who composed and performed his own work rather than performing officially sanctioned pieces produced by the government. The guitar-poet typically addressed the feelings of the individual and often spoke to the socially alienated. Audiences at underground venues were small, but through the use of the tape recorder their work could be spread to a wider audience. *Magnitizdat*, or tape recorder self-publishing, was a constant headache for the authorities.

Nonconformity during the Brezhnev years

The replacement of Khrushchev with Brezhnev in 1964 did not see a return to the strict application of Socialist Realism of Stalin's years, but it did narrow the boundaries of what was acceptable after the cultural thaw of the Khrushchev years. Many artists and writers found the new cultural climate easier to work in as there was more certainty over what was permissible but, nonetheless, continued to push the boundaries of what was acceptable.

Official culture continued to focus on propaganda and the achievements of socialism and the Soviet state, providing stirring themes for the population. The majority of the population preferred this style even if many artists and writers found it undemanding. To those wishing to stretch themselves creatively, this was, in the words of historian Richard Stites 'the graveyard of ideas, openness and free expression'.

Aspects of nonconformity include the following.

- By the 1970s, Soviet culture had become conservative, and artists and writers were more likely to get into trouble by touching on sexual themes than political ones.

- The *derevenshchiki* school of village prose highlighted the values of simple rural life. These accounts were often romanticised and featured a longing for a lost world of the past. It caused the government unease because it could be read as a critique of urban life in the Soviet Union.

- Russian nationalism received some encouragement from the government, but writers who took up the theme, the so-called 'Russites', alienated non-Russians and often came close to criticising the Soviet Union.

- The increasing influence of popular music. Soviet youth continued to be drawn towards cultural trends in the West. Vladimir Vysotsky emerged as an influential guitar-poet whose songs of sex and delinquency were popular with young people. His funeral in 1980 saw an outpouring of grief that worried the government. He had not been their idea of a role model for Soviet youth. It seemed to indicate the growing alienation of young people from Soviet society. The elderly men in the Politburo struggled to understand the appeal of rock and disco music, but realised that they could not suppress it. Control was exercised over record production and radio airtime, but undermined by the development of the cassette recorder, which was, by the early 1980s, widely available for personal recording and distribution.

By the early 1980s, nonconformity in the cultural sphere had continued to cause the government irritation. Artists and writers continued to use a range of responses to avoid conforming to the role expected of them by the government. Some chose emigration or were forced into exile, others refused to work. However, the Brezhnev years had made it easier to undermine the system by using subtexts in their work. Readers and audiences became skilful at grasping the messages behind the work.

Clashes between artists and the government to 1985

Although cultural restrictions were lessened after 1953, the boundaries of what was permissible were constantly tested by artists and writers. Nonconformity may no longer have automatically resulted in a prison sentence, but clampdowns by the authorities often produced clashes with the government.

Clashes with Khrushchev

The limits of Khrushchev's cultural thaw were shown by the treatment of Boris Pasternak over his novel *Doctor Zhivago*. The book, which was an epic story set during the Russian Civil War, contained criticisms of the Revolution. Soviet publishers were undecided over whether or not it should be published until Khrushchev intervened and, without reading the full text, decided that the book should be banned. However, the novel was smuggled abroad and an edition first appeared in Italy in 1957.

The reception it gained was extremely positive and, to Khrushchev's embarrassment, Pasternak was awarded the 1958 Nobel Prize for Literature. Khrushchev refused to allow Pasternak to travel to Sweden to receive his prize. The whole affair was a cause of international embarrassment for the Soviet government and Khrushchev later regretted his actions.

Abstract art was another area where nonconformity was not encouraged. It was a pet hate of Khrushchev's, as demonstrated in 1962 when he visited the exhibition hall in the Kremlin to view a collection of work by young artists. On seeing the pieces of art, Khrushchev fumed with rage, proclaiming that 'a donkey could smear better art with its tail'. The artists were harangued in full view of the cameras and left the exhibition in fear of arrest and imprisonment. But change had occurred and, despite Khrushchev's fury, no action was taken against the artists.

SOURCE

Khrushchev shows his disapproval when confronted with abstract art at the Manege gallery in Moscow, 1962.

Khrushchev's anger was also aroused by jazz music.

SOURCE

Khrushchev speaking at the 1962 Manege exhibition of art, Moscow.

When I hear jazz it's as if I have gas in my stomach... these new dances which are so fashionable now... You wiggle a certain part of your anatomy... it's indecent.

Komsomol groups were employed to patrol the streets and dance halls to report on young people whose behaviour was deemed unacceptable. In 1961, the government had gone as far as to hold a conference that decided on which dance moves were permissible. Enforcing the decision was a complete failure.

Khrushchev's cultural policy reflected his personality in that it was subject to mood swings. He became less tolerant of nonconformity in his last months as leader and this attitude was entrenched by his successors.

Both boys and girls had equality of access to education and by the 1980s the number of female students continuing to higher education matched that of males. Schools in large urban areas tended to attract better teachers, especially in residential areas occupied by the elite. Thus, education played a key role in perpetuating a Soviet elite.

- **Youth groups**
  These also provided opportunities to mould the young, both boys and girls, into committed communists. Progression from the Octobrists, for those aged five to nine, through the Pioneers (for ages 10 to 14) to Komsomol (for those aged up to 28) was important if you wanted to join the Party and therefore secure better promotion prospects.

- **The provision and range of social security benefits**
  Between 1950 and 1980, state welfare spending increased fivefold. Pensions, maternity benefits and housing all received more attention and did much to relieve poverty. In 1956 the pension scheme for the old, sick and disabled was expanded and the retirement age was reduced. Pensions rose at a higher rate than wages during the Brezhnev period but remained insufficient, for example 40 roubles a month in 1980. This encouraged many to continue to work part-time after reaching retirement age. The armies of street sweepers who cleared the pavements of winter snow were recruited from the elderly. Peasants did not receive a pension until the Brezhnev era.

- **Housing**
  Many Soviet lives were improved by Khrushchev's extensive housing programme. The annual amount of housing space provided by the state increased from 178 million square metres in 1951 to 394 million square metres in 1961. Most of this new housing was provided directly by the state or through co-operatives assisted by government credits. The edges of many Soviet cities resembled building sites, with endless housing blocks erected in a sea of mud. Housing blocks were nicknamed *khrushchoby* (Khrushchev's slums). The housing was based on prefabricated panels built to a standard design. This process helped the speed and cost of building but resulted in drab, uniform housing that was often poorly finished in the rush to meet targets. Occupants often complained that concrete blocks were left inside their apartments and that finishing touches, such as plastering, were left for them to do. Despite these problems, waiting lists for apartments were still long as many had been living in far worse conditions beforehand.

- **Health care**
  There was considerable growth in the provision of health care during the period 1950 to 1980. Availability of health care was not a problem for the Soviet population, but the quality of the provision was much more problematic. Polyclinics provided all-purpose health care in the first instance with referral to specialists where deemed necessary. Many workers made use of these services, partly encouraged by the right to time off work to see a doctor. A Russian tradition was the use of sanatoria, a sort of rest home with medical facilities. In 1978, there were over 2,000 sanatoria and over 1,000 rest homes linked to medical care. Workers were entitled to take time at one of these establishments for a wide range of conditions that included high blood pressure, heart problems and stomach complaints.

Most places were allocated by trade unions. The best medical services were available in Moscow, with Leningrad and other major cities not far behind. Provincial cities had fewer services and those in rural areas were primitive. The Central Asian republics of the USSR were particularly badly served; even as recently as 1988 some hospitals did not have heating or running water. Equipment in most hospitals was poorly made, outdated and often in need of repair.

- **Living conditions in the countryside**
  The increased investment in agriculture, which had occurred under Khrushchev, was continued by Brezhnev. Some of this investment was used to build schools, housing and health services in rural areas. Incomes of collective farmers were increased in 1966 when the government introduced regular wages rather than payment based on a share of the farm's income. By the mid-1970s, the wages of rural workers were only ten percent less than their urban counterparts. Collective farmers could also supplement their wage with the produce from their private plot.

By the 1970s, the majority of the Soviet population were experiencing benefits from the great Soviet experiment. State control over the economy and social welfare provision meant that they had a stake in keeping the system as it was and this helped create the underlying stability of developed socialism.

How stable was society under developed socialism?

With the increase in living standards there had been a rise in the expectations of the Soviet population. These greater expectations provided occasional problems for the government and show that the apparent stability of Soviet society could be undermined.

That the Soviet government feared social instability is shown by its nervous reaction to developments in its **satellite states** in Eastern Europe. There had been an uprising against Soviet rule in Hungary in 1956, which had resulted in Soviet tanks invading the country to maintain communist rule. Soviet military intervention had also been used in Czechoslovakia in 1968 to quell serious unrest. Soviet intervention to deal with popular unrest in Poland was avoided in 1980 when the Polish government declared martial law to prop up the communist regime. The Polish protests were over food prices and echoed many of the issues causing discontent in the Soviet Union itself.

Open protest caused by workers' discontent was rare in the Soviet Union, but it did occur. It was usually caused by changes to living or working conditions but tended to encompass wider aspects of life for which the government could be deemed responsible.

KEY TERM

Satellite state
Those states of Eastern Europe, such as Poland, Czechoslovakia, East Germany, Hungary and Bulgaria, that had communism imposed on them by the USSR after the Second World War. They were tightly controlled through political and economic ties with the USSR.

Evidence of protest

- There was serious unrest in Temirtau in 1959. Temirtau was a new industrial centre in Kazakhstan. The Party had encouraged enthusiastic Komsomol members to flock to the town in order to help build the new metal works. Many responded, but their enthusiasm was quickly dented by the appalling living conditions they were expected to endure, a lack of clean water and few supplies of food. To add insult to injury, they discovered that East German and Polish workers at the site were being paid more. In protest, the young workers burnt down the workplace canteen and hanged the local police chief. KGB troops were used to restore order and several dozen protestors were killed.

- There was a wave of protests over food prices in 1962, when the government increased the price of meat and dairy products. At Novocherkassk, the protests developed into serious unrest when the local factory manager reduced wages at the same time. The workers blamed the government, in particular Khrushchev. Their slogan was 'Cut up Khrushchev for sausages'. At least 70 people were killed before order was restored. The seriousness of the affair was indicated by the fact that members of the *presidium* (Politburo) were sent to the town to investigate. Extra food supplies were rushed to the area to quell further trouble.

- There were strikes and riots over food shortages in Sverdlovsk in 1969 and Gorki in 1980. Unrest over poor housing provision occurred in Kiev in 1969. In each case, the situation tended to escalate due to clumsy actions by the local police before order was finally restored. Incidents like these made the government nervous, but they were spontaneous and improvised demonstrations. The setting up of the Free Trade Union Association in 1977 was different. The association sought to represent the real grievances of Soviet workers rather than them having to rely on the government-controlled, and therefore restricted, trade unions that already existed. The government took action quickly and the organisation's leader, Vladimir Klebanov, was dismissed from his job and evicted from his flat. The point was made: what the state had provided, it could take away. The Association gained little open support and came to nothing.

- Terrorist actions were rare, but not unknown: in 1977, a bomb on the Moscow Metro killed several passengers. In 1969, there was an assassination attempt on Brezhnev when his motorcade was fired at. The assassin fired at the wrong car, killing the driver but leaving Brezhnev untouched. The assassin had no political motive and the official explanation was that he was mentally unstable. These incidents did not indicate a broader revolutionary movement aimed at overthrowing the government.

Soviet society was predominantly stable, but this does not mean that it was without social problems, which had a detrimental effect on social cohesion.

- The Second World War had killed a disproportionate number of young men and that led to a generation growing up without a father figure in the home. The lack of good role models for young men was possibly one of the causes of the high rate of divorce in the Soviet Union. In 1979, the divorce rate was 340 for every 1,000 marriages.

- Alcoholism, especially among men, was a serious problem. Between 1940 and 1980, when the Soviet population grew by 25 percent, alcohol consumption increased by 600 percent. There were an estimated 20 million alcoholics in the USSR in 1987.

- Hooliganism, while never on the scale of that in other countries in the developed world, was a cause of concern. In the 1970s, commuters in Moscow complained about being robbed by young thugs on evening trains. In 1975, the government introduced a one-year course on 'Principles of the Soviet State and Law' to make young Soviet citizens aware of their obligations. The gangs of *stilyagi* (nonconformists) may have been harmless, but their liking for the music of protest and nonconformist fashions worried the older generation.

Thus, beneath the surface of social stability lay social ills that threatened the cohesion of the family and, with it, society as a whole. What also undermined the stability of society in the longer term was the fact that it was based on an increasingly inefficient economic basis. There may have been full employment and considerable provision of social welfare, but it was based on poor productivity and corrupt practices. In the end, this system could not be sustained.

A Level Exam-Style Question Section A

Was the provision of full employment the main reason for social stability in the USSR during the years 1953–85? (20 marks)

Tip

Explain how the government's policy of full employment promoted social stability. What other factors helped create social stability? Give reasons why you think full employment may or may not have been the main reason. Are the factors linked?

ACTIVITY
KNOWLEDGE CHECK

Social stability under developed socialism

1 List the factors that provided stability in Soviet society under the Khrushchev and Brezhnev years.

2 Explain how each of these reasons helped create stability.

3 How far would you agree that Soviet society under developed socialism was stable?

4 Did this stability have any negative consequences?

TO WHAT EXTENT DID THE ROLE OF WOMEN AND THE FAMILY CHANGE BETWEEN 1917 AND 1985?

The **emancipation** of women had been a goal of most Russian radicals since the middle of the 19th century and the position of women was one area where the communists made important developments on coming to power. Lenin had written of the 'bourgeois' nature of marriage as a form of slavery, tying the woman to the male-dominated institution of family. A woman's role as a housewife was perceived as suppression into a life of drudgery. Radical communists called for sweeping reforms to liberate women, but their ideas did not always find favour with more conservative Party members. The circumstances of war and industrialisation meant that the position of women within society did not always improve and, where policies did attempt to bring positive changes, attitudes were often resistant to change. A return to more traditional attitudes to the family after 1935 meant that the liberation of women that radicals had hoped for did not materialise. It marked a move away from the ideals of Lenin.

KEY TERM

Emancipation
The process of setting free groups or individuals. In respect to the role of women, Russian laws before the Bolshevik Revolution had given women a position that was subordinate to men. Russian radicals wanted to change this by giving women greater rights and equality under the law.

TIMELINE FOR WOMEN AND THE FAMILY

1917
Bolsheviks establish Zhenotdel, Women's Department, headed by Alexandra Kollontai
Equal pay for men and women
Divorce is made easier

1918
Soviet Constitution gives men and women equality under the law
Family Code gives women greater rights within marriage

1918–21
Russian civil war: women conscripted into the workplace

1926
'Postcard' divorces allowed

1927
Campaign for the unveiling of women
Unregistered marriages given equal status with registered marriages

1930s
Women enter workforce in large numbers

1936
Stalin's 'Great Retreat': traditional family values reasserted, e.g. abortion banned

1941–45
Women conscripted into factories during Second World War

1944
Further measures to support traditional family values, e.g. tax on single people

1955
Abortion legalised

1957
Ekaterina Furtseva becomes full candidate member of the *presidium* (Politburo), first woman to do so

1968
Family Code places restrictions on divorce

HOW SUCCESSFUL WAS THE SOVIET GOVERNMENT'S ATTEMPTS TO IMPROVE THE PROVISION OF EDUCATION?

Education is often seen as one of the great successes of Soviet social policy: historians have highlighted the enormous expansion of educational provision at all levels and the reduction in illiteracy. Much of this success was achieved in spite of a lack of resources. The Soviet government attached a great deal of significance to education as a transformative force in society and as a method of instilling socialist values and attitudes into the general population from an early age. With the entire educational system in the hands of the state, the Party could exercise control over the curriculum for its own advantage.

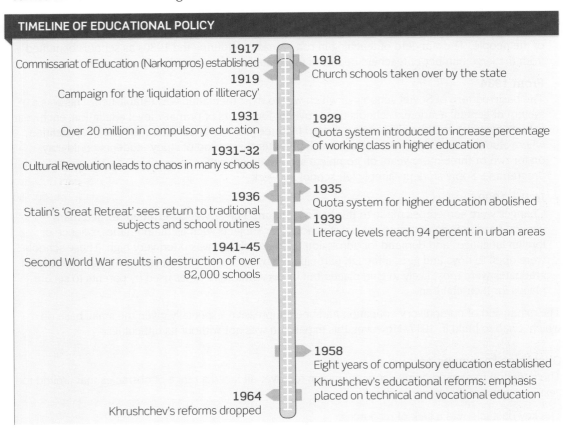

TIMELINE OF EDUCATIONAL POLICY

1917
Commissariat of Education (Narkompros) established

1918
Church schools taken over by the state

1919
Campaign for the 'liquidation of illiteracy'

1931
Over 20 million in compulsory education

1929
Quota system introduced to increase percentage of working class in higher education

1931–32
Cultural Revolution leads to chaos in many schools

1936
Stalin's 'Great Retreat' sees return to traditional subjects and school routines

1935
Quota system for higher education abolished

1939
Literacy levels reach 94 percent in urban areas

1941–45
Second World War results in destruction of over 82,000 schools

1958
Eight years of compulsory education established

Khrushchev's educational reforms: emphasis placed on technical and vocational education

1964
Khrushchev's reforms dropped

The growth of primary, secondary and higher education

Education in Tsarist Russia had been largely limited to the rich, especially at secondary and university level. Technical schools aimed at the children of the middle class were small in number and confined to the larger cities. At primary level, many schools were provided by the Russian Orthodox Church and there were several thousand peasant-run schools, but for many children school was not considered an important part of their life. The Tsarist government never made school attendance compulsory and many of those who did attend school dropped out before completing four years. In rural areas, 88 percent of children failed to complete primary education. In this context, the progress made by the Soviet government was all the more impressive.

The expansion of compulsory education
- **Under Lunachevsky**
  In 1917, control of education was given to the Commissariat of Education (*Narkompros*), headed by Anatoly Lunachevsky, and the Bolsheviks launched an ambitious programme to provide free, universal and compulsory education for all children aged 7 to 17, with a simultaneous expansion in higher education. In 1918, existing church schools were taken over by the government and education at primary and secondary level was based on the comprehensive model: schools took children of all abilities and all received the same education, at least until the last few years of secondary level provision.

The aim of universal compulsory education did not materialise during Lunachevsky's lifetime due to the lack of resources caused by the civil war of 1918–21. *Narkompros* could only supply one pencil for every 60 students. Shortages left students using pieces of coal to write with. Teachers were poorly paid and often expected to teach classes of 40 or more as well as devote unpaid time to cleaning the school. Conditions were not conducive to a good educational experience and drop-out rates were very high. In 1926, the average child had only attended school for 2.77 years.

- **During the 1930s**
  The goal of providing universal compulsory education was largely achieved, particularly in urban areas. The number of children in education increased from 14 million in 1929 to over 20 million in 1931. Nonetheless, most school children failed to continue their education beyond the first two years of secondary education. The 1930s saw access to education extended to children of 'alien social elements', that is, those whose parents were from the aristocracy, bourgeoisie or 'enemies of the people'. The standard of teaching in rural areas rose during the 1930s as schools benefited from the large number of teachers deported to isolated areas during the Great Terror.

- **From 1934**
  The basic pattern of Soviet schooling, which was to exist thereafter, was established. This was a system of general academic schools that provided four years of primary-level education, each year with its own class teacher. This was followed by three years of 'incomplete secondary education', where students were taught by subject teachers. After this period of study, students could stay on for two or three more years of 'complete secondary education' or transfer to a vocational programme. Some students simply left school for work.

- **In the 1980s**
  Changes were sometimes made to this basic structure. The Soviet government turned many general academic schools into specialist schools, for subjects such as mathematics, science or foreign languages and demand for admission to these schools was often very high. These schools were open to boys and girls, although participation by girls tended to decline with age. Children of graduates were most likely to gain places, but bribery was sometimes used by parents to secure places for their children.

The expansion of compulsory education had been impressive, especially given the small base on which it had to build in 1917. However, this expansion was not without its difficulties.

Obstacles to expansion
The intention to expand compulsory education to cover all faced a range of obstacles that limited the best intentions of the government.

The key obstacle was a lack of resources.

- In the 1920s, this was largely a consequence of the impact of the civil war, but it remained a limiting factor thereafter. Under the NEP, state spending on schools declined and the numbers attending school shrank, only recovering at the end of the 1920s. The lack of resources meant that many schools closed during the winter because there was no heating. It was not only economic resources that were in short supply.

- Low wages discouraged many people from entering the teaching profession, as did the low status attached to teachers in the 1920s. Rural schools were especially affected by a lack of teachers, poor teaching and inadequate facilities.

- School transport was underfunded and, until 1965, the cost had to be borne by parents.

- In 1940, tuition fees, albeit low, had been introduced for the last years of secondary education. These fees were withdrawn in 1956, after which no fees were required to attend either primary or secondary education. However, parents were expected to pay for textbooks, individual equipment and uniforms. For poor rural families, these costs could force children to leave school before the final years of secondary education.

- Resources were also severely stretched by the impact of the Second World War. A large number of teachers were killed in action, and 82,000 schools were physically destroyed in the fighting. Post-war recovery was difficult. Many schools worked a two- or even three-shift day to cope with the lack of classrooms.

- By 1951, the government felt able to move forward with further expansion. The Fifth Five-Year Plan (1951–55) set a target of implementing a ten-year compulsory education for urban schools by 1955 and rural schools by 1960. This proved to be over-optimistic and, after 1958, schools delivered an eight-year programme of compulsory education (ages 7 to 15), after which students could choose to attend a further two years of academic education, transfer to a vocational college or go directly into the workplace.

Traditional attitudes towards the importance of education were often hard to overcome. Attendance at rural schools was often problematic, especially at harvest time. Khrushchev was concerned about the different levels of education experienced by rural children compared with those who lived in towns and implemented a programme of affirmative action. This involved collective farmers being sent to colleges for specialised education and reserving college places for those who had two years of work experience on collectives. These policies failed to have much impact before they were withdrawn after Khrushchev's dismissal in 1964. Even when competing for places at colleges specialising in agricultural sciences, students from a rural background remained at a disadvantage. Two-thirds of students came from urban schools and possessed good academic qualifications. Rural customs remained difficult to break: in 1981, a head teacher from a school in Kirghizstan complained in *Pravda* that his students never turned up for the new school term until November.

Cultural influences also played a part in limiting the expansion of education. State education was viewed by many from the ethnic minorities as a vehicle for **Russification**. All schoolchildren had to learn Russian, even if other subjects were taught in the ethnic language of the region. Teachers were usually Russian and were often regarded with suspicion by minority communities. In Muslim areas, women teachers commanded very little respect. Cultural attitudes also limited the number of Muslim women entering the higher levels of secondary education. In the Uzbek Republic in 1955, girls made up only 26 percent of the school population in the final two years of secondary education.

Actions by the government in areas of policy other than education could have a negative impact on schooling. The forced collectivisation of agriculture after 1928 removed many teachers from village schools. They were often seen as elements of the 'old world' to be swept away in the name of socialist progress. Many were labelled as kulaks and deported to labour camps. This trend was accelerated during the chaos caused by the Cultural Revolution of 1931–32. Education in many rural areas was brought to a standstill as attacks on 'bourgeois' elements saw many teachers removed from schools. Students keen to see the back of unpopular teachers informed on them to Party officials. The result was that some schools ended up with no teachers at all.

Attempts to expand education, especially at secondary level, were aimed at helping the creation of a classless society, but changes were often limited or influenced by a Soviet elite, which preferred a system that separated their children from those of the masses. An academic education (rather than a technical or vocational one) that involved the completion of secondary schooling remained the desired route for those who wished their children to better themselves. This academic route may have been open to all, but the reality was that it remained dominated by the children of a white-collar and managerial elite.

Adult education

When the Bolsheviks took power they were aware that they were dealing with a population where most adults had not received a secondary education. Therefore, the government recognised that there was a need to address the educational needs of its adults as well as its children. Short courses were offered to teach adults basic literacy and numeracy, and evening classes were offered to those in work.

Khrushchev's background as a former **rabfak** student made him appreciate the importance of providing opportunities for those who had dropped out of education at an early age. Under his leadership, there was an expansion in opportunities to enable others to return to education as part-time or correspondence students. By 1964, over two million were attending such courses.

By the 1970s, adults could continue their education through an extensive programme of adult education. Diplomas and degrees were offered by vocational colleges and provided a useful strategy for updating workers' skills as well as offering a route to higher education for those who had dropped out of secondary school early. By the 1980s, such courses were sometimes supported by television and radio programmes. These courses were usually studied part-time in the evenings, which put additional demands on the worker. Correspondence courses were also popular, again a sign that many saw education as a way of securing a more fulfilling job and improving their status.

KEY TERM

Russification
The policy of imposing Russian language and culture on the ethnic minorities of the USSR in order to provide a greater sense of unity throughout the country.

KEY TERM

Rabfak
Schools set up after the Bolshevik Revolution to teach basic literacy and numeracy to those who had dropped out of education.

The suddenness of the collapse suggests that short-term factors played the dominant role, but it would seem that any one of these need not have been catastrophic for the USSR. It was the combination of these factors working together that produced the process of unravelling that broke the Soviet system. The links between these factors and their relative importance have formed the main focus of debate between historians.

Figure 5.1 The 15 republics of the USSR in 1985.

March 1989 – Elections to Congress of People's Deputies

April 1989 – Demonstrations in Tbilisi, Georgia

May 1989 – Gorbachev elected Chairman of the Supreme Soviet

March 1990 – Article 6 repealed: way opened for new political parties to be established

March 1990 – Lithuania proclaims independence from the USSR

July 1990 – Yeltsin resigns from the Communist Party

1989 1990 1991

October 1989 – 500 Days Programme calls for rapid transition to a market economy

Nov 1989 – Fall of the Berlin Wall

April 1991 – Georgia declares independence

June 1991 – Yeltsin becomes President of Russia

August 1991 – Coup by conservatives in the Party attempts to seize power Soviet Union recognises independence of the Baltic States

November 1991 – Yeltsin rejects Gorbachev's new Union Treaty

December 1991 – Dissolution of the USSR

EVALUATING INTERPRETATIONS OF HISTORY

Historians are concerned with more than merely describing the course of past events; they aim to explain why events happened. It is at this level that engaging with the past becomes really interesting. Historians approach the past in different ways, often with their own perspective on what drives change forward. Are individuals important in the big scheme of history? Do their intentions and actions shape the course of history? Other historians see individuals as less influential in determining events. Are individuals prisoners of their circumstances with very limited room for manoeuvre? These philosophical debates often underpin the way that historians consider the past.

Although historians may come to a topic with a particular perspective, their aim is to form an interpretation of events that is convincing because it can be supported by evidence. But evidence can be found in a range of forms and with varying degrees of value. This range includes accounts by individuals involved in events and statistical evidence of economic performance. All types of evidence needs to be subjected to the analytical skills of the historian.

The issue of what caused the collapse of the Soviet Union is subject to these issues of interpretation and has generated a range of views. When considering these interpretations, it is important to think about the following features:

- What is the perspective of the historian?

- How does the historian develop their interpretation?

- What evidence does the historian use to support their interpretation?

- Do you find their interpretation valid? Do you accept the judgements they make based on the evidence they use?

It is important to distinguish fact from opinion. There is nothing wrong with opinion – it would be a dull historian who did not have one! But opinions need to be supported and be convincing.

 THINKING HISTORICALLY Interpretations (5a)

What I believe is how I see

Below are three descriptions of the perspectives of very famous historians.

Herodotus	Leopold von Ranke	Karl Marx
• His research consisted of conversations • Identified that accounts had to be judged on their merits • Some believe that certain passages in his writing are inventions to complete the narrative	• Believed in an evidence-based approach and relied heavily on primary sources • Desired to find out the 'facts' and discover the connections between them • Stressed the role of the individual in shaping history	• Believed that history would go through stages leading to a state where everybody was equal • Believed that historical changes were ultimately determined by changes to the economy • Often driven by political considerations and looked for evidence to support his point of view

Work in groups of between three and six. Each member or pair will take the perspective of one of the above historians and argue from that perspective. Work through the questions as a group and answer the last one individually.

1 Herodotus did not use written evidence to construct his history. Does this mean that his history is less useful than the others?

2 Ranke based his writing almost exclusively on primary sources from the time he was investigating, rather than secondary sources. How might this affect his ability to see larger patterns in history as opposed to the other two?

3 Marx put his philosophy of history, and perhaps politics, first and research second. Would this make his history weaker than the others?

4 'Colourful' individuals populate the writing of Herodotus and Ranke, while Marx concentrates on the difference between classes. Write three historical questions that each historian might ask.

5 The three historians mentioned above all had different methods and motivations and yet their writing has been valued ever since it was created. Explain how the prior knowledge that we bring to the history that we write does not invalidate it.

HOW IMPORTANT WERE ECONOMIC WEAKNESSES IN BRINGING ABOUT THE FALL OF THE USSR?

The Soviet government had justified its legitimacy to rule by demonstrating its ability to meet the material needs of its people. This principle had become more important with the reduction in terror after 1953: the acquiescence of the population was based on the government ensuring the provision of their material and welfare needs. But this could only be achieved if the Soviet economy performed well enough to deliver these.

Long-term economic weakness

When Gorbachev became General Secretary in 1985, the Soviet economy was in decline. The weaknesses of the Soviet economic system had been highlighted in the Novosibirsk Report of 1983. Compiled by the leading economic sociologist, Tatyana Zaslavskaya, the report drew attention to the growing crisis in agriculture caused by state inefficiency and inflexibility. The report, which was known by its heading 'For internal use only', was distributed to the Politburo, but most of its ageing members did not understand the conclusions of the report or simply chose to ignore them. The exception was Gorbachev, who realised that reform was needed. He was less clear about the solution required. A period of trial and error followed, which ended with the dismantling of the Soviet economic system, and the result was to plunge the economy into disruption and chaos. Without the economic underpinning needed to sustain an improvement in the lives of the population, the Soviet government was placed in a weak and vulnerable position.

Gorbachev's initial economic reforms: discipline and acceleration

Gorbachev's initial steps were cautious and began with the positioning of like-minded reformers into key positions. One of his main rivals in the Politburo, Grigory Romanov, was dismissed in July 1985. Key reformers were brought into the Politburo: Yegor Ligachev and Nikolai Ryzhkov. Boris Yeltsin (the First Secretary of the Party in Moscow) and Alexander Yakovlev (both of whom were leading figures in the push for reform) were promoted to the Central Committee in 1986.

Gorbachev was now ready to launch reforms that would improve the economy. His initial approach echoed that of his mentor, Andropov. There was a campaign to attack the problem of rampant alcoholism. As well as improving the health of the Soviet population, the campaign against alcohol would help improve the productivity of the Soviet workforce. By the mid-1980s, alcohol accounted for 15 percent of all household spending. This was partly explained by the lack of other goods in the shops but, whatever the cause, it had a detrimental effect on the workforce, many of whom regularly turned up to work drunk. As Gorbachev put it in a statement in April 1985, 'We can't build Communism on vodka.'

The government introduced a series of measures to curb drinking: the legal age for the consumption of alcohol was raised to 21; the number of retail outlets where alcohol could be bought was reduced; vineyards were destroyed and distilleries closed. The cost of vodka in the shops tripled. The campaign produced some benefits, at least at first, but the tax revenues that the government gained from alcohol fell markedly and caused a serious shortfall in the budget. Drinking levels started to rise after a while as illegal moonshine liquor was produced in large quantities and often in unhygienic conditions. It soon became clear that relying on the workforce to become more disciplined and sober would not solve the underlying problems of the Soviet economy.

Twelfth Five-Year Plan

The key issue remained of how to improve the level of growth in the economy. The government fell back on the traditional Soviet method of increasing investment, controlled by central planning, to push the economy to greater production. It was hoped that this would accelerate growth in the economy. The focus of investment would be science and research, especially in engineering. This approach was to be implemented through the Twelfth (and last) Five-Year Plan (1986–90). The Plan, like Soviet planning before it, contained key weaknesses.

- Investment in the Soviet Union was heavily skewed towards construction projects, but these had a habit of leading to extra spending which was needed to equip the factories constructed. Therefore these projects tended to lead to overspends and sucked in far more investment than originally intended.

- Soviet industry had become notorious for using equipment that was out of date and prone to breaking down. Old factories relied on old equipment and became increasingly unproductive.

- Soviet industry was slow to use new technology, and imports of foreign technology were a drain on valuable foreign exchange, which was often used to import food.

- The agricultural sector was swallowing vast sums of investment that were not leading to improvements in productivity. The government had reached the point where it realised that there was little to be gained in terms of production growth from diverting additional sums to agriculture.

- The focus remained on quantity rather than quality. The traditional Soviet emphasis on meeting numerical targets meant that the quality was often poor, sometimes so poor the products were unusable.

Thus, Gorbachev's policy of acceleration did little to address the fundamental weaknesses of the Soviet economy. Part of the problem was the level of opposition to any real change and the fact that much of this opposition came from the Party and state economic planning apparatus. In June 1986, Gorbachev admitted, 'Take Gosplan… What they want, they do.'

Under the Twelfth Five-Year Plan, Gorbachev tried to streamline the state apparatus in an attempt to avoid waste through duplication and to cut rivalry by competing interests for available resources. Rather than decentralise economic decision-making, 'superministries' were set up to achieve better co-ordination of economic activity and reduce waste. However, the superministries were unable to bring about these changes.

Interpretations of Gorbachev's failure to bring about political reform

Historians are generally agreed that the failure of Gorbachev to reform the Communist Party damaged his authority and that of the Party, but there is less agreement over whether this left him severely weakened. Western historians have generally viewed Gorbachev's political reforms as well-meaning although unlikely to have ever brought success. So-called 'essentialist' historians take the view that communism and the Communist Party were impossible to reform because they were, in essence, incapable of producing anything other than a totalitarian state, where freedom was not allowed and a one-party state could only be sustained through force. More recent research has questioned the inevitability of failure, viewing Gorbachev's political reforms as potentially workable, but undermined by both conservatives and liberals within the Party.

EXTRACT

From O. Figes, *Revolutionary Russia 1891–1991,* published in 2014.

To explain the speed with which it all collapsed, we need to look, not at the structural problems of the Soviet Union, but the way the regime unravelled from the top. There was no pressing need for the radical restructuring of the system. If there was a 'crisis', it was in the minds of Gorbachev and other reformers who sensed it in the growing divergence between Soviet realities and socialist ideals. It was Gorbachev's reforms that brought about the real crisis: the disintegration of the Party's power and authority. The conceptual revolution begun by glasnost allowed people to question the regime and demand an alternative.

Glasnost was the really revolutionary element of the Gorbachev reforms, the means by which the system unravelled ideologically. The Soviet leader intended it to bring transparency to government and break the power-hold of the Brezhnevite conservatives opposed to his reforms... But the consequences of glasnost quickly spiralled beyond Gorbachev's control.

By relaxing censorship, glasnost meant that the Party lost its grip on the mass media, which exposed social problems previously concealed by the government (poor housing, criminality, ecological catastrophes, etc.), thereby undermining public confidence in the Soviet system.

EXTRACT

6

An interpretation of Gorbachev by historian Dmitri Volkogonov, from *The Rise and Fall of the Soviet Empire*, published in 1998. Volkogonov was a member of the Soviet army's Political Administration and had access to the Soviet leadership. After August 1991, he became one of Boris Yeltsin's advisers.

[Gorbachev] wanted to restructure 'everything' without touching the socialist foundations of state ownership, the Party's 'leading role', and the regime's Communist goals. It is not hard to see that these goals were not attainable. To restructure everything, and yet to leave intact the foundations laid by Lenin, was a logical impossibility. The Communist system was not reformable. Either it exists, or it does not. This was something that Gorbachev, who was after all General Secretary of the Communist Party, either could not or did not want to understand.

... He began a process of democratic reforms over which he soon lost control. The culmination of perestroika, despite his intentions, was the total disintegration of the Communist system. It was not Gorbachev who brought this about; but he did nothing to prevent it from happening. The events which he launched developed according to their own logic and in complete disregard of the command mentality of the Central Committee.

AS Level Exam-Style Question Section C

Study Extracts 5 and 6 before you answer this question.

Historians have different views about the reasons for the fall of the Soviet Union. Analyse and evaluate the extracts and use your knowledge of the issues to explain your answer to the following question.

How far do you agree with the view that the collapse of the Soviet Union came about because Gorbachev failed to reform the Communist Party? (20 marks)

Tip

Remember you are assessing different interpretations. Integrate your own knowledge with the material in the extracts so that you test the validity of their interpretations. Note that the focus of the question is on 'the failure of Gorbachev's reform programme'. Do not forget to make reference to the extracts in your answer. Make sure you come to a reasoned judgement of your own.

WHAT IMPACT DID THE RESURGENCE OF NATIONALISM PLAY IN THE COLLAPSE OF THE USSR?

The Soviet Union had contained a large number of different nationalities besides Russians, as recognised in part by the fact that the Union was divided into 15 different republics and many republics contained semi-autonomous regions. When the Soviet Union collapsed it was replaced by 15 different independent states, a fact that in itself implies that nationalism may have played a large role in bringing about the end of the Soviet Union. The pattern of events tells a rather different story.

The ending of the Brezhnev Doctrine

Soviet control over Eastern Europe had been enforced by military action under what became known as the Brezhnev Doctrine. This Doctrine had been formulated after the Soviet intervention in Czechoslovakia in 1968 to prevent the Czech communist government introducing liberal reforms in response to popular protests. Brezhnev had made it clear that, 'Whenever internal and external forces hostile to Socialism try to reverse the development of a Socialist country towards the restoration of capitalism … this becomes the concern of all Socialist countries.' The threat of a Soviet intervention had played an important role in the Polish government's response to popular protests in 1980–81. In order to avoid a Soviet invasion, the leader of the communist government in Poland, General Jarulzelski, imposed martial law. The unrest was suppressed. However, Gorbachev decided that he would not uphold the right of the USSR to intervene in the affairs of other socialist countries.

The funeral of the Soviet leader, Konstantin Chernenko, in March 1985 provided the new General Secretary, Gorbachev, with the opportunity to meet every leader of the communist regimes of Eastern Europe. Each in turn was informed by Gorbachev that he would not intervene in their internal affairs. They were free to choose their own path of socialism.

Supporting satellite states had become increasingly expensive. The USSR spent approximately $40 billion annually on propping up communist governments around the world. This money could be used to promote domestic reform. Gorbachev hoped that many would follow his lead in economic reforms. He had a genuine belief that this was the way to rejuvenate socialism. Gorbachev refused to use force to keep the population under control. He believed the use of armed intervention was, in most cases, morally wrong. Instead of seeing foreign policy as a tool of class struggle against the forces of capitalism, Gorbachev focused on universal values of human rights to promote the interests of all peoples. The end of the Brezhnev Doctrine meant the peoples of Eastern Europe could choose their own governments. The consequences of this change were to be spectacular.

The consequences of the ending of the Brezhnev Doctrine in Eastern Europe

Gorbachev's reforms in the USSR led to attempts by some governments in Eastern Europe to reform in response to the new Soviet lead, as well as increasing the pressure for change from the public. Much of this pressure was driven by nationalist sentiments: communist rule had been imposed on Eastern Europe after the Second World War and was associated with Soviet control. Now there was an opportunity for each nation to decide its own future. This trend gathered momentum and the pace of events took many by surprise. Those governments that resisted these trends became quickly isolated.

The ending of the Brezhnev Doctrine posed a particular problem for those Eastern European leaders who wanted to resist reform. They could no longer rely on Soviet military intervention to buttress their regimes. Evidence that Gorbachev meant what he said came in 1989 when Hungary adopted a multiparty system and Polish elections returned a non-communist government. The USSR took no action; Gorbachev even offered his encouragement. The result was the collapse of communist regimes in Eastern Europe as national groups asserted their independence.

Poland

In Poland the communist government yielded to pressure from the independent workers' organisation, Solidarity, in 1989 and decided to allow it and any other political groups to stand in elections. In the general elections that followed, Solidarity was able to defeat the Communist Party in a landslide victory. In the face of this lack of support, the Communist Party collapsed as an organisation.

The USSR had done nothing to stop these events happening, indeed Gorbachev seemed to approve of the Poles deciding on their own future.

The message was clear to all those pressing for change in other east European states: the USSR no longer had any wish to impose itself on the internal affairs of Eastern Europe.

The communist collapse spreads

Hungary

In Hungary the pressure for reform came from within the Communist Party, and in 1988 Janos Kadar, the hardline leader since 1956, was sacked. The government, now dominated by reformers, decided to allow other political parties to contest elections.

East Germany

The end of the Brezhnev Doctrine was of particular concern to the East German regime. The creation of East Germany had been a result of superpower tension and hostility after the Second World War. As an artificial country, East Germany was more reliant on Soviet support than the other regimes of the region. Gorbachev's visit to East Berlin in October 1989 encouraged those who wished to push for reforms. With mass demonstrations on the streets of East German cities, the pressure for reform became unstoppable. Egon Krenz, who became East German leader in October 1989, refused to sanction widespread repression and, amid the growing chaos, decided to open access across the Berlin Wall. On 9 November, the Berlin Wall, the symbol of Cold War Europe, was dismantled by 'people power'.

Czechoslovakia

Also in November 1989, the communist regime in Czechoslovakia was forced to make concessions in response to public demonstrations calling for reforms. An organisation called Civic Forum emerged to co-ordinate the campaign to get rid of the communist government. Under severe public pressure, the communists caved in, reforms were introduced, and in December 1989 Václav Havel, a leading playwright and opponent of communism, was elected President.

Romania

Romania was afflicted by the weaknesses seen elsewhere: a discontented population tired of food shortages, a lack of consumer goods, a repressive government and a lack of real democracy. When demonstrations against the communist government started at the end of 1989, support for the regime collapsed. Nicolae Ceaușescu, Romania's leader, used the army to open fire on the demonstrators, but this merely increased the unpopularity of the regime. By December even the army was unwilling to support Ceaușescu and he was forced to flee Bucharest by helicopter. His arrest and subsequent execution on Christmas Day sealed the end of communism in Romania.

The impact of the collapse of communist regimes in Eastern Europe

In June 1979, Pope John Paul II had visited Poland. During his visit, he had addressed those living under communist rule with the words, 'Do not be afraid.' His words encouraged those who sought change. Nationalism had played a significant role in mobilising people power against Soviet-imposed communism. Where people power had been less significant, such as in Hungary and Bulgaria, reformers within the ranks of the Communist Parties had taken the lead in asserting national independence. Across Eastern Europe, the forces of communism had collapsed. It had been a swift and largely peaceful process, with the exceptions of Romania and Yugoslavia, where a bloody civil war accompanied the break-up of the country.

By the end of 1989, every pro-Soviet communist government in Eastern Europe had disintegrated. The role of Gorbachev was vital in changing the context in which these regimes operated. Gorbachev's foreign policy was, therefore, a key factor in encouraging the assertion of independence by the satellite states. This trend was to have an impact on the different nationalities within the Soviet Union.

ACTIVITY
KNOWLEDGE CHECK

The collapse of communism in Eastern Europe
The year 1989 was very exciting to live through. How might the events in Eastern Europe influence the perspective of historians writing about communism?

SOURCE

6 British Ambassador Rodric Braithwaite's telegram from 19 August 1991.

[The next few days] will determine whether Russia is relapsing into sullen acquiescence or that she is once again entering a time of troubles, as our friends here have so long feared. I do not think that this is foregone, even though what has already happened is far more ominous, far-reaching and potentially bloody, than the events in Lithuania in January. But whatever now happens, the prescriptions for policy are much the same now as they were in the winter... The difference is, of course, that last January we could signify our support for 'Gorbachev the Reformer,' and hope to influence the man. It may be a long time before another such figure appears in Russia to catch the imagination and personify the hopes of foreigners. And Moscow already resounds to the keening of liberal intellectuals who now regret that they did not support Gorbachev while he was still there.

The coup lasted four days. It had been poorly planned and implemented without the whole-hearted backing of the armed forces. The leaders of the coup were unsure how to proceed.

EXTRACT

11 An interpretation by Peter Kenez, from *A History of the Soviet Union from Beginning to End* (2006).

The putschists [plotters] accomplished the opposite of what they had intended: by their actions they demonstrated there was no force behind them, and that the old order could not be reconstructed. Their press conference, in which they allowed themselves to be ridiculed and showed themselves to be helpless, drunken and fearful men, was a demonstration of the bankruptcy of the old order. Although the regime managed to hold on for four more months, this ill-considered conspiracy was the real end of the Soviet era...

THINKING HISTORICALLY Change (4a)

Significance

Look at the two accounts of the August Coup in the Soviet Union in 1991 (Source 6 and Extract 11).

1 In what ways does British Ambassador Rodric Braithwaite think that the coup might be significant?

2 How significant does Braithwaite seem to think the coup might be in the long run?

3 Compare this to historian Peter Kenez's interpretation. What significance does Kenez ascribe to the August Coup of 1991?

4 Why do you think these views might differ so greatly?

The key impacts of the August Coup on developments were as follows.

- Yeltsin's stand against the plotters greatly enhanced his reputation as a defender of freedom and reform. His demand that Gorbachev be released from house arrest and returned to his position as President of the USSR had the advantage of making his stance seem less like he was using the coup as an opportunity for self-seeking publicity.

- Emboldened by his enhanced position after the failure of the August Coup, Yeltsin quickly introduced a series of measures that speeded up the collapse of the Soviet Union. He launched a programme of market reform in the economy. By the summer of 1991, the monopoly of the Communist Party had been legally ended, and Yeltsin and other reformers from the Communist Party were free to establish the Democratic Reform Movement as a political party. In November he banned the Communist Party of the Soviet Union within Russia.

- Yeltsin then undermined the new Union Treaty. It is doubtful whether the Union Treaty would have survived after the August Coup. The plot had shown the dangers of action by conservatives in the Soviet government. An opportunity to finally kill the Treaty was presented when Ukrainian President Leonid Kravchuk refused to sign it and asked for further negotiations. Yeltsin decided to follow suit in November. In its place, Yeltsin organised the Commonwealth of Independent States, a much looser arrangement that required no central Soviet government. When this was implemented in December 1991, the Soviet Union was no more.

SOURCE 7

Yeltsin outside the White House, the Russian Parliament building in Moscow, during the August Coup, 1991. He personally confronted the soldiers in the tanks and asked them to return to their barracks.

ACTIVITY
KNOWLEDGE CHECK

1 List the strengths and weaknesses of both Gorbachev and Yeltsin as leaders.

2 Who do you think was most responsible for bringing about the collapse of the USSR? Explain your answer.

ACTIVITY
WRITING

Gorbachev and Yeltsin

Use the words in the list below to complete the sentences so that they best describe the issues facing Gorbachev and Yeltsin.

> fundamental; ingrained; superficial; integral; endeavoured; entrenched

Gorbachev found it difficult to address the economic weaknesses of the Soviet Union. Corruption and nepotism were .... in the system. They had become so .... that they were considered key features of the regime. When he attempted to reform the Party, these problems were to pose an enormous challenge. Gorbachev .... to bring life back into the system, but, at heart, socialism remained .... to his vision of the Soviet Union. For Yeltsin, reform was impossible; the changes required would need to be more .... than ....

Interpretations of Yeltsin's role in the collapse of the Soviet Union

Interpretations of Yeltsin's role have varied depending on the personal view of the writer towards the more liberal reforms Yeltsin put forward. His supporters saw him as the leader who had the solutions to the problems of his time. Yet as leader of Russia after the collapse of the Soviet Union, Yeltsin was unable to deal effectively with the economic problems that faced Gorbachev. As the years have passed, interpretations of Yeltsin have been less kind to him. They have focused on the following issues.

- Was Yeltsin more interested in his own power than principles? Was Yeltsin prepared to sacrifice the Soviet Union for the sake of boosting his own political position?

- Did Yeltsin control events or simply make use of them? Divisions between conservatives and reformers would have existed without Yeltsin. Nationalist movements in the non-Russian republics did not rely on Yeltsin for the growth in their support. However, Yeltsin was extremely well placed to take advantage of Gorbachev's weakness and the growing fragility of the Soviet Union to deliver the final blow.

EXTRACT

12

An interpretation of Boris Yeltsin by Vitaly Tretiakov, head of the weekly paper, *Moskosvskiie Novosti* (2006, No. 4–6).

... Despised by the majority of citizens in the country, Yeltsin will go down in history as ... having corrupted (the country) to the breaking point, not by his virtues and or by his defects, but rather by his dullness, primitiveness, and unbridled power lust of a hooligan...

EXTRACT

13

An interpretation by George W. Breslauer, in an article, 'Evaluating Gorbachev and Yeltsin as Leaders', in A. Brown and L. Shevtsova (eds), *Gorbachev, Yeltsin and Putin*, published in 2001.

During 1988–1991, Boris Yeltsin established himself as the hero of the anti-communist opposition to Soviet rule. After his overwhelming electoral victories of March 1989 and June 1991, followed by his facing down of the coup plotters in August 1991, his authority at home and abroad had become legendary. He had evolved into a charismatic leader of almost mythic proportions, especially among those who had assumed that the Soviet and communist control structures were unassailable. Thus, as an oppositional leader, Yeltsin is likely to go down in History as a uniquely courageous and effective figure who managed to prevail against seemingly overwhelming odds...

Moreover, his success during 1990–1991 in decoupling the concept of 'Russian' from that of 'Soviet' was both intellectually and politically inspired, as was his insistence in March 1991 that Russia choose a president by popular election for the first time in its thousand-year history. Yeltsin was a revolutionary hero who achieved what he did through his extraordinary personal traits...

Those who approve of Yeltsin's role in destroying the communist and soviet systems acclaim his leadership in this period, while those who disapprove of these ends censure him accordingly. But neither side would contest the observation, which is value-neutral, that Yeltsin was, in his leadership role, an 'event-making man'.

 THINKING HISTORICALLY   Interpretations (4b)

Method is everything

Bad history	Extract 1	Good history
• Based on gut feeling • Argument does not progress logically • No supporting evidence	*An except from a history book with quotes making a point about an event*	• Based on an interpretation of evidence • Argument progresses logically • Evidence deployed to support argument

Work in pairs.

Historical writing can reveal much about the methods by which it was constructed. Read Extracts 12 and 13 and answer the questions.

1 Look carefully at the spectrum of methodology above.

　a) Where would you place each source on the spectrum of historical practice?

　b) What evidence would you use to support your choice?

2 Look at Extract 12. How would you change it to make it the same quality of historical writing as Extract 13?

3 Use a dictionary. Explain the following words in their relation to historical writing: substantiation, deduction, inference, cross-reference.

4 How important is it that historians understand and evaluate the methods used by other historians?

The Second World War put additional demands on women. Women took over jobs previously held by men who had been conscripted into the Red Army. Women also joined the Red Army; 800,000 women served in the armed forces during the Second World War, most in medical units, but also as pilots, machine-gunners and tank crews. Eighty-nine women received the Soviet Union's highest military award, Hero of the Soviet Union. Although many women were removed from their jobs after the war when the men returned to civilian life, women were beginning to be seen in a different light. The line between what was considered to be male and female work was now blurred, far more so than in the developed capitalist countries of the West. This marked a change in how women were seen in the workplace.

> This section is still taking a chronological approach, but there is some awareness of 'change'. A better approach would have been to start the paragraph with the sentence, 'Traditional views of the status of women started to break down during the Second World War.'

By the 1950s, the status of women had changed a lot since 1917. Women were expected to work and could do so in a wide range of occupations. The government had taken the lead in this change by directing women into work during times of war and to support the programme of rapid industrialisation of the Five-Year Plans. Yet change was not always positive for women. Life remained harsh and women were still expected to play the key role in looking after the home and providing for the husband and children. This double burden put considerable pressure on women and made career progression difficult. The Bolshevik Party may have promoted the ideology of gender equality, but the reality was that policy towards women was decided on the basis of practicality rather than equality. The fact that there were only seven women on the Central Committee of the Party before the Second World War reflected the fact that men dominated the Party.

> This section is better because it is starting to address the issue of change more explicitly. It would be even better if it explored the issue of changing status by looking at different groups of women. This answer is weakened because it tends to assume that all women experienced the same changes.

Thus, the status of women had changed since 1917. Traditional attitudes had broken down and, although the ideas of gender equality promoted by Alexandra Kollontai proved to be rather idealistic, many of the changes to women's lives raised their status and role in Soviet society.

> The concluding paragraph makes a judgement that is relevant, but it lacks reasoning to make this judgement convincing. The judgement needs to be explored more to nail the point.

Verdict

This is an average answer because:

- it lacks a direct focus on the key words 'status' and 'change' in the question
- it adopts a descriptive, chronological approach
- it does not come to a strong reasoned judgement
- the analysis is generalised.

Use the feedback on this answer to rewrite it, making as many improvements as you can.

Paper 1: AS Level sample answer with comments

Section B

These questions assess your understanding of the course in breadth and will cover a period of 30 years or more. They will ask you about the content you learned about in the four key themes, and may ask about more than one theme. The questions will also require you to explore a range of concepts, such as change over time, similarity and difference, as well as significance. For these questions remember to:

- identify the focus of the question
- consider the concepts you will need to explore
- support your points with evidence from across the time period specified in the question
- develop the evidence you deploy to build up your overall judgement
- come to a substantiated judgement that directly addresses the question set.

How far did the status of women in Soviet society change between 1917 and the death of Stalin in 1953? (20 marks)

Strong student answer

Alexander Samokhalov's famous poster of 'Woman Metro builder with pneumatic drill' gives an image of a strong, powerful female worker, taking an active role in the building of socialism. This image, although propaganda, signalled the change that had occurred during Stalin's rule to the status of many women. It was starkly different from the traditional view of subservient Russian women who were little more than punchbags for their husbands. An improved status for women was promoted by communist ideology, but this was not always the key factor in bringing about change. Industrialisation and war were to exert considerable change on women's lives. By 1953, the status of different groups of women depended on the role they played in the economic structure of the country rather than on the fact that they were women.

> This is a strong introduction because it provides a clear definition of the issue. It focuses on change and status and gives a sense of change through the period specified in the question.

Communist ideology promoted female equality with men and, on seizing power in 1917, the Bolsheviks were quick to attempt to change traditional Russian attitudes to the status of women. Zhenotdel, the Women's branch of the Central Committee, introduced a series of measures that included allowing abortion, making divorce easier and giving women equal status with men under the law. Despite their intention, these measures did not always raise the status of women and, in fact, often made it worse. It was hoped that by making divorce easier many women could escape a violent or neglectful husband. The reality was that most divorces were initiated by men, seeking to get out of marriages they no longer wanted. The result was that many women were abandoned by husbands who had merely to inform their wife of their divorce by postcard. By 1926, 50 percent of all marriages in Moscow were ending in divorce. The so-called 'Great Retreat' of 1936 re-established traditional family policy by tightening up on divorce and abortion. The status of women within the traditional family was raised by the government's use of awards for 'mother-heroines', the introduction of guaranteed job security for pregnant women and the extension of maternity leave to 16 weeks.

> This answer is effective because it focuses on status and change rather than merely stating what the Bolsheviks did.

Urban women were likely to see the greatest change in their status through the period 1917 to 1953. The demands of war and industrialisation required more labour in the factories and this had an important impact on the status of women. During the civil war, millions of women were recruited into the factories and over 70,000 women joined the Red Army. They played a crucial role in ensuring the Red Army was well supplied with weapons and clothing. Women gained greater independence from their husbands because they were receiving wages of their own. Attitudes towards women in work changed and it became more acceptable for women to engage in industry. Nonetheless, these attitudes had limits. Many women lost their jobs after

> This section focuses on the degree of change experienced by urban women and highlights that change varied through time.

the civil war as soldiers returned from the army and reclaimed their old jobs. This pattern was repeated during the Second World War, when 800,000 women served in the armed forces, most in medical units, but also as pilots, machine-gunners and tank crews. Yet this time attitudes showed some change since the civil war. What was considered women's and men's work had become blurred and this was due in part to the use of female labour during the industrialisation programme of the 1930s. The number of female workers had risen substantially in the 1930s, from three million in 1928 to over 13 million in 1940. Women dominated the workforce in light industry, especially textiles, but were increasingly found in occupations previously considered to be the preserve of male workers. Women entered the construction industry and worked in lumbering and engineering. Parts of the Moscow underground were built by brigades of female workers. The accumulation of these developments had changed attitudes towards the status of women in the towns.

Even within the urban population, the status of women could vary. The 1930s saw the emergence of a more privileged group of women, the wives of the Soviet elite. Those married to managers or Party officials did not have to enter the workforce and were encouraged, instead, to do 'social work'. This included activities such as providing curtains in workers' dormitories, providing classes on hygiene and organising cultural productions in the workplace. There was even a magazine aimed at this group, entitled 'The Socially Active Woman'. It was a subtle way of reinforcing social divisions among women and indicated that capitalist notions of class could define the status of groups of women.

This section is effective because it draws attention to the different groups of women within the urban population. This is a sophisticated way of dealing with change.

Women in the countryside did not experience the same changes in their status as women in urban areas. Attitudes in rural areas were much more resistant to change, often a consequence of a lack of educational provision. Women in the countryside also suffered from the low priority given by the government to agriculture. Collectivisation was designed to make agriculture subservient to the interests of industry and the rural population in general was given less status than that of the cities. Many men had moved from the countryside to the towns in search of employment, leaving women as the majority on most collective farms. Conditions for these women remained primitive. The Second World War exacerbated the problem of a lack of men on the collectives and even as late as 1950 it was possible to find villages with no adult males.

The answer is now examining the different changes affecting rural women. The focus is sustained on 'change' and the degree of change.

Particularly resistant to change were the Muslim areas of Central Asia, where the polygamous, male-dominated family was well entrenched. The Bolsheviks attempted to break down these traditional attitudes and the campaign against the veiling of women in 1927 met with some success. Opportunities for Islamic women increased and female brigade leaders and tractor drivers were celebrated through films and posters. Despite these changes, traditional Islamic attitudes were slow to change and resistance was often violent.

This section is strong because it continues to explore the issue of changing status of women by considering different groups. It does not assume all women experienced the same changes.

The status of women had changed by 1953 and government policy had taken an important role in breaking down traditional social attitudes towards women. Women were less likely to be restricted to a specific, defined women's role, but this did not mean that their lives were always improved. Changes in status were also uneven: urban women, especially the wives of Party officials, saw the greatest changes. The status of women in rural areas was little changed, a reflection of not just traditional attitudes, but of the government's low priority for agriculture.

The concluding paragraph makes a judgement that stems from the explanation given in the answer. It addresses the key words 'how far' in a more sophisticated manner by considering the degree of change on the various groups of Soviet women.

Verdict

This is a strong answer because:

- it focuses on 'status' and 'change'
- it addresses 'how far' by looking at the degree of change and the experience of different groups of women
- it has precise examples to make the points convincing
- the conclusion makes a clear, reasoned judgement
- the quality of written communication, logical coherence and conceptual understanding are all excellent.

Russian Association of Proletarian Writers (RAPP) made increasingly bitter attacks on the Fellow Travellers and condemned the decadent individualism of writers who adopted new experimental techniques. The type of writing preferred by the regime included Kataev's novel 'Time Forward' (1932), about a record-breaking shift at Magnitogorsk steel works. Works like this were used to support the programme of rapid industrialisation that had been started by Stalin's First Five-Year Plan. As the demands of industrialisation increased, Stalin realised that greater control was needed to ensure the Soviet population rose to the severe challenges faced during the enormous economic changes of the 1930s. The result was a tightening of control through the imposition of Socialist Realism on all aspects of culture and the arts. Art was used by the regime to project ideal images of life under the Five-Year Plans. Socialist Realism produced posters, paintings and sculptures that presented images of the worker and peasant, often together, working for socialism and gaining strength through their endeavours. Socialist Realism combined with Stalin's growing cult of personality. Thus, images of Stalin were linked to the great projects of the Five-Year Plans, such as the White Sea Canal and Dneiper Dam. Stalin was promoted as the architect of industrialisation and the moderniser of the Soviet Union. It is difficult to judge the full success of Socialist Realism, but there is plenty of evidence of young Communist Party members joining projects to help build a new socialist future. The huge Magnitogorsk industrial centre was one of many projects swamped by volunteers inspired by Soviet propaganda.

> These sections continue the explanation. There is good use of precise examples and success is discussed. Government policy is placed in its wider context.

Culture and the arts worked best when the interests of the Party built upon attitudes and values already existing in the population and a good example of this is when the government tapped into feelings of patriotism and Russian nationalism during the Second World War. Eisenstein's film 'Alexander Nevsky' became a hit with the public. Its story of Nevsky's successful stand against an invasion by Teutonic Knights in the 13th century inspired the Soviet population to stand firm against the Nazi invasion of 1941. Given the huge losses (over 20 million) endured by the Soviet people, this was no mean feat. Public concerns over the threat of invasion and war were reinforced after 1945. The government built on these fears during the Cold War to promote attacks on foreigners through the arts, which became known as the Zhdanovschina. Rigid control over the arts and culture was firmly maintained and artists, such as Shostakovich, were heavily restricted. Fear of foreign invasion and war, after Russia's experience of the First World War, civil war and the Nazi invasion, was a potent force that the regime could use to serve its own foreign policy against the West during the Cold War.

> The concluding paragraph makes a relevant and reasoned judgement. It addresses the key words 'interests' and 'success' and explores them in some depth and with some sophistication.

Given the excessive use of terror that the Soviet regime became infamous for, it is tempting to think that Soviet control was all-pervasive. In reality, not all artists were prepared to go along with the dictates of the Communist Party. Some artists criticised the regime, often at considerable personal cost. Others refused to play the game and opted for what Isaac Babel called the genre of silence. One of Russia's greatest poets, Anna Akhamatova, gave up writing poetry for publication during Stalin's rule. Works critical of the regime had little choice but to become part of an underground network, operating out of the eyes of the secret police. Nonetheless, it would be a fair assessment to state that, as a result of the rigid state control exercised over culture and the arts, the Communist Party was to ensure that its political and economic interests were served with considerable success.

Verdict

This is strong answer because:

- it considers the precise focus of the question by explaining how culture and the arts were used to 'serve the interests of the Communist Party'
- it gives a reasoned judgement on whether cultural policy was a success
- it places culture and the arts into their wider context
- although the answer is not thorough in its use of detail, each point has precise examples to make it convincing
- it displays high-level thinking skills
- the quality of written communication, logical coherence and conceptual understanding are all excellent.

Paper 1: A Level sample answer with comments

Section B

These questions assess your understanding of the course in breadth and will cover a period of 30 years or more. They will ask you about the content you learned about in the four key themes, and may ask about more than one theme. The questions will also require you to explore a range of concepts, such as change over time, similarity and difference, as well as significance. For these questions remember to:

- identify the focus of the question
- consider the concepts you will need to explore
- support your points with evidence from across the time period specified in the question
- develop the evidence you deploy to build up your overall judgement
- come to a substantiated judgement that directly addresses the question set.

To what extent did the economic reforms of Khrushchev and Brezhnev address the fundamental weaknesses of the Soviet economy between 1955 and 1982? (20 marks)

Average student answer

Both Khrushchev and Brezhnev tried to reform the economy of the Soviet Union. Under Khrushchev this involved the launching of the Virgin Lands Scheme in agriculture and the Seven-Year Plan of 1959–65, which focused on the promotion of light industry. Under Brezhnev, the focus on agriculture and light industry continued. Consumer goods became more plentiful, leading to a rise in Soviet living standards. Not all proposed reforms were implemented, or were successful when they were. The Kosygin reforms of 1965 were watered down to the point where their impact was extremely limited.

In 1957, Khrushchev set up 105 Regional Economic Councils to supervise enterprises. It was an attempt to move some decision-making from the centre to regional bases, which, it was hoped, would be able to take more account of local circumstances. Managers of industrial enterprises were given more influence in their factories. Khrushchev disliked the fact that they were merely 'robots of Moscow'. To encourage initiative they were allowed to keep 40 percent of the profits made by their factory to invest as they wished in their enterprise. Many of these reforms were promoted by the Liberman Plan of 1962, which called for greater autonomy for local managers. The influence of Khrushchev on economic policy was evident in the Seven-Year Plan. The government pushed ahead with transforming the fuel and chemical industries. This involved a shift of emphasis from coal to oil and gas. The focus on the chemical industry was linked to the increased targets for consumer goods. The production of synthetic fibres was to rise from 166,000 tons in 1958 to a target of 666,000 tons by 1965. Substantial rises were also targeted in footwear, natural fabrics and housing. The annual growth rate of the Soviet economy in the 1950s was 7.1 percent. This seemed impressive compared with the US growth rate of 2.9 percent, but the Soviet economy still lagged behind because its economic base was smaller.

Agriculture received a lot of attention from Khrushchev. In 1955, individual collectives were given greater powers to make decisions at local level. Flexibility over how directions from the Ministry of Agriculture were implemented was allowed. The MTS were abolished. Collectives were increased in size, many becoming large agro-industrial villages that linked food production with food processing. These units made some sense in terms of creating greater economies of scale. They also enabled much greater investment in agriculture to take place. There was a rapid increase in mechanisation, fertilisers and irrigation. Nonetheless, these much larger farming units proved deeply unpopular with the peasants, who felt more divorced from the land they worked.

This introduction shows some awareness of the whole period and identifies some of the key economic reforms that need to be explored in the answer. Unfortunately, the introduction does not define the economic weaknesses of the Soviet economy.

It would be better to start to open up the issue by defining these weaknesses and considering the extent to which economic reforms addressed them.

These paragraphs have a lot of good, precise detail, but they do not use this information to explain how the reforms tackled key economic weaknesses.

It would be better to start each paragraph by identifying the economic weaknesses that the reforms were trying to address.

The most famous of Khrushchev's agricultural initiatives was the Virgin Lands Scheme. Introduced in 1954, it encouraged the opening up of new areas to agricultural production. Six million acres of land were brought under cultivation with considerable investment. Over 120,000 tractors were provided for the scheme.

Attempts to reform the economy were continued under Brezhnev. In 1965, Alexei Kosygin, the Prime Minister, launched a series of reforms that aimed to improve productivity. His reforms, like those of Khrushchev, gave incentives to enterprise managers to use their resources more productively. He also attempted to make central planning take more notice of cost and profit rather than the Stalinist approach of using quantity produced as the main indicator of economic success. Kosygin's reforms had much to commend them, but little was achieved. The reforms were blocked by the officials who had to implement them. These officials were too conservative in their attitude to take risks and managers preferred to stay with safe and tried methods. On a more positive note, Brezhnev encouraged greater use of scientific research to ensure the latest technology was applied to production. Khrushchev's push for greater consumer goods was continued by Brezhnev, and the Ninth Five-Year Plan placed a particular emphasis on this. Goals were not fulfilled, but the growth achieved was still impressive and living standards rose.

In agriculture, Brezhnev reversed Khrushchev's decentralising schemes for agriculture. Power was returned to the Ministry of Agriculture and the Virgin Lands Scheme was dropped. The Politburo did accept that agriculture needed heavy investment and this feature of previous policy continued. By 1976, 26 percent of all investment was in agriculture, but this investment was producing fewer returns.

Both Khrushchev and Brezhnev recognised that the Soviet economy needed to be improved, and introduced reforms to try to address this. These reforms did mark a shift away from the focus on heavy industry and central control that had dominated the economic system under Stalin, but their success in raising production and productivity was limited.

> These sections are less detailed, but contain good points that could have been explored further. The use of incentives is mentioned. This could have provided an opportunity to explore the problems of central planning.

> The concluding paragraph makes a straightforward, relevant judgement and reveals that the student's understanding is much better than their answer indicates. The shift from heavy industry and central control – two fundamental weaknesses – could have been explored in depth in the essay.

Verdict

This is an average answer because:

- it has limited focus on 'fundamental weaknesses'
- it does not use precise detail to explain points
- it does not explore the central issue in the question in any depth.

Use the feedback on this answer to rewrite it, making as many improvements as you can.

Figure 1.1 Political map of China, 1949.

HOW SUCCESSFUL WERE THE COMMUNISTS IN CREATING A POLITICAL SYSTEM THAT WOULD GIVE THEM CONTROL OF POWER WITHIN THE PRC?

It was important for the Communists to act quickly to establish a new political system. If they waited too long, they could have lost their gains and China could have slipped into anarchy. It was also vital to give the new regime an air of legitimacy, so that people accepted its authority.

Therefore, preparations for the new China began as soon as Beijing fell, at the end of January 1949, although it was not until October that the new republic could be declared officially. Collaborating over the planning with other groups who were opposed to the GMD, not only helped to split the nationalist opposition, but also gave the new regime an appearance of wider popularity. The Communists kept up this pretence of unity until they were strong enough to stand alone in the early 1950s.

Temporary bodies were set up to run the country and a provisional constitution was adopted, until, by 1954, it was possible to adopt more permanent political institutions. Even though the constitutional details were not finalised until 1954, it was immediately made clear that the Communist Party would be leading the government, and that its power would be based on a continuing partnership with the PLA.

Government control of the press, which was already considered normal before 1949, was continued through Xinhua, the government-controlled press agency. This ensured that all of the mass circulation daily newspapers reported favourably on government policies and party initiatives, and therefore the new system received positive publicity from the outset.

The organisation of the government

In September 1949, with victory in the civil war imminent, the Communist Party arranged a meeting of the **Chinese People's Political Consultative Conference (CPPCC)**, which took the first steps in preparing a new political system to replace that of Chiang and the Nationalists once they surrendered.

It was composed mainly of Communist sympathisers, but its 600 delegates included a range of other minority groups, such as the China Democratic League, giving it a broader appearance and therefore a greater claim to legitimacy. The CPPCC appointed the new **Central People's Government** as the supreme state body and approved the **Common Program**, a temporary constitution to steer China through the next five years. It also decided the various state symbols that would be used, such as the flag, national anthem, calendar and choice of capital city.

The Common Program declared that China had been transformed into a new society based on an alliance between the workers and peasants, whose interests would be represented by the Communist Party. It guaranteed a wide range of personal freedoms, as well as gender equality, making China theoretically one of the freest countries in the world. The reality, in practice, was of course very different, as the Common Program also gave the army and the police the right to suppress all counter-revolutionary activity, powers they used to great effect in the years that followed.

As China was not yet thought ready for full socialism, it was conceded that there would have to be a transitional period of co-operation between the working class and the existing capitalist elements of society. However, the long-term future of these capitalist elements was clearly insecure, as Source 2 illustrates. In his speech 'On the People's Democratic Dictatorship', Mao had identified the four classes of people who should be allowed to have rights in the new China. Everyone else (he called them 'the five black categories') was to be repressed.

SOURCE

2 From 'On the People's Democratic Dictatorship', *Selected Works of Mao Tse-tung*. These are excerpts from a much longer speech to the public by Mao on 30 June 1949, in which he looked back on the lessons that the Communist Party had learned over the previous 28 years (it was founded in 1921), and looked ahead to the way they hoped to organise the political system in China once final victory over the GMD had been achieved.

All the experience the Chinese people have accumulated through several decades teaches us to enforce the people's democratic dictatorship, that is, to deprive the reactionaries[*] of the right to speak and let the people alone have that right...

Who are the people? At the present stage in China, they are the working class, the peasantry, the urban petty bourgeoisie, and the national bourgeoisie. These classes, led by the working class and the Communist Party, unite to form their own state and elect their own government; they enforce their dictatorship over the running dogs[**] of imperialism – they suppress them and allow them only to behave themselves. If they speak or act in an unruly way, they will be promptly stopped and punished. Democracy is practised within the ranks of the people, who enjoy the rights of freedom of speech, assembly, association and so on. The right to vote belongs only to the people, not to the reactionaries. The combination of these two aspects, democracy for the people and dictatorship over the reactionaries, is the people's democratic dictatorship.

[*Reactionaries prefer to keep things as they are, and are therefore considered as standing in the way of progress. It was a label frequently used to discredit political opponents who were not being co-operative.

**Running dog was a demeaning term frequently used by the Communists to put down the USA and its friends.]

Mao referred to this approach as 'New Democracy', but it was a very different type of democracy from that practised in the UK, and the way it worked is often referred to as democratic centralism (explained below).

When it came to passing legislation, the central government simply rubber-stamped proposals put in front of it by the **Politburo**. The CPPCC began to draft the future constitution and, until this was published, it acted as the **legislature**. All existing laws that had been passed by the GMD were abolished, as was the old judicial system.

China was divided into six regions (bureaux) so that decisions taken at a national level could be imposed throughout the country, and the creation of regional congresses at least gave each region the impression that Beijing (the new capital) was listening to them. However, by putting four senior Communist officials in place over each region (a military commander, an army **political commissar**, a government chairman and, most powerful of all, a Party secretary), the CCP was clearly taking no chances. In some regions, this power was highly concentrated. For example, in the north-eastern Bureau of Manchuria, one man – Gao Gang – held all four posts, while elsewhere, three Party leaders (Deng Xiaoping, Lin Biao and Peng Dehuai) all held multiple posts. Such a level of central control was intended to prevent China from reverting to the warlord years of the 1920s, when powerful regional leaders had fought each other while the central government stood by, powerless.

EXTEND YOUR KNOWLEDGE

At this stage (1949–54), Deng Xiaoping was vice-premier to Zhou Enlai and minister of finance: Lin Biao was one of the leading marshals in the PLA, soon to be elevated to the Politburo; and Peng Dehuai was China's senior military leader, who became defence minister in 1954.

The 1954 constitution and increasing bureaucracy

In 1954, the new constitution was duly published, at which point China was officially confirmed as a Communist country. It was very much based on the 1936 Soviet Russian Constitution. The National People's Congress was created as the new legislature, and the State Council took over the functions of the Central People's Government. Although again couched in democratic terms, with various references to elections, the Communist Party retained control of the entire electoral process. Real power remained in the highest Party bodies, where decisions were taken before being endorsed by the state bodies.

The administrative composition of China also changed at this point. The six regions were now subdivided into 21 provinces, five autonomous border regions and two urban centres (Beijing and Shanghai).

This constitution was modified in 1975, but remains essentially based on that of 1954.

KEY TERMS

Politburo
The key decision-making body of the CCP, just as in the Soviet Russian Communist Party (CP). There were 14 members when it met for a plenary session, but in between these meetings, decisions were taken by the five-man standing committee of Mao Zedong, Liu Shaoqi, Zhou Enlai, Chen Yun and Zhu De. Such decisions became laws when the legislature (known as the National People's Congress from 1954) approved them, which it always did.

Legislature
The government body responsible for passing laws (legislation).

Political commissar
Responsible for monitoring people's loyalty to the Party at a local level and enforcing control as necessary.

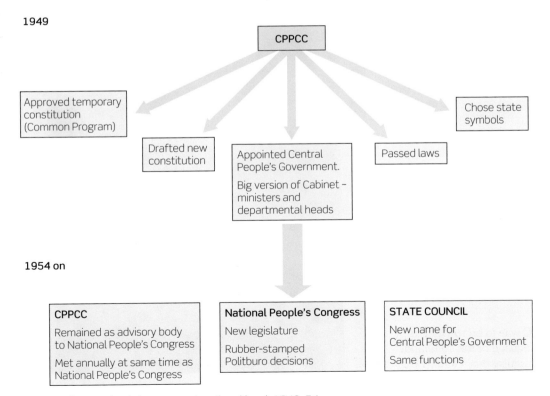

Figure 1.2 Changes in state organs at national level, 1949–54.

According to the historian Frank Dikotter, roughly one percent of victims were shot, another one percent were sent to labour camps for life, three percent were jailed for more than ten years and the rest were fined, although the fear of humiliation drove many to commit suicide. This in itself was difficult, as suspects were closely supervised. Nets were attached to break people's falls from high buildings, and parks were patrolled to prevent people hanging themselves from trees. One person who succeeded in committing suicide was the Dean of the Shanghai Law College, who threw himself into a river to drown as a result of the treatment he was receiving (see Source 7).

SOURCE

Robert Loh, *Escape from Red China* (2007). This comes from Loh's account of his own life in China, written after his flight to the USA. Here he is describing the fate of a colleague from the time he worked at Shanghai University.

He was made into the janitor at the trade association he had previously headed. He was paid 18 yuan a month and could live only by selling his household furnishings. His employers addressed him only to give him orders and wrote weekly reports on his behaviour. He himself had to go once a week to the police with a written expression of his gratitude to the party for the leniency of the people's justice; if his gratitude was not expressed in terms sufficiently abject, he was made to rewrite his paper until it was found acceptable. No one else dared speak to him, let alone try to help or comfort him.

He was supposed to be kept under surveillance like this for three years, but killed himself half way through his sentence.

A Level Exam-Style Question Section A

Study Sources 6 and 7 before you answer this question.

How far could the historian make use of Sources 6 and 7 together to investigate the impact of the 'anti' campaigns of 1951–57?

Explain your answer using both sources, the information about them and your own knowledge of the historical context. (20 marks)

Tip
Make sure to cover the full chronological range and be prepared to look at longer-term aspects of the impact that go beyond 1957.

Fines were a way of destroying the old business class by removing their wealth, and also contributed to the financing of the Korean War – although it may be argued that the chaos caused to normal economic activity by the movement did more harm than good to the economy.

The focus of the 'antis' movements had been on corrupt practices within the management levels of the Party and businesses. However, the top level of the Party was also purged by the attack on **Gao Gang** and Rao Shushi in late 1953, who were accused of infringing the ban on factions and building up their own empires inside the Party. Rather than face humiliation, Gao committed suicide; Rao was arrested and died in jail in 1975, over 20 years later.

KEY PERSON

Gao Gang (1905–54)
Rose to favour as a force in economic planning, but had over-reached himself and began plotting to replace Zhou Enlai as vice-chairman of the Party.

The affair reinforced Mao's position at the top and made the cadres lower down realise that it was dangerous to take opposition too far. This was a lesson that would become even more obvious during the Hundred Flowers campaign.

ACTIVITY
KNOWLEDGE CHECK

The terror
1 Why do you think the authorities encouraged people to denounce each other? Explain three reasons.

2 What was the point of making it hard to commit suicide?

The development of the *laogai* system

The official explanation of the *laogai* camps was that they were places of re-education rather than of punishment. Misguided people who had failed to grasp the benefits that Communism had brought would be shown the error of their ways, before being eventually reintegrated as useful citizens. In reality, the system supplied the terror that the regime depended on in order to frighten most of the population into conformity.

Just as in Russia, where the gulag system developed, the existing Chinese prison system simply could not cope with the extra number of inmates produced by the Great Terror. Soviet experts were brought in to provide guidance on the management of a new labour camp system. By 1953, there were two million prisoners, over half of whom were working as forced labourers in *laogai*. As well as serving a political purpose, the camps were also of significant economic value, contributing some 700 million **yuan** in industrial products and 350,000 tonnes of grain to the state each year by 1955. Under the Great Leap Forward, prisoners were used as a convenient means of getting the most hazardous jobs done, such as mining and clearing malaria-infested swamps.

KEY TERM

Yuan
Also known as renminbi, the new currency introduced in 1950.

Socially, the prison population represented a cross-section of Chinese society, ranging from poor farmers in debt to the state, to technical experts accused of being counter-revolutionaries. However, nine out of ten inmates were political prisoners, and such was the backlog of cases that many had been working in them for years before they were formally charged. At village level, many farmers were sent to prison without any trial at all, and while it was widely accepted that a significant proportion of prisoners had been wrongly accused, there was no means of redress.

Prison conditions varied according to local circumstances, but were predictably brutal, involving constant fear of violence and frequent use of sleep deprivation and other forms of torture, not to mention the hard labour and poor diet.

Added to this was the psychological effect of **thought reform**, which involved endless self-criticism and indoctrination meetings, designed to make prisoners lose their previous identity.

The prison population ballooned again in 1955, when there was a further purge of counter-revolutionaries. A new layer of imprisonment, known as re-education through labour, was added to absorb a further 300,000 inmates. This system bypassed judicial procedures entirely: victims were sent without trial and could be held indefinitely in prison until the police, or local militia, who ran them decided they had been sufficiently 're-educated'. It was through this system that many people disappeared without trace in subsequent years.

Statistics for the numbers who died in the camps vary enormously, but it may have been as high as 25 million over the whole period, 1949–76. Even those fortunate enough to be released could rarely slot back into normal life, because they were frequently ostracised by others, who feared being branded as guilty by association.

Placing people under public supervision (*guanzhi*) was an additional way of responding to prison congestion. It involved placing convicts under the control of local cadres, who could use them to perform whatever menial tasks were required, and as handy scapegoats to be paraded around during public campaigns. It was a device used far more widely in rural areas. Luo Ruiqing spoke of 740,000 people under this system in 1953, but the figure is likely to be higher, as local cadres took the law into their own hands and could call on the local militia to back them up if required.

ACTIVITY
KNOWLEDGE CHECK

The *laogai*

1 Explain two reasons why it was necessary to change the penal system as time went by.

2 Why do you think the *laogai* were such an effective means of exerting political control?

The Hundred Flowers campaign (1957) and its aftermath

By 1956, with the First **Five-Year Plan** coming to a close, Mao surprised everyone by calling for an open debate about its results and the future pace of change.

In April 1956, in an address to the CCP, Mao called on delegates to 'let a hundred flowers bloom, and a hundred schools of thought contend'. This apparent call for an open debate was at least partly influenced by recent events in Russia, where **de-Stalinisation** was leading to uncertainty.

Mao's call for a debate may have been prompted by his desire not to expose himself to the same criticisms that were being levelled at Stalin. However, the outbreak of the Hungarian rising later that year must also have made Mao realise that appearing too open-minded might backfire, by encouraging challenges to Communist rule. Although Mao had never trusted intellectuals as a group, he knew that they had a valuable contribution to make to the economy of China, and he may have been trying to win them over by giving them some opportunity to make constructive criticisms.

Mao continued to promote the need for a debate to the CCP Congress in November 1956, but still got no support, and repeated his hundred flowers theme in a major speech in February 1957. Given the trouble that anyone even accused of counter-revolutionary activity got into, it is little wonder that critics were slow to surface – particularly as the media campaign against **Hu Feng** had led to the arrest of a hundred or so intellectuals only two years earlier.

Frustrated with the lack of response, Mao summoned the editor of the *People's Daily* newspaper to demand news coverage be given to the debate, and then embarked on a stage-managed railway tour to 'engage' with the peasants and hear their views for himself. Finally, a trickle of comments did surface, which, as people gained confidence, developed into a flood of criticisms. Suggestions for improvement became denunciations of policies and even of individual leaders.

Suddenly – and the speed with which Mao acted may suggest he had been planning to do this all along – a halt to the debate was announced and Mao rounded on his critics, branding them as '**Rightists**', whose intention was to destroy the revolution. An anti-Rightist campaign was launched 'to squeeze the pus out of the abscess'. What began as a call for open expression became another exercise in Thought Control, which produced around half a million new inmates for the 're-education camps'. He accused them of wanting to turn back the clock by overthrowing the Communists and returning China to the rule of the nationalist bourgeoisie.

Mao's grip on the CCP tightened further, but the goodwill of intellectuals was lost for ever.

KEY TERM

Rightist
A blanket term that was applied to anyone Mao wanted to get rid of. The implication was that they had betrayed the principles of the revolution by being too far to the political right.

THINKING HISTORICALLY   Evidence (3a)

Comparing accounts of the Hundred Flowers campaign
Read Source 5 and Extract 1 and then complete your own copy of the table below.

	According to Cheo	According to Short
Reasons why Mao invited criticisms		
Reasons why it can be seen as a blunder		
What it tells us about Mao's political methods		

EXTRACT 1
From Philip Short, *Mao: A Life* (1999). Short worked as a BBC foreign correspondent for 30 years and has written several books on China.

The Hundred Flowers was not, as Mao's victims and supporters both claimed, a carefully contrived trap from the start, an example of the Chairman's cunning in 'luring the snake out of its hole'. Nor was it a colossal blunder, as most western scholars argue.

Mao had always mistrusted intellectuals; their behaviour at Yanan had strengthened his conviction that they were fundamentally unreliable, and nothing that had happened since had done anything to alter that view. He didn't suddenly decide, in the spring of 1957 that they were trustworthy after all. He believed there would be a few 'extremists' who would have to be uprooted. Hence his refusal to give a blanket assurance that there would be no retaliation. Hence, too, a revealing slip of the tongue at a Party conference in March before the movement began, when he referred to intellectuals as the enemy, rather than potential allies to be won over.

On the other hand, the economic base of Chinese society had been transformed, and therefore in Marxist theory, the ideological 'superstructure' should follow suit. Throughout the campaign, Mao used the metaphor of hair and skin, arguing that now the old, bourgeois economic 'skin' had died, the intellectuals, the ideological 'hair', had no choice but to graft themselves on to the new 'skin' of the proletarian economy.

Mao misjudged the volume and bitterness of the criticisms, and what started as an attempt to bridge the gap between the Party and the people was turned on its head. It became a trap, not for the few, but for the many - for the hundreds of thousands of loyal citizens who had taken the Party at its word.

The tragedy was that Mao genuinely did want the intellectuals to 'think for themselves' and join the revolution of their own free will, rather than being forced to do so. He could not comprehend that if people had the freedom to think for themselves, they would think what THEY wanted, not what HE wanted.

Party-led work teams put considerable time and effort into whipping up anti-landlord paranoia in villages, by digging up old grievances against better-off individuals and by offering the prospect of a share in the confiscated spoils of those found guilty of being landlords.

Putting power in the hands of the poor and middle-ranking peasants, who had conducted these 'speak bitterness' meetings and passed the sentences against landlords, enabled the Party to underline its claims that this was a peasant-led revolution against the old landlord class. By making sure that it was the villagers themselves who carried out the killings, the Communists were implicating them to such an extent that there was no turning back.

EXTRACT

2 P. Short, *Mao: A Life* (1999).

... peasants who killed with their bare hands the landlords who oppressed them were wedded to the new revolutionary order in a way that passive spectators could never be.

ACTIVITY
KNOWLEDGE CHECK

Land redistribution

1 Explain why the idea of land redistribution was popular with:

   a) the peasantry

   b) the Party.

2 What do you think was the main danger for the Party of redistributing land?

3 What was the overriding aim behind all of the changes to land ownership?

4 What was the point of directly involving the villagers in dealing with landlords?

5 Why do you think it was necessary for the work teams to stir up old grievances?

Moves towards agricultural co-operation

The Party never intended the peasantry to become established as a new class of landowners, and therefore moves towards **collectivisation** began rapidly.

Mao hoped that a measured approach to this, taken before the peasants got used to owning more land, would avoid a repeat of the disastrous situation experienced by Stalin in Russia. Stalin had encountered so much resistance to collectivisation that he ended up eliminating the *kulaks* (better-off peasants) as a class. However, in Russia, the peasants had already been in possession of the land for ten years and had become used to life under the **New Economic Policy**, so there was bound to be resistance to change there.

The moves towards collectivisation passed through several stages because the party improvised as they went along, depending on circumstances. Mao said that it would take about 15 years to complete.

From 1951, groups of ten or so families were encouraged to unite to form Mutual Aid Teams (MATs), in which they could pool their labour, animals and equipment, while retaining their rights of private ownership. This happened anyway at busy times of year, but it was now being formalised as a permanent arrangement and managed by the **peasant associations**. While membership was voluntary, it soon became apparent that individuals who remained outside the MAT would find it hard to get hold of resources, and villagers who stayed out on their own ran the risk of persecution.

KEY TERMS

Collectivisation
The process whereby the state takes over the ownership of land and equipment that was previously in private hands. Collective farms are managed by the state, which supplies the peasants with food and accommodation in return for their labour.

New Economic Policy (NEP, 1921–28)
Russia had become so short of food during the civil war (1918–21) that Lenin had decided to restore capitalist practices to the Russian countryside by introducing the NEP. This allowed peasants to sell their produce and keep the profits once they had paid their taxes to the state. While the NEP did feed the countryside, it did not produce a sufficiently regular surplus with which to feed the urban industrial workers who were required for industrialisation. This was a major reason why Stalin ended it in 1928, replacing it with collective farming.

Peasant associations
Organisations originally created in the 1920s to help peasants to defend their rights and campaign for lower rents. They were revived in the 1950s by the work teams in order to get the villagers used to the idea of collective activity.

EXTEND YOUR KNOWLEDGE

Peasant associations
Peng Pai (an early pioneer of the revolutionary peasant movement, who was killed by the GMD in 1929) created the peasant associations in the 1920s in Guangdong province. The associations had been so successful that the Party had backed away from them. At this point in time, the Communists were still working with the GMD in the United Front and had not yet decided whether to focus on the industrial workers or the peasants. They were afraid that the associations would commit them too closely to the peasants. By the 1950s, it was clear that the peasants came first.

In 1952, successful MATs were encouraged to combine and form Agricultural Producers' Co-operatives (APCs) of 40–50 families. In APCs, land could also be pooled and could therefore be consolidated into larger units and cultivated more efficiently than in traditional strips. Families with larger holdings were still allowed to keep back some land for their personal use, while renting the rest to the APC, which was a strong incentive for richer families to join. Profits were shared out at the end of the year, according to resources contributed and food produced.

The change from voluntary to enforced collectivisation

Mao was frustrated at the slow pace at which the APC system was developing (only 14 percent of rural households were in APCs by March 1955), but he continued to follow a cautious approach until 1955, responding to circumstances as they arose and frequently changing tack.

In their desire to respond to Mao's wishes for faster change, many local officials had rushed into creating APCs before they had been properly planned. Consequently, these APCs had gone into debt because they had to borrow money to buy equipment, prompting Mao to call for a slowdown in the spring of 1953.

However, once things stabilised again in 1954, peasants started buying and selling their land and food, just as they would under capitalism. This apparent rejection of revolutionary values infuriated Mao, who then condemned the previous slowdown as a 'rash retreat', and renewed the pressure on peasants to join APCs. However, even when better-off peasants did bow to local pressure and reluctantly joined the local APC, they often slaughtered their animals and ate them rather than handing them over, in scenes reminiscent of forced collectivisation in Russia. When the 1954 harvest was poor, this prompted the government to requisition grain in order to get enough to feed the cities. However, this caused so much rural protest that, in January 1955, Mao did another U-turn and announced a policy of 'Stop, Contract and Develop', calling for a halt to APC development for the next 18 months.

Then, only six months later, in July 1955, Mao made up his mind to go for all-out collectivisation when he announced to a Conference of Local Party Secretaries that a full-scale drive would be started immediately. This time, there was to be no turning back. From 17 million households in APCs in July 1955, the figure grew to 75 million by January 1956, until, by the end of the year, only three percent of peasants were still farming as individuals. The official reason given for the drive to collectivisation was that it was in response to the demands of the peasantry, an illusion that Mao helped foster by publishing 'Socialist Upsurge in the Countryside', a selectively edited compilation of favourable reports on collectives written by local activists. The real reason was more likely to have been Mao's fear that supplies to the cities would continue to be unreliable as long as peasants still owned the land. Like Stalin, he saw the peasants as so instinctively reactionary that they needed to be forced into collectives, where the state would operate as their landlord, otherwise they would revert to capitalism at the first opportunity. Mao summed up the situation when he said, 'the peasants want freedom, but we want socialism.'

EXTEND YOUR KNOWLEDGE

Mao's skill at political manipulation
Announcing the decision to collectivise to a Conference of Local Party Secretaries was a means of bypassing the higher bodies within the Party that such decisions would normally have gone through. Inside the higher echelons of the Party there was considerable opposition to moving so fast, but if Mao could publically announce it elsewhere, it would be very hard for the decision to be rescinded.

Most of these new APCs were classed as 'higher' (HPCs), and consisted of 200–300 households. In an HPC, peasant families no longer owned the land or the equipment, and the profits at the end of the year were shared out according to work points earned by the labour contributed. This meant that those who contributed the most land and other assets might find themselves receiving the same rewards for their labour as those who had surrendered the least in terms of material possessions.

EXTEND YOUR KNOWLEDGE

Why peasants joined co-operatives
It may seem odd that some peasants, especially the richer ones with the most to lose, joined APCs or HPCs when they clearly did not want to. The explanation was that the Party had become so well entrenched at a grass-roots level that they were able to apply intolerable levels of pressure on reluctant individuals, using a combination of fear and ridicule to isolate them from the mainstream. Only the very thick-skinned could withstand this, and only a tiny minority of three percent did so. The other reason was financial: banks had been nationalised in 1949 and would not lend money to individual peasants who stayed outside the co-operative.

Ideologically, collectivisation was a tremendous success for Mao because the state now owned the means of production of food, the land, on which 90 percent of the population worked. This was Chinese Marxism in action. Politically, it was more of a mixed blessing for Mao: the fact that it had been carried out far more quickly than imagined was a tribute to his authority within the Party, and his ability to outmanoeuvre powerful conservative opponents such as the premier, Zhou Enlai. Furthermore, the actual process of carrying out the changes greatly increased the control the party exerted over local people at grass-roots level. However, collectivisation also marked a distinct change in the relationship between the CCP and the peasantry, who now became servants of the Party, rather than loyal allies whose support had to be earned. In addition, the speed with which the big surge towards higher-level APCs was achieved made Mao dangerously overconfident. He no longer worried about practical obstacles that stood in the way of change, and this was soon to lead to catastrophic mistakes in the Great Leap Forward of 1958.

In economic terms, the impact of collectivisation was disappointing. Over the period of the First Five-Year Plan, food production had increased by 3.8 percent per annum, but this was still insufficient to sustain the growing industrial workforce, which was growing even faster. The basic problem was that the amount of cultivated land per head of the population was so low. Yields per hectare were quite high, but labour productivity was low, and it would have been hard for the peasants to produce a surplus, whether collectivised or not. The situation was worsened by the lack of state investment in agriculture and the demotivating effect created by the fact that people no longer owned their own land, so they did not directly benefit from the work they put in.

Collectivisation

1 Fill in a timeline like this to check your understanding of the sequence of events between 1950 and 1957. Allocate one row to each year.

Year	Main development and brief explanation of what it entailed
1950	Agrarian Reform Law – enabled redistribution of land to be organised at village level. 'Landowners' identified, property shared out, punishments inflicted.
1951	
1952	

2 How easy was it to collectivise agriculture? Put each of the factors below into a table. Next to each factor, explain why it made collectivisation easier or harder to organise (or possibly both).

Factors to consider: Communist experience of land reform in Yanan in the1930s and 1940s; the zeal of Party activists; regional variations in land ownership; internal Party disputes about the pace of change; the war years making people accustomed to higher levels of violence; fear of US invasion from Korea, 1951–53; the shortage of industrial goods; the Soviet Union's experience of collectivisation; shortages of land in some regions (such as Sichuan); the strong links between the CCP and the peasantry that had been forged before 1949; the huge number of peasants.

3 Was collectivisation supposed to be more productive than private ownership? Identify and explain at least three reasons for each side of the argument.

WHAT WAS THE IMPACT OF THE PEOPLE'S COMMUNES AFTER 1958?

Mao returned from his second visit to Moscow in November 1957, impressed by the Russians' achievement in launching a **sputnik** into space, but nevertheless determined to modernise China independently in the future. While in Moscow, he had already announced plans to overtake Britain as an industrial power within 15 years, but the question he faced on his return was how to do this. His answer was by merging the collectives into much larger units and making them responsible for a wide range of activities in addition to farming – industrial production, education, welfare provision and local defence.

Reasons for launching the Communes

Mao had been delighted with the speed at which collectivisation had been carried out, and he continued to seek ways to maximise food production in order to accelerate industrial growth. The idea of bigger collectives, in the form of communes, had an obvious appeal, since they ought to enable the pooling of even larger resources of equipment and labour. This should mean higher food yields and more peasants being freed up to work on construction schemes.

The initial steps came from enthusiastic cadres in Henan, who claimed that the local APCs were asking to merge so they could share their resources and therefore release more manpower for the water control projects that were being launched in the winter of 1957–58. Such initiatives impressed Mao, who had embarked on a fact-finding tour of the countryside in the spring of 1958. Mao returned to Beijing determined to press ahead with radical solutions, convinced that he had the backing of both the peasantry and the local Party activists for a more ambitious collective scheme. Armed with first-hand evidence, even if it was of questionable accuracy, he was able to get both Liu Shaoqi, the vice chairman of the CCP, and Deng Xiaoping, the CCP secretary general, to put their support behind the idea of People's Communes.

A further, ideological, reason for wanting to press ahead with the communes was Mao's determination to prevent the revolution losing impetus. If collectives were simply allowed to evolve at their own pace, he feared the revolution would be in danger of becoming becalmed by the bureaucrats, who preferred to keep the status quo because it was less trouble. If 600 million people could be mobilised as active participants in the Great Leap Forward, there would be no chance of this happening.

How the Communes were organised

It was for the above reasons, therefore, that a radical new policy initiative (officially known at the time as the Three Red Banners, but normally referred to as the Great Leap Forward) was announced at the Eighth CCP Congress of May 1958. The Great Leap Forward would involve developing industry and agriculture at the same time, in what Mao referred to as '**walking on two legs**'. The People's Communes that had already been created were to be expanded, and the labour force was to be mobilised on water conservancy and other civil engineering schemes. Mao had faced bitter opposition from conservatives within the CCP leadership during the previous months, but he had now succeeded in getting this new direction endorsed by the Congress, where he also repeated his claim that China would overtake Britain as an economic power, reducing the time it would require to do so to seven and a half years.

Production of steel and grain were to be given equal priority. It was the task of the farmers to produce the grain in order to feed the workers, who would make the steel. As the planners liked to put it, 'General Grain' would produce the food, and 'General Steel'

HOW SUCCESSFUL WAS THE FIRST FIVE-YEAR PLAN, 1952–56?

Why it was not immediately introduced

Although Mao regarded the establishment of a much stronger industrial base as vital if China was to develop as a world power, no major economic plan could be launched until more immediate problems had been solved. First, the Communists had to consolidate their political control by mopping up the remnants of Nationalist opposition and conquering the outlying provinces. Second, they had to reduce the annual inflation rate from the staggering 1,000 percent that they inherited. It was also necessary to reward the peasants for their support by arranging for land redistribution to take place as soon as possible, so this took priority. Further delay in detailed planning was also caused by the high level of military spending and the disruption caused by participation in the Korean War from October 1950.

The USSR's financial and technical support

Why they used the Soviet model

By 1951, the annual inflation rate had been cut to a manageable 15 percent, by a combination of cuts to public spending, increases in taxation and the replacement of the old Chinese dollar with the yuan (or renminbi). The first of what Mao envisaged would be three Five-Year Plans was launched the following year. It was based on the Soviet model. Despite the difficulties of the relationship between the CCP and the Russian Communist Party over the previous 25 years, Soviet Russia was still, at this stage, an inspiration to the Chinese Communists, and Mao had made it clear in 1949 that he would 'lean to one side', by aligning China with Russia rather than looking towards the West for help. Also, despite its problems, the centrally planned Soviet system had enabled Stalin to defeat Nazi Germany, so it was regarded as the best, albeit only, available option for China to copy. Mao's task in introducing a centrally planned economy was made easier by the fact that there had been some degree of state involvement in Chinese industry since imperial times, and this had accelerated under Chiang Kai-shek, who had established a National Resources Committee (NRC) to control industrial investment and encourage migration from the countryside to the cities. Mao was able to take advantage of the expertise of the managers of the NRC, many of whom remained after the fall of the GMD.

The nature of Soviet help

A vital part of the Sino-Soviet Treaty of 1950 was the arrangement for Soviet advisers to come to China and teach them how to run a Communist state. Over 10,000 civilian technicians brought their specialist knowledge of civil engineering, industry, governmental organisation and higher education. Their expertise came at a cost, however: their high salaries were paid by the Chinese, and they were housed, at China's expense, in closely guarded compounds outside the main cities, in an odd throwback to the situation in imperial times, when **European concessions** had enjoyed similar special privileges. Russia also agreed to lend China $300 million, as security for which the Chinese had to hand over a large part

of their bullion stocks. Furthermore, the credit was not a gift: the loans were to be repaid with interest. Chinese delegations also visited Moscow, particularly to be trained in propaganda techniques and in aspects of governmental organisation.

> **KEY TERM**
>
> **European concessions**
> Areas in 19th-century China where the European powers were allowed to run affairs their own way, beyond Chinese jurisdiction.

The influence of the Soviet Union soon became clear to see in the cities, where critics complained that classical Chinese buildings were being cleared to make way for new office blocks and construction projects built in 'Soviet brutalist' style. Russian ideas also penetrated education, where Russian was the only foreign language taught in schools, and the lunch hour was pushed back to three in the afternoon, to copy the Russian practice of having six consecutive morning classes. TASS, the official Soviet news agency, became the main source from which the Chinese newspapers gathered their information. 'The Soviet Union's today is our tomorrow' soon became a slogan familiar to all in the cities.

While Soviet influence may have made more visual impact in urban areas, it also exerted a profound influence on the lives of those in the rural communes through the adoption of Lysenkoism.

The plan's targets

The overall aim was to make the PRC as self-sufficient in food and manufactured goods as possible, in order to protect China in a potentially hostile capitalist world. Although detailed plans for each industry could not be finalised until the Korean War was over, the principles were already in place by 1952. Targets would be set from above by economic planners, rather than in response to consumer demand, and heavy industry (iron and steel, transport and communications, energy supply, industrial machinery and chemicals) would come first. In addition, several spectacular public works projects, like new bridges across the Yangtze at Nanjing, were added for their propaganda value. The basic ideas were given a preliminary dry-run in Manchuria, where heavy industry was already well established, before being applied to the entire nation. The targets for specific industries can be seen in Source 4.

The aim was also to channel resources into these heavy industries, away from consumer goods, which were regarded as less important. Also, it was hoped that people would be more willing to invest in patriotic savings schemes, which the government could then direct into industrial investment, if there were few consumer goods to tempt them into spending on alternatives. By forcing the collective farms to sell food at low prices to the government, it was hoped to keep industrial workers' wages low, because cheap food would be readily available in the urban areas.

Initially, not all industries were nationalised – only those belonging to foreigners and those in the banking, gas, electricity and transport sectors of the economy were taken under state control in 1949. However, the fear generated by the 'five antis' campaign (see Chapter 1) made it possible, in early 1956, to bring an end to private ownership entirely. For business owners, it was easier to accept compensation from the state for their enterprises than to run the risk of being denounced as 'rightists' and suffer the inevitable punishment that would have incurred.

As well as by food requisitioning from the APCs and patriotic savings schemes, the plan was to be financed by higher levels of taxation in the cities and loans from the USSR.

Successes and failures of the plan

SOURCE 4

Production of key items during the First Five-Year Plan, 1952–57. From Robert Whitfield, *The Impact of Chairman Mao 1946–76* (2nd edition) (2008).

Industrial sector	1952 (actual)	1957 (target)	1957 (actual)	1957 (actual as percentage of target)
Coal (millions of tonnes)	68.50	113	130	115.00
Steel (millions of tonnes)	1.35	4.12	5.35	129.80
Cement (millions of tonnes)	2.86	6	6.86	114.30
Electrical power (millions of kWh)	7.26	15.90	19.34	121.60
Locomotives	20	200	167	83.50
Trucks	0	4,000	7,500	187.50
Insecticide (tonnes)	600	70,000	61,000	87.10
Machine tools	13,374	12,720	28,000	220.10
Bicycles (thousands)	80	555	1,174	211.50

According to the official statistics, most sectors of the economy succeeded in reaching their targets. The annual growth rate was about nine percent per year during the plan, a figure that compared favourably with the Russian experience in the 1930s, particularly when it is remembered that the war in Korea disrupted long-term planning early on. Urban living standards improved in terms of wages and job security, though at the expense of a loss of freedom to change jobs or travel. More people were migrating to the cities, where the population grew from 57 million in 1949 to 100 million by 1957.

However, despite the overall success of the plan, the figures are unlikely to be completely reliable, because officials had an obvious vested interest in exaggerating levels of production in order to please their superiors, in the same way, although not to the same extent, as cadres in the communes covered up the true state of affairs. The emphasis on reaching targets also inevitably put the emphasis on quantity over quality.

There were also other negative aspects to the plan. While Soviet guidance was invaluable, it exposed shortcomings in the skill and literacy levels of Chinese workers that would only improve when the education system was updated. However, by the time the plan ended, less than half the children under 16 were in full-time education, so this was a long way from happening. At a managerial level, many of the economic planners who worked for the Nationalists had remained in place after 1949, but by the time the plan began, the 'anti' campaigns of 1951–52 had driven out many of them, and the standard of bureaucratic administration suffered as a result. Finally, there was competition for resources between private and state-owned enterprises (SOEs), which was not resolved until the ending of private ownership in 1956.

In the countryside, the plan had more negative than positive influences. Here, the peasants in the communes were going short of food because it was being exported to Russia to pay for the Soviet advice, and sold cheaply to the cities to feed the urban workers. It was an ironic twist that Lysenkoism, which formed part of the Soviet advice that they were paying for, was actually making peasants' lives much worse.

SOURCE 5

From an article in *China Pictorial*, published in April 1958. This was a weekly magazine that was first published in 1950. Calligraphy for the title was done by Mao himself, and it was one of the few publications allowed to continue during the Cultural Revolution.

Last December (1957) Liu Shaoqi issued a call for China to catch up or surpass Britain in output of iron and steel within fifteen years. It should be remembered that China's first five year plan began in 1953, nearly two hundred years after the industrial revolution in Britain. But the Chinese people have displayed amazing ability in building up their country.

In the first plan, the targets for total output value of industrial and agricultural production were over-fulfilled. The output of steel increased on average by 31.2% a year... there was a new and large factory or mine coming into operation every two days.

Inspired by the success of the first five year plan, the Chinese people are launching a new nationwide upsurge in industrial and agricultural production. China's second five year plan is even more awe inspiring than her first. In 1962, when the plan will be completed, the yearly output of steel will reach twelve million tons.

ACTIVITY
KNOWLEDGE CHECK

The First Five-Year Plan, 1952–56

1 Draw up a balance sheet to show the successful and unsuccessful aspects of the First Five-Year Plan.

2 Using the above list, decide which aspects were successful or otherwise from the point of view of each of the following: the Chinese economy; the urban population; the rural population; Mao.

WHAT WAS THE IMPACT OF THE SECOND FIVE-YEAR PLAN, 1958–62?

The Second Five-Year Plan formed part of the Great Leap Forward, which was announced at the Eighth CCP Congress in May 1958. While agriculture was to be modernised by the development of the People's Communes, ambitious new targets for industrial growth were to be pursued at the same time. Mao called this 'the Great Leap' because he was impatient at the relatively slow pace of economic progress made so far. He now wanted China to become a modern industrial power without bothering to go through the normal phases of development that other leading powers had experienced.

In February, the responsibility for economic planning had been moved from the state to the Party, which partly explains why this Five-Year Plan was not a 'plan' in the strict sense of the word. It did not involve planners announcing carefully thought-out targets that specific industrial sectors were supposed to reach by a certain time. Instead, the organisational details were often left to the initiative of local cadres, and direction from above came in the form of slogans urging people on to greater efforts, mixed with threats against those who did not pull their weight. Targets were constantly being revised upwards, sometimes by Mao himself, sometimes from below, by keen officials trying to create a good impression.

Mao's reasons for launching it

Although the decision to launch the Great Leap Forward can be explained by a combination of reasons – economic, political, personal and ideological – in the final analysis, it was political considerations that were paramount.

On an economic level, industrialisation depended on agriculture becoming more productive and efficient in order to feed the industrial workforce. This would free up peasants, who would migrate to the cities to become urban workers themselves. The speed with which farming had been collectivised and the encouraging early signs from the new People's Communes seemed to indicate that agriculture was progressing sufficiently rapidly by 1958 to encourage Mao to accelerate the demands on industry. However, it was not as simple as that, because there was still a vigorous debate going on between conservatives and radicals in the Party. Conservatives, like Zhou Enlai and **Chen Yun**, advocated a 'carrot' approach of rewarding high food producers with material incentives (in the form of more consumer goods and higher food prices), while radical hardliners called for punitive measures against low producers and the requisitioning of food (the 'stick'). Mao initially considered this latter approach too risky, given that 70 percent of Party members were peasants. Yet the problem with the cautious approach was that industry was not yet producing large amounts of consumer goods to offer the peasants, and the state simply could not afford to pay generous prices for the food. It would therefore be wrong to see the launch of the Great Leap as purely the result of rational economic logic, because the arguments about the best way forward had not yet been won.

KEY PERSON

Chen Yun (1905–95)
A long-time Politburo member with significant influence over economic planning. Partly because he had been trained in Russia, he retained a strong preference for centralised control over the economy. He later helped draw up the Third Five-Year Pan, which restored central control.

More important were personal and political factors. On a personal level, Mao's confidence was at a high: collectivisation had been achieved more rapidly than expected, there had been an impressive burst of activity on water conservancy schemes during the winter of 1957–58, and his provincial tour of early 1958 had been enthusiastically received. Anxious to prove their credentials against the backdrop of the latest anti-rightist campaign, local cadres were eager to demonstrate the revolutionary fervour of the peasants in their locality, all of which helped to convince Mao that more ambitious schemes would be possible.

On a political level, Mao had just returned from Moscow determined to show the Soviet Union that he could act independently of them. By moving from socialism to communism along the 'Chinese road', rather than following the Russian model, Mao hoped to demonstrate his credentials as the next leader of the communist world. The Great Leap Forward, with its commitment to developing industry and agriculture simultaneously, while also mobilising the peasantry en masse on construction projects, would do just that.

Liu Shaoqi, Deng Xiaoping and economic reform, 1962–65 (the Third Five-Year Plan)

The retreat from the Great Leap Forward, which had begun in late 1960, speeded up in 1962, when Liu and Deng were put in charge. As well as allowing the communes to be broken up, they also closed down thousands of inefficient projects that had been set up in the Great Leap and announced more realistic coal and steel targets. To help with this, there was a relaxation of the persecution of scientists and intellectuals, previously attacked as 'rightists', but whose contribution was now regarded as desirable.

Much of this more pragmatic approach to economic planning came from Chen Yun, who was mainly responsible for drawing up the Third Five-Year Plan in 1962.

The third plan marked a decisive shift back to centralised control, with production targets being reviewed annually and made more realistic. Experts were back in favour and financial incentives were restored to encourage workers to greater efforts. The results were positive across all sectors of the economy: agricultural production recovered to 1957 levels, oil and natural gas production rocketed, and manufactured goods were produced in much greater quantities.

It was during this period (1964) that Chinese scientists succeeded in exploding China's own atom bomb, having pieced together the documents that the Soviet advisers had hurriedly shredded when they were withdrawn in 1959. Mao was jubilant, and contemptuously 'thanked' Khrushchev for 'helping' the Chinese to develop nuclear weapons independently by withdrawing.

Although Mao welcomed the economic improvements of the early 1960s, he was reluctant to attribute them to the retreat from the Great Leap Forward, which he described as dangerous **revisionism**.

In an attempt to prevent any further drift away from strict communist principles, Mao had summoned a conference of 7,000 cadres in January 1962. However, the result had not been as he had hoped, because Liu Shaoqi, while praising Mao for his correct leadership, had gone on to imply that Mao should share some of the blame with the other leaders at the centre of government for China's past mistakes. After Lushan, this was a risky tone to take, but Liu knew he had the approval of the conference and Mao accepted responsibility as chairman of the Party, though he stopped short of admitting any personal mistakes. This was significant, because it was the first time that Mao's aura of infallibility had been damaged, and for the next few months, he withdrew from public life, leaving Liu, Deng and Zhou in charge.

A clear difference of views over how the economy should be run was now becoming apparent. On the right of the Party were Liu, Deng and Chen Yun, who took the pragmatic view that ideological concessions would be necessary to restore the economy: mass mobilisation was no substitute for expertise and planning, and private trade was justified if it motivated people to work harder. On the left, Mao was arguing that continuing revolution should be the key: without mass mobilisation, there would always be the danger of a new bourgeoisie emerging inside the Party and destroying the gains of the revolution. Mao returned to the political fray in the summer of 1962 at the annual Party conference, where he went on the attack, demanding to know whether China was going to take 'the socialist road or the capitalist road', and condemning the revisionism of Liu and Deng. The result was an uneasy compromise, whereby Liu and Deng outwardly agreed with Mao's analysis of the situation, while continuing to do things their own way. They criticised rural capitalism, but did nothing to stop farmers owning their own private plots and selling their produce for profit.

Liu and Deng's pragmatic economic approach continued for the time being, but a political power struggle inside the Party was building up, which would explode in the Cultural Revolution from 1966.

> **KEY TERM**
>
> **Revisionism**
> A term of criticism used by Communists to describe any course of action that they felt betrayed communist principles. Mao frequently used it against his enemies, notably Khrushchev.

ACTIVITY
KNOWLEDGE CHECK

Differences between the Five-Year Plans

1 Create a table showing the aims, methods and results of the three Five-Year Plans, to illustrate the key similarities and differences between them.

2 Identify and then explain two differences between the first and second plans.

3 Identify and then explain two differences between the second and third plans.

THINKING HISTORICALLY   Cause and consequence (6b)

Attitudes and actions

Individuals can only make choices based on their context. Prevalent attitudes combine with individual experience and natural temperament to frame the individual's perception of what is going on around them. Nobody can know the future or see into the minds of others.

Action	Context
At the CCP Central Committee meeting, held at Wuhan in December 1958, Mao announced that he was stepping down as Chairman of the PRC. He handed over the responsibilities of this post to Liu Shaoqi.	Mao had claimed for some time that he was becoming increasingly unhappy with the formal duties that went with the chairmanship of the country and wanted more time to devote himself to ideological matters.
	Mao stayed on in his role as chairman of the CCP.
	At the same meeting, Mao announced a record harvest for that year of 430 million tonnes of grain, a figure that stretched the credulity of the Central Committee, which scaled it down before announcing it.
	The Great Leap Forward had been announced in May 1958, which involved meeting ambitious industrial production targets and making rapid progress towards establishing the People's Communes.
	During 1958, Mao had been on two tours of the provinces, to see for himself how the communes were working.
	In July 1959, a special conference was called at Lushan to discuss the progress of the Great Leap Forward.

Answer the following questions individually, and then discuss your answers in a group:

1 Why did Mao decide to step down at this particular point in time?

2 Why did he step down from that particular role?

3 Apart from the reason given above, what other reasons explain his decision?

4 What evidence can you find from subsequent developments that his decision to step down succeeded, or caused him problems?

5 How far should the historian try to understand the context of the beliefs and values of people in the past when explaining why individuals make choices in history?

A Level Exam-Style Question Section B

How accurate is it to state that, as far as industry was concerned, the First Five-Year Plan was a success and the Second Five-Year Plan was a failure? (20 marks)

Tip

The question requires you to assess the relative success of each of these Five-Year Plans, so you need to ensure you examine positive and negative features of each. You cannot do this effectively unless you first establish the criteria on which you can judge them, so make these clear at the outset: meeting targets, increasing output of key goods, etc.

ACTIVITY
SUMMARY

The economy

1 Make a table with three columns, one for the aspects listed below, one for success and the other for failure:

   Land redistribution; collectivisation; the People's Communes; SOEs; water conservancy projects; backyard furnaces; the Lushan Conference of 1959; the Third Five-Year Plan.

   For each of the eight aspects, put the strongest piece of evidence in support of seeing it as a success, and then for seeing it as a failure. Explain each choice.

2 In what ways did the Soviet experts make a positive contribution to China's economic progress?

3 Compile a list of examples from the period that show that political rather than economic considerations mattered more to Mao.

WIDER READING

Becker, J. *Hungry Ghosts*, Henry Holt (1998)

Dikotter, F. *Mao's Great Famine*, Bloomsbury (2010)

Dikotter, F. 'The Great Leap Backward', *History Today* (November 2010)

Priestland, D. *The Red Flag – A History of Communism*, Grove Press (2009)

Short, P. *Mao – A Life*, Hodder and Stoughton (1999)

Yang, J. *Tombstone: The Great Chinese Famine, 1958–62*, Farrar, Straus and Giroux (2008)

The attacks on the 'four olds'

While it was Mao who had identified the 'four olds' (old culture, old ideas, old customs and old habits) that needed to be dealt with in order to root out revisionism, it was Lin Biao who instructed the Red Guards to attack them in his speech to the 18 August rally. These categories are impossible to separate and were kept deliberately vague, so that they could be stretched to cover any element that suited Mao. By labelling them as 'olds', he hoped to give the young extra incentive to eradicate them, as it was made clear that nothing in China's past was worth preserving. Anything representing past values was denounced under the blanket term of '**Confucius** and Co.', and fit for destruction. Only the future mattered.

KEY TERM

Confucius
Lived in the 6th century BC, and is generally regarded as China's most influential philosopher. His ideas, which focused on the importance of harmony, respect for legitimate authority and order, had become accepted as fundamental to Chinese life, but were regarded with contempt by the Communists because they had helped preserve the status quo for so long.

SOURCE

6 Nien Cheng, *Life and Death in Shanghai* (1986). Nien Cheng survived over six years in prison, where she was sent because she was the widow of a manager who had worked for Shell. She emigrated to the USA in 1980, where she wrote her autobiography.

In the days after Mao reviewed the first group of Red Guards in Beijing, and gave them his blessing, the Red Guards in Shanghai took over the streets. The newspaper announced that the mission of the Red Guards was to rid the country of the 'Four Olds'... There was no clear definition of 'old'. It was left to the Red Guards to decide. First of all they changed street names. The main thoroughfare of Shanghai along the waterfront, the Bund, was renamed Revolution Boulevard... the road on which the Soviet Union had its Consulate was re-named Anti-Revisionist Street... They smashed flower and curio shops because, they said, only the rich had the money to spend on such frivolities. The other shops were examined and goods they considered offensive or unsuitable for a socialist society they destroyed or confiscated. Because they did not think a socialist man should sit on a sofa, all sofas became taboo.

AS Level Exam-Style Question Section A

Study Source 6 before you answer this question.

How much weight do you give the evidence of Source 6 for an enquiry into the attack on the 'four olds' launched by the Red Guards in August 1966?

Explain your answer using the source, the information about it and your own knowledge of the historical context. (12 marks)

Tip
Make sure you use the date, the level of detail and the tone of the language when you are examining what the source reveals. For example, does the fact it was written some 20 years after the events appear to be reflected in the detail of her recollections?

The Red Guards were quick to take up the call, particularly targeting Western influences in fashion, such as high heels, winkle-pickers and so-called 'Hong Kong style' clothing and hairstyles. Correction stations were set up on street corners, and offenders had their heads shaved there. Street names were changed to reflect new values: the address of the British Embassy in Beijing became Anti-Imperialist Street. Some people adopted new given names, such as 'Red Hero' or 'Militant', reflecting their revolutionary ideals. It took all of Zhou Enlai's diplomatic skills to dissuade the Red Guards from changing the colours of the traffic lights. They reasoned that, if red was the colour of the revolution, then it should mean go not stop, but accepted Zhou's argument that red was stopping threats to the revolution.

While such actions were relatively harmless, many were not: houses were ransacked in search of bourgeois possessions, such as musical instruments, jewellery, antiques and paintings, which were dragged out and destroyed. Books considered to have been written by bourgeois authors were burned in street bonfires or pulped. Even if their owners could avoid the ritual struggle sessions, they were often the victims of impromptu beatings that sometimes had fatal consequences.

Religion was deemed to fall into an 'old' category, and attacks on it intensified to such an extent that no public worship or ceremonies were allowed. Clergy who had survived earlier persecutions were rounded up and imprisoned, prompting criticism from the outside world.

The traditional nuclear family of parents and children also came under attack, as young people were urged to treat Mao and the newly cleansed CCP as their true parents, to whom they owed obedience. It was expected that children would inform the Red Guards of parents or relatives who clung on to old attitudes.

The physical destruction of cultural sites is covered below (page 226), but all cultural activity was subjected to scrutiny by the CCRG, where Jiang Qing was given responsibility to 'purify' the nation's culture. With her former career as an actress, and strong links with Shanghai radical writers, she set about the task with fanatical zeal. Culture was not seen by Mao as a peripheral matter; to him, the culture of a nation should reflect its political priorities, so it was important to 'cleanse' cultural activity of inappropriate values and make it truly socialist.

Although the campaign against the 'four olds' was intense and violent, where it focused on deeply ingrained and long-held attitudes its effects were short-lived, and many traditional views reappeared. For example, the survival of the 'old' attitude of

---

ACTIVITY
KNOWLEDGE CHECK

Attacking the 'four olds'

1 Why did Mao package the values to be attacked as the 'four olds'?

2 Use the sources and the other material to draw up a list of things that came under attack, putting each in the most appropriate of the 'four olds' categories.

3 Why do you think Western ideas and culture came under such attack?

showing respect for the dead was clearly shown when thousands of mourners attended a huge Festival of the Dead ceremony in April 1976, in tribute to the recently deceased Zhou Enlai. This happened while Mao was still alive.

The growth of anarchy and the use of terror

Given free rein to attack figures of authority, and egged on by wall posters in the universities and articles in the press, students turned first on unpopular teachers, and then on anyone whose lifestyle suggested wealth, privilege or an adherence to old or foreign ideas. Because Mao had described chaos as more virtuous than order, and the police and army stood aside, there were few restrictions on what the Red Guards could do. Those accused were subjected to lengthy struggle sessions in which they were often physically attacked, tortured and forced to confess to 'crimes' against the Chinese people. Previous contributions to the revolution or military achievements did not guarantee immunity from attack, as was shown by the cruel treatment meted out to Huang Xinting, the military leader of the Chengdu region. He was seen as a potential barrier to Lin Biao's continued advancement, a 'crime' that was compounded by having been too close to a friend of Peng Dehuai.

Examples of savage brutality were apparently endless, but what started as random attacks in August and September 1966 soon became more systematic, as officials in the Ministry of Public Security passed names of members of the **bad classes** on to the Red Guards.

KEY TERM

Bad classes
These were usually listed as: landlords, rich peasants, reactionaries, bad elements and rightists.

The Babaoshan crematorium in Beijing disposed of 2,000 bodies in a two-week period in 1966. Reliable statistics are inevitably hard to come by, but some idea of the scale of the killings can be seen from the trial of the Gang of Four in 1980, who were accused of having sanctioned the deaths of over half a million people. The violence was not confined to the principal cities: in the southern province of Guangxi, 67,000 killings were recorded over the ten years 1966–76, while in the outlying provinces of Sichuan, Tibet and Mongolia, the figure ran into hundreds of thousands.

The formation of new Red Guard units by radical factory and office workers in November 1966 escalated the violence, as did the appearance of new units from students who came from non-Party bourgeois backgrounds, which ironically turned out to be among the most militant. Previously denied the opportunity to participate in revolutionary activity due to their background, they seized the chance to demonstrate their credentials.

As the movement widened, splits and rivalries emerged, particularly in Shanghai, which degenerated into chaotic infighting between different factions during January 1967. Eventually, Mao intervened, with the help of the PLA, to end what became known as the January Storm, and the city was placed under the control

of the Shanghai Revolutionary Committee, a combination of PLA representatives, Party officials and revolutionaries. This became the model that was applied to other cities and provinces over the next year.

As the Cultural Revolution began to penetrate more sections of society, arguments broke out between the PLA, anxious to be exempted from the same struggle sessions as civilian society, and the CCRG, which wanted the same criteria to apply to every institution, without exception. When Mao failed to give a clear lead, the PLA took matters into its own hands to suppress radicals in some provinces in the February Crackdown. Leading Politburo members appeared to support this action, when they also called on the Red Guards to calm down their activities, so it looked as though the excesses of the Cultural Revolution would be ended early in 1967.

However, in typically perverse fashion, Mao dug his heels in and called for the CCRG to override both the Politburo and the PLA, and China drifted further into factional disputes and chaos. Only in August 1967, when Mao realised that the PLA might be so seriously undermined that it would be incapable of defending the country, did Mao make another U-turn, by authorising the PLA to crack down on radical groups when it needed to. This decision marked a watershed and, from that point on, the radical phase gave way to consolidation.

EXTEND YOUR KNOWLEDGE

Defending the country
At this time, China's southern and northern borders were under threat. To the south, the increased American involvement in the Vietnam War posed a risk. Meanwhile, relations with Russia had deteriorated to such an extent that border disputes over Xinjiang in the north-west and Manchuria in the north-east were worsening, and would almost lead to war in 1969. Mao could not allow national security to be jeopardised by subjecting the army to the same level of scrutiny as the Party had endured.

Cultural destruction

As part of their attack on the 'four olds', the Red Guards embarked on a frenzy of destruction of cultural objects between mid-August and late September 1966. According to official documents, they destroyed two-thirds of the 7,000 places of historical and cultural importance in Beijing, where they also broke into over 100,000 homes in search of 'old' artefacts. However, support for their actions was by no means universal. Zhou Enlai prevented them from attacking **the Forbidden City**, by bringing in a PLA unit to defend it, and even Chen Boda, on the radical left of the Party, expressed reservations about the scale of cultural vandalism.

KEY TERM

The Forbidden City
Beijing's best-known monument, the walled inner city that had been the home of the emperors for 500 years, until their overthrow in 1911. It is now a World Heritage Site.

Perhaps their greatest single act of desecration was the attack on Confucius' home town of Qufu in Shandong province, where Red Guards spent four weeks vandalising countless books, paintings, statues, graves and monuments with connections to Confucius. But here, as in Beijing, local people intervened to protect some historical treasures from destruction.

ACTIVITY
KNOWLEDGE CHECK

The Red Guards

1 Why did 1966–67 contain so much violence?

2 Identify and explain three reasons why the most radically destructive period of the Cultural Revolution was relatively short.

3 Why do you think divisions emerged in the Red Guard movement?

4 Construct a timeline in as much detail as you can to cover the events of 1966–67.

5 Why did Mao eventually decide to let the PLA clamp down properly on the Red Guards in August 1967, and not earlier in the year?

HOW WAS THE CULTURAL REVOLUTION USED TO ATTACK MAO'S POLITICAL AND CLASS ENEMIES?

The attacks on Liu Shaoqi and Deng Xiaoping

Essentially, both President Liu and Party General Secretary Deng were removed from their posts for ideological reasons. The pragmatic approach they had used to good effect in extricating China from the Great Leap Forward was tolerated by Mao as a means to an end, but when they continued to advocate pragmatic policies, Mao became convinced that the future of the revolution was not safe in their hands. However, he could not act against them while both remained popular in the Politburo, and by entrusting Liu and Deng to oversee the ending of the rural crisis, Mao had ceded some of his grip on power to them.

Liu and Deng supported pragmatic economic policies and were less committed than Mao to a collectivist approach, which is why they had no qualms about allowing the restoration of private farming. Mao, however, continued to put great faith in advancing the revolution by mass mobilisation campaigns from below, unlike Liu and Deng, who preferred a top-down approach, where policies were imposed from above. This difference, which became clear during the Socialist Education Movement of 1963–64, was to resurface when student unrest took off in 1966.

By late 1964, Mao was accusing Liu of taking the 'capitalist road', and Deng of acting independently, and although on the surface they appeared to be working together, once Mao felt he had built up enough support outside the Politburo, he was looking for the opportunity to strike against them.

By the end of 1965, Mao had the support he needed. He knew he could count on Lin Biao and the PLA, Jiang Qing and the Shanghai radicals, Chen Boda (who had control of propaganda) and Kang Sheng, the security chief. It was at this point, therefore, that he instigated the attack on Wu Han, to see if the power of Liu and Deng in Beijing could be shaken.

By the time of the Party Central Committee meeting that criticised them in August 1966, Liu and Deng must have realised they had been outmanoeuvred. Although they both appeared with Mao on the balcony at the rally on 18 August, it was clear from their position in the background that they no longer held high influence. In October 1966, following a Red Guard demonstration directed specifically at them, they were both formally dismissed from their positions within the government and Party. Wall posters appeared, naming and denouncing both Liu and Deng for betraying the revolution. The position of president, which Liu had held, was left vacant until being officially scrapped in 1969.

Liu and his wife, Wang Guangmei, were dragged from their house and beaten by a jeering mob. Liu was then forced to undergo a series of brutal struggle sessions, before being imprisoned in conditions deliberately intended to break his already fragile health. He had diabetes, but when he also contracted pneumonia, he was refused permission to go to hospital. He died in November 1969.

Wang was subjected to a humiliating interrogation before being paraded before a large crowd wearing a necklace of table tennis balls and a revealing skirt, which she was accused of having worn on a recent trip to Indonesia in order to seduce President Sukarno. She was sentenced to death, but the verdict was not carried out because Mao intervened to save her.

Deng was less harshly treated, but was also subjected to public humiliation before being sent to perform corrective labour in a tractor factory in Jiangxi province. He survived the experience and, thanks partly to his links with Zhou, he was rehabilitated into the Party in 1973. His son, however, was left permanently paralysed when Red Guards threw him from an upstairs window.

The attack on Lin Biao

While the reasons behind the fall of Liu and Deng are clear, the explanation of Lin Biao's fall in 1971 is more controversial.

Lin had played a pivotal role in the Communist victory in the civil war, after which he had slowly risen up the political pecking order. Only Mao stood above him in the army command structure after he replaced Peng Dehuai as defence minister in 1959, and he had used this power to politicise the PLA, abolishing ranks and using *The Little Red Book* to increase the level of political indoctrination. Lin was the principal architect of the personality cult, and the PLA played a significant role in orchestrating the huge 1966 rallies. Under Lin's guidance, the PLA became an even more radical force, which Mao could use to advance the revolution, and Mao showed his gratitude by insisting that Lin become his designated successor when Liu fell later that year.

However, Lin's rise to political prominence may not have been driven purely by personal ambition, because he was often swept along with the tide of events. It was only with reluctance that

HOW AND WHY WAS THE CULTURAL REVOLUTION WOUND DOWN AFTER 1968?

TIMELINE OF KEY EVENTS IN THE WINDING DOWN OF THE CULTURAL REVOLUTION

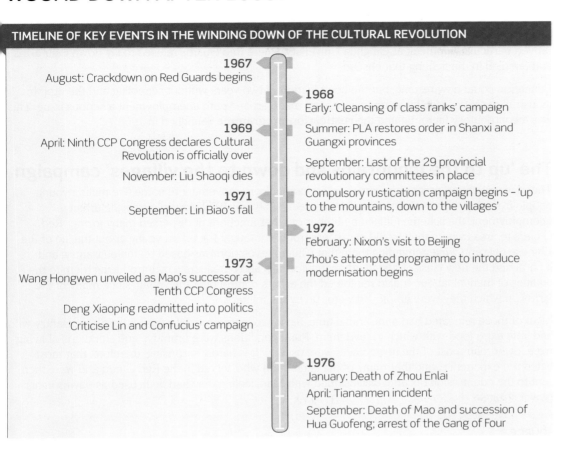

1967
August: Crackdown on Red Guards begins

1968
Early: 'Cleansing of class ranks' campaign

Summer: PLA restores order in Shanxi and Guangxi provinces

September: Last of the 29 provincial revolutionary committees in place

Compulsory rustication campaign begins – 'up to the mountains, down to the villages'

1969
April: Ninth CCP Congress declares Cultural Revolution is officially over

November: Liu Shaoqi dies

1971
September: Lin Biao's fall

1972
February: Nixon's visit to Beijing

Zhou's attempted programme to introduce modernisation begins

1973
Wang Hongwen unveiled as Mao's successor at Tenth CCP Congress

Deng Xiaoping readmitted into politics

'Criticise Lin and Confucius' campaign

1976
January: Death of Zhou Enlai

April: Tiananmen incident

September: Death of Mao and succession of Hua Guofeng; arrest of the Gang of Four

The restoration of order by the PLA

In August 1967, Mao finally decided to allow the PLA to clamp down on the Red Guards. The fact that he had almost decided to do this in February, before changing his mind to give them longer to wreak havoc, and the ease with which the PLA did restore order after August, suggests that Mao had always been in control of events, and was confident that the PLA would be willing and able to carry out his wishes. Mao had no objection to the violence of the Red Guards, but by this time they were undermining the army's role and were inflicting unsustainable damage on China's economic and educational systems.

For their part, the PLA was anxious to end the Red Guard violence because it did not want to open itself up to the self-criticism and struggle sessions that radicals were pushing for. Neither did the PLA want to risk jeopardising its status as the creator and defender of the revolution, which the Red Guards might eventually challenge if allowed to continue unchecked indefinitely. Once Mao had removed four of the most radical members of the CCRG, which was pushing for the radical action of the Red Guards to be extended, it proved straightforward for the army to restore order.

Mao ordered the rival Red Guard and workers' factions to form alliances and stop fighting each other. He speeded up the creation of the new revolutionary committees, which were henceforth to run the cities and provinces. Significantly, membership of these committees was dominated by PLA officers at provincial, county and local level, giving the military the main influence over the new political structures. The last of the 29 provincial committees was in place by September 1968, prompting the CCRG to declare that the entire country was now red.

Then the PLA began a full-scale purge of the Red Guards, disbanding the last Red Guard units and closing down their newspapers by the end of 1968. The army had already shown that it had taken over Red Guard revolutionary tasks, by launching the campaign to 'cleanse the class ranks'.

It took military action to end the most serious unrest, the full-scale civil war in Shanxi and the looting of weapons bound for Vietnam in Guangxi, but both provinces were eventually pacified in the summer of 1968.

The PLA was also entrusted with re-establishing discipline in the schools and universities, which had been closed for two years. Although the threat of force was usually sufficient to accomplish this, it proved particularly difficult at Qinghua University, where Red Guards refused to lay down their arms and ten died in the fighting that ensued.

Education could now resume, but the combination of two years without schooling and the drop in industrial output caused by so much infighting made urban youth unemployment a serious issue. This was a contributory factor behind the **rustication programme**, launched in 1968.

KEY TERM

Rustication programme
There had been an earlier, voluntary rustication programme, under which urban school leavers were encouraged to relocate to the countryside and work there, in order to help restore food production levels immediately after the famine. This new programme was compulsory.

The 'up to the mountains and down to the villages' campaign

The new rustication programme involved the compulsory movement of some five million young people from the cities to the countryside between 1968 and 1970. As well as easing urban unemployment, the scheme fulfilled a number of other functions: it dispersed many former Red Guards to areas where they would cause less trouble; it taught the urban young about the life of the Chinese peasant, while reminding them that China's revolution was based on the peasantry; and it hardened the new class of young urban intellectuals and bureaucrats by introducing them to the realities of manual labour. It also reinforced the army's control over the young, since many of the farms on which they were employed were run by the military.

Most of those relocated had a miserable time, having to learn new skills from a hostile peasantry who had little extra food with which to feed them. Rural conditions were primitive and standards of living were lower than most of the newcomers were used to. It is hardly surprising, therefore, that most hated the experience, and that many of the generation who served in the Red Guard and were then sent to the countryside became disillusioned with Mao, feeling they had been used as pawns in his power struggle.

SOURCE
 13

Jung Chang, *Wild Swans* (1992). Jung Chang was a keen Red Guard as a teenager, in the early years of the Cultural Revolution, but her opinions of Mao altered when her parents became victims of persecution and she realised how her generation was being used. After rustication, she was able to resume her university course, and left China to study in England two years after Mao's death. *Wild Swans* is an account of the lives of three generations of her family and won her international acclaim as a writer.

I was not very popular in the village, although the peasants largely left me alone. They disapproved of me for not working as hard as they thought I should. Work was their whole life, and the major criterion by which they judged anyone. Their eye for hard work was both uncompromising and fair, and it was clear to them that I hated physical labour and took every opportunity to stay at home and read my books. Virtually every day I had some sort of diarrhoea and my legs broke out in infected sores. I constantly felt weak and dizzy, but it was no good complaining to the peasants; their harsh life had made them regard all non-fatal illnesses as trivial.

SOURCE
 14

Anchee Min, *The Cooked Seed* (2013). She was only 17 when she was sent 'down to the villages' in the rustication campaign. The campaign had been launched in 1968, but was still operational in 1974, which is the year she is writing about here.

Mao had won the Cultural Revolution. Using the students, calling them the Red Guards, he had successfully eliminated his political opponents. But the youth had started to cause unrest in the cities, so Mao sent them to the countryside. He told us to get a 'real education by learning from peasants'.

It didn't take long for us to realise that we were in hell. We thought we were growing rice to support Vietnam, but we could barely grow enough to feed ourselves. The salt-saturated land was hostile. We worked eighteen hours a day during planting seasons. There were a hundred thousand youths between seventeen and twenty-five in the camps near the East China Sea. The Communist Party ruled with an iron fist. Harsh punishment, including execution, applied to those who dared to disobey the rules. There were no weekends, holidays, sick days or dating. We lived in army-style barracks without showers or toilets. We worked like slaves. Since childhood we had been taught that we owed our lives to the Communist Party.

A Level Exam-Style Question Section A

Study Sources 13 and 14 before you answer this question.

How far could the historian make use of Sources 13 and 14 together to investigate the consequences of the rustication campaign?

Explain your answer using both sources, the information about them and your own knowledge of the historical context. (20 marks)

Tip
The sources focus on the consequences for the young people involved. Try to extend the range of the answer by considering wider consequences – on agriculture, the urban situation and so on.

The return to power of Deng Xiaoping and Zhou Enlai

Zhou Enlai, who held the post of Prime Minister from 1949 until his death in 1976, was the ultimate survivor. Although he got into trouble on a number of occasions, he was never purged because he was far too useful to Mao and was skilful at distancing himself from awkward situations. His pragmatic stance had made him a target of the radicals during the early phase of the Cultural Revolution, but Lin Biao's demise helped to restore his credibility.

His role in uncovering the alleged assassination plot, and in foiling Lin's escape by closing China's airports, emphasised his personal loyalty to Mao. The fact that it was to Zhou that Lin's daughter had leaked news of the plot was testament to the trust in which he was widely held. In the years immediately after the plot, Zhou's moderate approach seemed appropriate, because Mao was still unsure how to present Liao's treachery to the public: should he be condemned as a traitor on the far left (which is what his conduct as PLA commander appeared to indicate) or on the far right (which is where his plotting seemed to put him)? Zhou used the opportunity presented by this uncertainty to revive his call for the **Four Modernisations**, which he had been advocating since 1963.

A fundamental part of this was to establish closer links with the West in order to acquire more technological expertise, and Zhou played the key role in facilitating US President Nixon's visit to China in 1972. Although full diplomatic relations were not to be activated until 1979, the tone of more conciliatory relations had been set in place. Common enmity with Russia had convinced the USA of the value of treating China as an equal, and Mao had now adopted the more limited ambition of guaranteeing China's survival as a communist state, rather than trying to make it the launching pad for the spread of world communism.

Encouraged by the success of the Nixon visit and Mao's continued uncertainty over how to interpret Lin's behaviour, Zhou embarked on a concerted effort to restore economic production and stability after the disruption of the Cultural Revolution. Chen Yun (the veteran economic planner), while too old to resume work, at least appeared in public to endorse Zhou's policies. The introduction of university entrance exams also did something to raise standards in further education.

However, Zhou was unable to remove the radicals from their positions of power in the CCRG, and Mao swung his support back behind them in 1973, when he eventually decided that Lin had in fact been a rightist pretending to be on the far left. This slowed Zhou's progress with his policies and led to him becoming the renewed target of attacks from the radicals, whose confidence had now been restored.

Despite this setback, Zhou did manage to get Deng Xiaoping brought back into the fold in 1973. Deng had been identified as a serious 'capitalist roader' in 1966, when he was sacked from his post and sent into exile to perform manual labour. However, as a pragmatist and as someone who could get things done, he too benefitted from the post-Lin need for moderation, and Zhou was able to persuade Mao to bring him back into the government. Mao's initial motive in restoring Deng was to employ him to help train his newly chosen successor, **Wang Hongwen**.

Mao's plan was for Deng and Wang to work together for a few years; if all went well, Wang would be able to go it alone after Mao's death. In this way, Deng played an important role in helping Mao to strike a balance between the radicals and the pragmatists between 1973 and 1976. Deng also led China's delegation to the United Nations, to which they had been admitted in 1971 when they gained US support, and he was appointed army chief of staff in order to keep the regional military

KEY TERM

Four Modernisations
Zhou had been advocating a pragmatic programme to develop agriculture, industry, defence and education on a more systematic basis for many years, but without much success. They became the future cornerstone of Deng's policies, when he assumed control after 1976.

KEY PERSON

Wang Hongwen (1935–92)
A member of the Gang of Four who had risen to prominence during the Shanghai disturbances of early 1967. His background as a worker, peasant and soldier ticked all the right boxes, and he was unveiled as Mao's choice to succeed him at the Tenth Party Congress of 1973.

had not brought them equality with men, and many old practices were still being followed at the time of the Communist revolution, particularly in rural areas, where change was inevitably slower.

Clause Six of the Communist Common Program of 1949 promised the abolition of restrictions affecting women and affirmed their right to equal treatment with men, in political, economic, cultural, educational and social spheres, and the freedom for both men and women to marry whoever they wanted. The Communists' commitment to eradicating all signs of China's **feudal** past also required destroying the concept of the family as the basic social unit. This was for two reasons:

- family relations embodied the Confucian values of obedience to parents and elders
- the existence of the family encouraged a bourgeois mindset, because it tempted people to attach too much importance to acquiring personal possessions.

KEY TERM

Feudal
In Chinese history, feudal refers to the time under the emperors before 1911. The rich got land in return for serving the emperor. Lower down the hierarchy, peasants without land were allowed to rent it from the landowners in return for working for them. To Communists, 'feudal' was a blanket term symbolising everything wrong with traditional China.

Without doubt, the status of women was significantly raised by the Communists. However, merely passing new laws is not enough to alter deeply ingrained attitudes, so the impact of the reforms was much more limited in practice than it was in theory.

Foot binding

Foot binding involved breaking the toes of young girls and folding them back under the foot, which was then tightly bound. This excruciatingly painful process had to be carried out before the feet were fully grown, and it restricted foot growth to about three inches, which was regarded by men as a sign of beauty and distinction. It was also a convenient way of restricting women's

movement. In her book *Wild Swans*, Jung Chang described how her grandmother had her feet bound at the age of two, having a cloth stuck into her mouth to gag her, while the arch of her foot was crushed by a large stone.

Although the practice came under challenge in the 19th century and was outlawed in 1911, it still persisted in some rural areas when the Communists came to power. Their decision to ban it brought it to a speedier end, but it was already on the way out.

The Marriage Law, 1950

The Communists had experimented with new marriage laws in the Jiangxi and Yanan areas under their control in the 1930s, and the Red Army was instructed to treat women with respect, in marked contrast to women's treatment at the hands of the Japanese invaders after 1937. Once the Communists acquired power over the whole country, the 1950 Marriage Law was one of the first changes they introduced. The new Marriage Law dramatically changed the basis of marriage, from a contractual arrangement between families to something freely entered into by two individuals.

Mao had been personally involved in opposing arranged marriages since his teens. As a 14-year-old, he had rebelled against his father by refusing to go through with his own marriage (which had been arranged with a woman seven years his senior), even though the **bride price** had already been paid. In 1919, he had become embroiled in a bitter controversy in Changsha that had flared up when an unhappy young bride had cut her own throat and bled to death in front of the guests, rather than go through with her wedding.

KEY TERM

Bride price
An amount paid by the family of the groom to the family of the bride, which reflects her perceived value. A dowry is a payment in the opposite direction.

This incident had inspired Mao to write a series of articles condemning arranged marriages and the marriage system in general, which he claimed turned women into slaves. It seems

1966 – Red Guards attack the 'four olds'
Schools and universities closed
Barefoot doctor scheme launched
Jiang Qing put in charge of cultural policy

1971 – Propaganda campaign to restrict family size

1976 – Death of Mao

| 1965 | 1970 | 1975 | 1980 |

1968 – Rustication campaign takes teenagers away from families

1973 – Zhou begins to restore stability to education system
Revival of anti-Confucius campaign in bid to discredit Lin Biao

to have sparked a genuine urge on his part to promote women's rights, and, as his power within the CCP grew, he made it clear that he regarded advancing women's rights as an integral part of the Communist programme. This idealism that first aroused Mao's interest in women's rights was also mixed with practical considerations. Women made up half of the population (he had referred to them as holding up half of the sky), and without at least their tacit support, revolution could not be achieved.

The new law was based on the principle that marriage should be a free choice between both partners and on equal rights for both sexes. The main clauses were as follows.

- The practice of arranged marriages and the payment of dowries to a husband or his family were outlawed.

- Men and women who had been forced to marry previously had the right to divorce their partners.

- All marriages and divorces had to be registered with local government.

- Divorce was to be available on equal terms, except that a man could not divorce his wife if she was pregnant or within a year of her giving birth.

- Children born out of wedlock had equal rights with other children.

- Women retained the right to keep the property they already owned when they married.

- **Concubinage** and **polygamy** were both outlawed.

The importance the Communists attached to the law is shown by the speed with which they tackled the issue, drafting it while the civil war was still going on. In order to enforce it effectively, they deluged the public with a huge propaganda campaign in the press, on the radio and through posters and leaflets. The Party organised thousands of drama troupes to take plays that publicised the new laws around the villages, and Party cadres were urged to check that the law was actually being applied.

KEY TERMS

Concubinage
The practice of financially supporting women as mistresses. Although now banned by law, this apparently did not apply to Mao himself, who always had access to a supply of women, officially designated as a PLA dance troupe.

Polygamy
The practice of having multiple wives at the same time.

SOURCE

1 Government posters publicised the changes made by the 1950 Marriage Law. The caption on this one, which was published in 1953, reads 'In marriage, keep an eye on your own interests, and return radiant after registration.'

婚姻自己作主張 登記回來喜洋洋

However, despite these efforts, the impact of the law was limited by traditional resistance, which was even more pronounced in the Muslim regions of the west. As a result, a second propaganda drive was launched in 1953, but this too was undermined by the outlook of the cadres, many of whom resented the changes. It would take time and a lot more education to shift traditional male attitudes to marriage and the status of women in general.

The impact of collectivisation and the communes on women's lives

The land redistribution campaign of 1950 appeared to have advanced the cause of women's emancipation significantly, as it gave women the chance to own land in their own name for the first time. Prior to this, all property dealings had been controlled by men. However, this gain was short-lived, because neither men nor women were allowed to own land privately once the new collectivisation scheme became compulsory a few years later.

In theory, the communes should have been beneficial for women, because it was envisaged that they would provide canteens, laundries and kindergartens to free women from domestic chores, enabling them to concentrate on working on the land or other enterprises in which the communes were engaged. However, since few communes could supply this range of support facilities, the reality was far less liberating. The poem below, written by women in a commune in Hsiancheng county for the propaganda monthly, *China Pictorial*, portrays the idealistic view.

SOURCE

2 This poem, which appeared in the magazine *China Pictorial* in 1958, was written by a woman living in a People's Commune.

Nurseries, kindergartens, tailor shops,
You don't do the cooking,
Or feed the pigs the slops.
Machines make the clothing
And grind the flour.
When you give birth to a baby
It's cared for every hour.
Freed from household drudgery,
Let's produce more by the day,
And drive ahead to communism,
It isn't far away!

While the introduction of the communes might appear to have been a step towards sexual equality, the actual working conditions in agriculture put women at a serious disadvantage. Typically, they earned fewer **work points** than men because the nature of much agricultural work involved heavy physical labour, and women's productive capacity was frequently lower than men's. Furthermore, the cadres responsible for enforcing discipline usually held traditional attitudes towards sexual equality, and were intolerant of requests for absence from women who were pregnant or during menstruation. This meant women were frequently treated more harshly than men.

KEY TERM

Work points
Awarded according to output. In theory, they were convertible into cash or material rewards, although they became increasingly irrelevant in communes where everyone ate communally and food was shared. Furthermore, there seemed little point earning work points when there was nothing to spend them on, which was often the case.

Women's vulnerability increased during the years of famine (1958–62), when food was even scarcer. As the most productive workers, men could claim more of the food rations. As mothers, women had the invidious task of deciding if they, or their children, were going to be fed first, if at all. Lack of food is often cited as driving more women into prostitution during the famine. It also caused a significant rise in the divorce rate in badly hit areas. When food ran out, either the husband or wife went elsewhere to seek work and maybe a new partner. In Gansu province, for example, the divorce rate rose by 60 percent in the famine years. Wife-selling was another desperate remedy adopted by some to make their resources go further.

SOURCE

9

From Nien Cheng, *Life and Death in Shanghai* (1987). This comes from Cheng's account of the day the Red Guards ransacked her house to destroy any evidence of the 'four olds'. She was the widow of a former manager at Shell, and lived with her daughter in a very comfortable house, where she still employed two servants, who also had rooms in the house. She had been expecting a visit for some time. It came on 3 July 1966.

The Red Guards pushed open the front door and entered the house. There were between thirty and forty senior high school students, aged between fifteen and twenty, led by two men and one woman much older. Although they all wore the arm bands of the Red Guards, I thought the three older people were the teachers who generally accompanied them when they looted private homes.

The lead Red Guard, a gangling youth with angry eyes, stepped forward and said to me, 'we are the Red Guards. We have come to take revolutionary action against you!' Though I knew I was doing something futile, I held up the copy of the Constitution and said calmly 'It's against the Constitution of the People's Republic of China to enter a private house without a search warrant.'

The young man snatched the document out of my hand and threw it on the floor. With his eyes blazing, he said, 'the Constitution is abolished. It was a document written by the Revisionists within the Communist Party. We recognise only the teachings of our Great Leader Chairman Mao.'

A girl came within a few inches of where I stood. She shook her fist in front of my nose and spat on the floor. Another young man used a stick to smash the mirror hanging over the chest facing the front door. Then he took from another Red Guard a small blackboard which he hung up on a hook. On it was written a quotation from Mao. It said, 'When the enemies with guns are annihilated, the enemies without guns still remain.' The Red Guards read the quotation aloud as if taking a solemn oath. Afterwards, they told me to read it. Then one of them shouted to me, 'an enemy without a gun! That's what you are. Hand over the keys!'

I placed my bunch of keys on the chest amidst the fragments of glass. One of them picked them up. All the Red Guards dispersed into various parts of the house. A girl pushed me into the dining room and locked the door.

 THINKING HISTORICALLY Cause and consequence (6a)

Seeing things differently

Different times and different places have a different set of ideas. Beliefs about how the world works, how human societies should be governed or the best way to achieve economic prosperity, can all be radically different from our own. It is important for the historian to take into account these different attitudes and be aware of the dangers of judging them against modern ideas.

The account in Source 9 describes a visit by the Red Guards. It goes on to describe how the author, having persuaded the students to let her out to visit the bathroom, tried to dissuade them from smashing various valuable antiques, suggesting they might sell them in Hong Kong to raise funds for their campaign to export the revolution abroad. Although this ploy was successful, it did not stop them smashing her collection of classical records. When she tried to argue that they were not 'the forbidden music of our dance halls and night clubs', she was told: 'You live in the past. Don't you know that our Great Leader has said that western music of any kind is decadent? Do the peasants and workers want Chopin, Mozart, Beethoven or Tchaikovsky? Of course not! We are going to compose our own proletarian music.'

Answer the following questions:

1 How would you describe the attitudes being shown by the Red Guards in this extract?

2 Why do you think they held these attitudes? (Think about longer-term as well as short-term reasons.)

3 How do you think it would have affected the students' attitudes if they had known that they would be sent up to the mountains and down to the countryside later in the year?

4 Are there any other attitudes towards things that people held in China in this period that strike you as very different from your own ways of seeing things?

5 How important is it for historians to deal with events in the context of the beliefs and values of people in the past, as well as seeing them as part of a greater pattern?

The role of Jiang Qing and the imposition of revolutionary art and culture

Interviewed after her arrest following Mao's death, Jiang Qing defended her behaviour by describing herself to the Public Prosecutor as 'Chairman Mao's dog – whoever he asked me to bite, I bit'. However, while she may not have initiated policy, she certainly carried it out ruthlessly. Believing that her previous career as an actress gave her a special insight into the performing arts, and supported by her radical allies in the CCRG, Jiang Qing set about her task of purifying Chinese culture, working closely with the Minister of Culture and a range of experienced singers, dancers and composers. A rigid form of censorship was established which prevented any work (across the entire field of the arts) from appearing in public until it had satisfied her criteria of cultural purity. While this led to strict control, it also resulted in some inconsistencies to accommodate her own arbitrary preferences. For example, while most Western cultural influences were banned because of their bourgeois origins, piano music and oil paintings were allowed because they suited her personal taste.

Only works that related to contemporary Chinese themes were permitted, so traditional stories had to be updated and put into a modern context. Creative artists unwilling to produce work that served the revolution found themselves at best unemployed, at worst sent for re-education to a labour camp.

Jiang Qing also took advantage of her power over culture to pursue personal vendettas against her many enemies from the past, including actresses who had won roles ahead of her in the 1930s and those who knew compromising details of her earlier career.

The main result of Jiang's control was to completely stifle creativity. In an effort to fill the void, and to satisfy her desire to dominate artistic output herself, she commissioned a set of eight opera ballets, each of which symbolised the triumph of the heroic workers over their class oppressors. Most of these involved reworking traditional stories into a modern setting to give them contemporary relevance. They were the only form of theatrical entertainment available and became very well known beyond Beijing, because they were broadcast so frequently over the radio and were much used in schools.

SOURCE 10

Anchee Min, *Red Azalea* (2006). This was the first part of her memoir (*The Cooked Seed* was the second – see Source 5), recalling her youth as a keen teenage Red Guard, before being rusticated along with thousands of other young people.

I became an opera fan. There were not many forms of entertainment. The word 'entertainment' was considered a dirty bourgeois word. The opera was something else. It was a proletarian statement. The revolutionary operas created by Madam Mao. To love or not to love the operas was a serious political attitude. It meant to be or not to be a revolutionary. The operas were taught on radio and in school, and were promoted by the neighbourhood organizations. For ten years. The same operas. I listened to the operas when I ate, walked and slept. I grew up with the operas. I decorated the porch with posters of my favourite opera heroines. I sang the operas wherever I went. My mother heard me singing in my dreams; she said that I was preserved by the operas. It was true. I could not go on a day without listening to the operas. I pasted my ear close to the radio, figuring out the singer's breaths. I imitated her. The aria was called 'I won't quit the battle until all the beasts are killed.' It was sung by Iron Plum a teenage character in an opera called *The Red Lantern*. I would not stop singing the aria until my vocal cords hurt. My father could not bear my loud wailing with the radio; he always yelled, 'Are you hanging yourself in the kitchen?'

AS Level Exam-Style Question Section A

Study Source 10 before you answer this question.

How much weight do you give the evidence of Source 10 for an enquiry into the impact of Jiang Qing's control of Chinese culture between 1966 and 1976?

Explain your answer using the source, the information about it and your own knowledge of the historical context. (12 marks)

Tip
You will need to extend the range of your answer to go beyond opera, which is the focus of the source.

These model works were played out before huge audiences, who dared not express anything but approval. US President Nixon recalled not looking forward to going to see the *Red Detachment of Women* during his visit in 1972, but being pleasantly surprised by its 'dazzling technical virtuosity' even if the story was 'emotionally and dramatically superficial'. Party secretary Deng Xiaoping was less complimentary, arguing that people wanted entertainment and variety, not battlefield scenes, but Jiang had her revenge when he was purged, not once, but twice.

Many of the eight model works were made into feature films, which were the main offerings of cinemas during the period 1966–73. It has been calculated that, by 1974, the film of the opera *Taking Tiger Mountain by Strategy* had received 7.3 billion viewings, which equates to seven viewings by every Chinese person. This probably owes more to the lack of choice (no other full-length films were made and foreign films were banned) than to its popularity, but the figure also reflects the growth of rural projection units taking films around the countryside.

SOURCE

Anchee Min, *The Cooked Seed* (2013). The events she is referring to occurred in 1976, shortly before Mao's death. Madame Mao is Jiang Qing.

I was handpicked by Madame Mao's talent scouts while hoeing weeds in a cotton field. Like a package, I was shipped to the Shanghai Film Studio. I was to be trained to play a leading role in Madame Mao's propaganda movies, although I knew nothing about acting. I was chosen only because my looks matched Madame Mao's image of a proletarian heroine. I had a weather-beaten face and a muscled body capable of carrying hundreds of pounds of manure. I froze the moment I heard the sound of a camera rolling, but I tried hard so that I could escape the labour camp.

It was not my fault that Madame Mao picked me. She wanted 'a piece of white paper on which to paint any colour she liked'. All I did was follow orders. I was even taught how to drink water 'in the proletarian style' at the Shanghai Film studio.

'No, you're drinking the water incorrectly, Comrade Min,' my instructor yelled. Your pinkie[*] is up, and that's Miss Bourgeois. You must grab the cup, gulp the water down in one breath, and wipe your mouth with both of your sleeves!'

I had no talent for acting. The camera assistant had to pin the corner of my costume down to hide my trembling. My back was soaked with sweat at the sound of 'Action!' I kept picturing myself being shipped back to the labour camp.

[*pinkie means little finger]

SOURCE

From Nien Cheng, *Life and Death in Shanghai* (1987). Here she is writing about her daughter, Meiping, who had already started work as a film actress when the Cultural Revolution took off. Because her work was seen as serving the revolution, she initially avoided being subjected to struggle sessions and jailed like her mother, but she was arrested as a 'class enemy' in 1967 and murdered by the Red Guards that year.

It had been somewhat of a surprise when my daughter told me that two well-known film actresses, currently teachers at the new Film School of Shanghai, had approached her to suggest that she try for the entrance examination as a specially selected 'talent' to enrol in the school. She said they had sent talent scouts all over the country to select students for the examination. 'There is bound to be a big response because everybody wants to live in Shanghai', she said.

So, she went to the Film School. Three years later she graduated and was given a job with the Film Studio, which was run by the Ministry of Culture. The acting profession was glamorous even in Communist China, but those who worked in it did not receive higher pay than factory workers. The function of an actress was to bring entertainment to the masses, so besides taking part in films, she often gave performances in factories, rural communes, coal-mines and oilfields, travelling far and wide with her unit all over China.

A Level Exam-Style Question Section A

Study Sources 11 and 12 before you answer this question.

How far could the historian make use of Sources 11 and 12 together to investigate Jiang Qing's efforts to create a new style of proletarian culture during the period 1966–76?

Explain your answer using both sources, the information given about them and your own knowledge of the historical context. (20 marks)

Tip
The sources show similarities and differences; also, you will need to widen your answer to include a wider range than the cinema, and pay attention to the dates.

Preparing for your AS Level Paper 2 exam

Advance planning

1. Draw up a timetable for your revision and try to keep to it. Spread your timetable over a number of weeks, and aim to cover four or five topics each week.
2. Spend longer on topics that you have found difficult, and revise them several times.
3. Above all, do not try to limit your revision by attempting to 'question spot'. Try to be confident about all aspects of your Paper 2 work, because this will ensure that you have a choice of questions in Section B.

Paper 2 overview:

AS Paper 2	Time: 1 hour 30 minutes	
Section A	Answer 1 compulsory two-part sources question	8+12 marks = 20 marks
Section B	Answer 1 question from a choice of 3	20 marks
	Total marks =	40 marks

You should familiarise yourself with the layout of the paper by looking at the examples published by Edexcel. The questions for each section are followed by eight pages of lined paper where you should write your answer.

Section A questions

Each of the two parts of the question will focus on one of the two contemporary sources provided. The sources together will total around 300 words. The (a) question, worth 8 marks, will be in the form of 'Why is Source 1 useful for an enquiry into…?' The (b) question, worth 12 marks, will be in the form of 'How much weight do you give the evidence of Source 2 for an enquiry into…?' In both your answers you should address the value of the content of the source, and then its nature, origin and purpose. Finally, you should use your own knowledge of the context of the source to assess its value.

Section B questions

These questions ask you to reach a judgement on an aspect of the topic studied. The questions will have the form, for example, of 'How far…', 'To what extent…' or 'How accurate is it to say…'. The questions can deal with historical concepts such as cause, consequence, change, continuity, similarity, difference and significance. You should consider the issue raised in the question, consider other relevant issues, and then conclude with an overall judgement.

The timescale of the questions could be as short as a single year or even a single event (an example from Option 2C.2 could be, 'To what extent was Russia's involvement in the First World War responsible for the fall of the Provisional Government in 1917?'). The timescale could be longer depending on the historical event or process being examined, but questions are likely to be shorter than those set for Sections A and B in Paper 1.

Use of time

This is an issue that you should discuss with your teachers and fellow students, but here are some suggestions for you.

1. Do not write solidly for 45 minutes on each question. For Section A it is essential that you have a clear understanding of the content of each source, the points being made, and the nature, origin and purpose of each source. You might decide to spend up to ten minutes reading the sources and drawing up your plan, and 35 minutes writing your answer.
2. For Section B answers you should spend a few minutes working out what the question is asking you to do, and drawing up a plan of your answer before you begin to write your response.

Preparing for your AS Level exams

Paper 2: AS Level sample answer with comments

Section A

Part A requires you to:

- identify key points in the source and explain them
- deploy your own knowledge of the context in which events took place
- make appropriate comments about the author/origin/purpose of the source.

Study Source 5 (Chapter 2, page 206) before you answer this question.

Why is Source 5 valuable to the historian for an enquiry into the reasons why the Second Five-Year Plan (1958–62) was so ambitious?

Explain your answer using the source, the information given about it and your own knowledge of the historical context. (8 marks)

Average student answer

The source is valuable to the historian because it shows how well China had performed in the First Five-Year Plan, and the second plan was the logical next step. It comes from a publication that supported the government.

> Opening paragraph is generalised. The observations made are valid, but are left undeveloped.

The article from 'China Pictorial' was written just after the first plan finished and is commenting on how successful it had been in increasing production. It boasts about steel production going up by 31.2% per year and the large number of new factories opening up, saying that the Chinese people showed 'amazing ability in building up the country'. As a result, the second plan will be 'even more awe-inspiring' and will produce 12 million tonnes of steel so that soon China will overtake Britain, even though its Industrial Revolution was so long ago. Therefore, because the first plan had been a success, there was every chance the second could go even further, and this comes across in the source.

> This shows understanding of the source content. However, there is no additional contextual knowledge. While the final sentence makes a valid inference, an example from the source to back it up would strengthen it.

The background to the source shows that 'China Pictorial' was on the side of the government because it featured Mao's calligraphy and was allowed to carry on during the Cultural Revolution. The timing of the source is significant because it was written just as the first plan finished, so the writer would be well placed to comment on its achievements, which of course is what influenced the government making the second plan so ambitious.

> The background is being examined here, but at a superficial level, without explaining relevance. The importance of the source as a means to inspire the public to work hard, and therefore make a more ambitious second plan succeed, has been overlooked.

Overall the source is valuable because it makes it clear that the government knew that China had the potential to develop further because the first plan had been such a success, and it was using the magazine to drive people forward to greater efforts.

> A useful conclusion that summarises the answer, but the value of the source as a piece of propaganda has been hinted at rather than explicitly explained.

Verdict

This is an average answer because:

- it is focused on the question
- it identifies evidence from the source that shows the success of the first plan, and makes the point that the second plan built on this – so the content of the source has been understood and used

- it makes some attempt to examine the nature of the source, but without explicitly explaining its role as propaganda – therefore, as a piece of historical evidence, the source has only been used superficially
- it lacks own supporting contextual knowledge.

Use the feedback on this answer to rewrite it, making as many improvements as you can.

Paper 2: AS Level sample answer with comments

Section A

Part B requires you to:

- interrogate the source
- draw reasoned inferences
- deploy your own knowledge to interpret the material in its context
- make judgements about the value (weight) of the source in terms of making judgements.

Study Source 7 (Chapter 4, page 249) before you answer this question.

How much weight do you give the evidence of Source 7 for an enquiry into the Communists' approach to health care reform, 1949–76?

Explain your answer using the source, the information given about it and your own knowledge of the historical context. (12 marks)

Average student answer

This source carries quite a lot of weight for an enquiry into health reform because it comes from an eyewitness who personally participated in some aspects of the reforms during part of this period. It highlights some of the problems that the Chinese faced in training the barefoot doctors and the hard work that they put into it.

> A reasonably focused start, but without reference to limitations of the source.

It is clear from what Horn has written that the Chinese authorities were not willing or able to invest much money into training the barefoot doctors, who lived in primitive conditions and had very little equipment to work with. He explains that they had to cram their training into four months of the year and the books they used had to be specially written by people like Horn in the mobile teams.

> Adequate understanding is shown of the source's contents and there is a brief, but undeveloped, contextual hint about the economic constraints.

The scenes Horn describes fit in well with the approach to reform that Mao wanted. Mao wanted to make health care much more widely available, and knew that diseases like dysentery, cholera and typhoid needed to be controlled in order to reduce the high death rates in the countryside. However, there was little money to spend on health because of the disasters of the Great Leap Forward (1958–62), which had ruined the economy. Also, it was Mao's preferred method to promote mass involvement in campaigns in order to keep the spirit of the revolution alive, so there was an ideological reason for making the training of new doctors a grass-roots scheme involving ordinary people like this.

> Context is provided more fully here to explain the nature of the scheme described by Horn.

However there is the problem that Horn was a Communist sympathiser so he has reasons to take a 'rose-tinted view' of the situation, and his account certainly conveys an optimistic view of the system, saying he was 'amazed' at how hard they studied. There is never any mention of the negative side of things, which does reduce the value of the source in such an enquiry.

> Limitations are briefly discussed, which run into a concluding judgment.

Verdict

This is an average answer because:

- there is some attempt to question the source in terms of Horn's wishful thinking
- the contents have been understood and some inferences about the reasons for training doctors in this way have been made
- there is some clear contextual awareness – economic and ideological
- a brief judgment has been reached.

Use the feedback on this answer to rewrite it, making as many improvements as you can.

Source 14 is useful because it tells us how the Communists went about persecuting Catholics ◄─── and it shows that the campaign worked because the Church was closed down and most of the Catholics gave in without a fight. Some Catholics even criticised their own Church, accusing it of 'enslaving them' and their numbers slumped from 400 to three overnight, so the campaign was successful in this area at least. The small number of Catholics who refused to give in ended up being sentenced to hard labour sometime later.

Valuable details have been extracted from both sources, and there is some attempt being made to draw inferences from them and to direct them at the question.

There is not so much detail about the campaign to destroy ancestral shrines, but it is clear in this case that they were destroyed to provide building materials for the backyard furnaces. Even Mao's parents' graves were ruined, which suggests that no one's graves or shrines were safe and therefore the campaign was a success, although Mao had personal misgivings, saying that the shrine should have been left alone and was useful in cheering people up.

Overall, therefore the two sources do provide a significant amount of useful material to the historian investigating the campaigns against religion, especially as they come from believable eyewitnesses.

Very brief as a concluding statement. The similarities and differences could be developed further, to much greater effect.

Verdict

This is an average answer because:

- it shows understanding of the content of the two sources, which is treated analytically
- evidence from the content is selected and linked to the focus of the question

- it makes only limited reference to the background context, which is left significantly undeveloped, and there is little attempt to bring in own knowledge
- it makes some attempt to establish the utility of the sources, in particular the credibility of Dr Li as an eyewitness.

Use the feedback on this answer to rewrite it, making as many improvements as you can.

Paper 2: A Level sample answer with comments

Section A

You will need to read and analyse two sources and use them in tandem to assess how useful they are in investigating an issue. For these questions remember to:

- spend time, up to ten minutes, reading and identifying the arguments and evidence present in the sources; then make a plan to ensure that your response will be rooted in these sources
- use specific references from the sources
- deploy your own knowledge to develop points made in the sources and establish appropriate context
- come to a substantiated judgement.

Study Sources 14 and 15 (Chapter 4, pages 259 and 260) before you answer this question.

How far could the historian make use of Sources 14 and 15 together to investigate the impact of the campaign to eradicate religion after 1949?

Explain your answer, using both sources, the information given about them and your knowledge of the historical context. (20 marks)

Strong student answer

Both sources would be useful to the historian investigating the campaign against religion because they both come from eyewitnesses with a good eye for detail. Zhang Yinxian says she 'will never forget 1952' and can remember what people said and some details, such as the rats taking over when everyone left. Even though she was over 100 when she was interviewed, and she had a clear motive for criticising the people who attacked her church, the detail makes her evidence seem convincing. In any case, even if some details are inaccurate, the fact remains that the church of which she was a member was closed down, and she and her two colleagues were put to hard labour. Moreover, her account was the product of a historian seeking out evidence from participants – Zhang herself was not seeking to publicise the events. The fact that Liao Yiwu is a critic of the regime in China does not detract from the value of the evidence at all because it is an interview and these are the words of Zhang, rather than the author's version of them.

> A direct opening, which explores the background to Source 14 in some detail and why this makes it useful, despite the obvious doubt raised by Zhang's age.

Dr Li also had a keen eye for detail, noticing how people in Mao's entourage responded to the situation and remembering Mao's reaction carefully. Li also wrote his account years after the event, from his new home in the USA, but he is resisting the temptation to attack Mao as a hypocrite who continued to take ancestor worship seriously, even though it was officially banned. It would have been easy to have mocked Mao, from the safety of his new home, for causing the destruction of his parents' shrine by his backyard furnace scheme, but the fact that Li does not do this suggests that his account is accurate.

> The background to Dr Li's account is explored, and again its value is established quite carefully.

Both sources provide useful details of the campaign against religion, but they are more explicitly stated in Source 14. This account explains the pressure that Catholics were put under as they underwent a 'political review process', and the impact is clear from the fact that they 'left in droves', some even going so far as to renounce the church and accuse it of 'enslaving them'. However, the actual wording of the renunciation makes it sound as though they may have merely been agreeing with a statement put in front of them because it sounds like one of the official slogans that the Communists often used.

> The value of the details provided in Source 14 is effectively weighed up here and linked to the wider context by some own knowledge of the anti-Catholic campaign.

The scale of the change is indicated by the statistics – 400 Catholics being reduced to a mere three. It is also apparent that the few, like the Bishop and Zhang, who did resist, were given a stay of execution before being dealt with. This ties in with the patriotic churches initiative which the government launched in a bid to appear more tolerant to the outside world, while retaining total control of the Christian Churches. Perhaps the resistance of Zhang, her aunt and the Bishop was partly accounted for by the Vatican's policy, which was not to yield to persecution.

Source 15 shows that ancestral shrines were sacrificed if they stood in the way of economic progress. If even Mao's mother's favourite Buddhist shrine and his parents' gravestones were demolished to provide the stone for backyard furnaces, then this suggests that the campaign was effective at least in removing the physical evidence of ancestor worship. However, Mao's personal sadness at the loss of his parents' graves shows that the campaign was less effective in changing people's attitudes. The same might be said of the campaign against the Catholic Church in Source 14, but to a lesser extent since only three people actively resisted and it looks as if most gave in quietly.

> The slightly more complicated scenario described in Source 15 is explained here, and there is a strong inference about the success of the campaign at a superficial level, since even Mao was in a sense a victim.

Taken together, the two sources do provide some useful evidence about the anti-religious campaigns, although they only cover two elements of the campaign which was also waged more widely against Buddhism, Islam, Confucianism and the Protestant Church. They show some similarities, in that both come from reasonably reliable and observant eyewitnesses. The fact that one (Source 14) comes from a victim of the campaign, while the other was written by a spectator adds something to their overall value.

> In this concluding paragraph, and at the end of the previous one, an attempt is being made to sum up by examining their joint value. Similarities and differences are being recognised and taken into account.

Verdict

This is a strong answer because:

- it shows understanding of the content provided by both sources and appropriate details are selected and made relevant to the enquiry
- it brings in accurate contextual information, which is linked to the material selected from the sources themselves

- it examines the nature of the two sources as eyewitness accounts quite closely, and makes careful inferences from this about their utility and limitations
- there is some attempt to assess the two sources as a pair.

Paper 2: A Level sample answer with comments

Section B

These questions assess your understanding of the period in some depth. They will ask you about the content you learned about in the four key themes, but may not ask about more than one theme. For these questions remember to:

- give an analytical, not a descriptive, response
- support your points with evidence
- cover the whole time period specified in the question
- come to a substantiated judgement.

How accurate is it to say that Mao's main motives for launching the Cultural Revolution in 1966 were ideological rather than political? (20 marks)

Average student answer

The Cultural Revolution began with the first great rally in Tiananmen Square, attended by a million Red Guards in August 1966. Mao was motivated to launch it by a mixture of both ideological and political motives.

> A weak opening because it gives no indication of how the answer will develop and provides only basic context.

Ideology was always important to Mao and one key element of this was his concern to prevent 'the revolution going to sleep'. He knew that if things were allowed to settle down for too long, then complacency would creep in and people would become more interested in preserving their vested interests than in creating a genuine communist state. Things had settled down in China since the Great Leap Forward was launched in 1958, mainly due to the appalling famine that it caused, but Mao knew it was time to start a new initiative before it was too late. Mao was also aware that there were a lot of young people who had not yet been involved in the revolution and it was the ideal time to get them involved so that they would feel that they had helped to create communism and would therefore be willing to defend it from future attack. This is why the Cultural Revolution gave such freedom of action to the Red Guards, who were told to go out and smash the 'four olds'.

> Two valid aspects of ideology as a motivating reason are introduced here, but the lack of factual development weakens it.

Another way in which Mao can be seen as ideologically motivated is because he was worried that ever since 1960 capitalism had been coming back into the economy. This was because Liu and Deng had been given the task of restoring economic stability after the famine, and to do so they had allowed many communes to disband and had restored private trade. China was even importing food from capitalist countries, which made it look to the rest of the world that communism was failing. Mao hated this and he had started accusing Liu in public of being a 'capitalist roader', who had chosen the wrong track for China.

> This point has much more factual support. However, the importance of these ideological factors in influencing Mao needs summing up before the argument moves on to the political motives.

However, Mao also had political motives for starting the Cultural Revolution. Liu Shaoqi and Deng Xiaoping, who were in charge of restoring economic stability, had become quite popular with peasants who preferred private ownership to the communes and inside the Communist Party. Mao easily got paranoid about threats to his leadership of the Party, and he had made the mistake of stepping down in favour of Liu as chairman of the Republic after the Great Leap Forward went wrong. Even though Liu probably was not plotting to take over, Mao thought he was and decided to get rid of him as soon as he could.

With this aim in mind, Mao started building up his personality cult, mainly with the help of the PLA leader, Lin Biao, who produced 'The Little Red Book' of Mao quotations and made it an essential part of army training. It was also much used by teachers in schools as a textbook to influence the younger generation the same way. Mao also got radical supporters from Shanghai, such as Chen Boda and Kang Sheng, into important politburo positions, so that by 1966 he felt he had enough support to launch an attack on Liu. Liu did not seem to realise what was happening until it was too late.

In 1966, Mao announced his return to politics by his much-publicised swim in the Yangtze and then his supporters in the politburo started a wall poster campaign to encourage the university students to rebel against teachers who were not revolutionary enough. When Liu made the mistake of trying to control the student unrest, it was easy to make him appear as a counter-revolutionary and to discredit him. He was sacked from his post soon after, and the Cultural Revolution had begun with the Red Guard students going out to destroy the 'four olds'.

Political factors, then, did also play a key part in Mao's decision to launch the Cultural Revolution, since Mao was determined he had to act to get rid of Liu and Deng, both of whom he saw as threats to his leadership. The Cultural Revolution actually got started because Mao wanted to discredit Liu, and he could do this once he had lined up enough support from the politburo and in the country as a whole, where the army and young people had become followers of the Mao cult. However, ideology was equally important because Mao took this very seriously having written a lot about it before he got to power. He was worried that the revolution would run out of steam if a big new mass mobilisation campaign was not launched soon, and the young people were ideal to carry this out.

> Mao's political motive for wanting to downgrade Liu is explained clearly enough, with adequate support provided. The point about Mao's paranoia could be strengthened by referring to other occasions when rivals were removed in pre-emptive strikes.

> The events leading to the start of the Cultural Revolution are described here. As it stands it looks like freestanding narrative, but it could easily be strengthened by making stronger links to the question. For example, a comment explaining that Mao dared not act against Liu, his political rival, until he had strengthened his own support base inside the key organ of the Party and in the country at large.

> The conclusion does bring both parts of the answer together, but there is still no answer to the question. Each part has merely been summed up and no overall judgement made.

Verdict

This is an average answer because:

- while it covers the key elements of the argument accurately, with some analysis, there are also some descriptive passages
- it shows understanding of what the question is driving at, but the paragraphs need linking more strongly to the wording of the question

- an overall judgement is lacking – the evidence in support of each viewpoint is summarised, but there is no overall answer to the question
- the answer is generally well organised and clearly written.

Use the feedback on this answer to rewrite it, making as many improvements as you can.

Paper 2: A Level sample answer with comments

Section B

These questions assess your understanding of the period in some depth. They will ask you about the content you learned about in the four key themes, but may not ask about more than one theme. For these questions remember to:

- give an analytical, not a descriptive response
- support your points with evidence
- cover the whole time period specified in the question
- come to a substantiated judgement.

How accurate is it to say that Mao's main motives for launching the Cultural Revolution in 1966 were ideological rather than political? (20 marks)

Strong student answer

Several aspects of Mao's ideology played a key role in his decision to launch the Cultural Revolution in 1966. Mao was concerned that true socialism was being undermined by the pragmatic economic policies followed by Liu and Deng since 1961. He was also anxious to prevent the revolution losing its impetus and therefore wanted to launch a new mass campaign as soon as possible. However, his motives were also political – he was determined to reassert his political power, which had slipped since he stepped down as leader of the PRC in 1959 – so he started the Cultural Revolution for a combination of both reasons.

Constantly renewing the revolution was vital to Mao for ideological reasons, because he feared that if the revolution stopped moving forward, then old bourgeois attitudes would start to resurface and the gains already made would be lost. This is what he thought had gone wrong in the Soviet Union. By the early 1960s, China had split from Russia and was portraying itself as the main Communist power in the world, so it suited Mao for this political reason to follow a different path from Russia. However, since the need to continue the revolution was so deeply entrenched in his thinking, it was inevitable that Mao would launch a new drive forward at some point in the mid-1960s. It is therefore fair to argue that ideology was at the forefront of his reasons for launching the Cultural Revolution.

Moreover, Mao was deeply worried that the dismantling of communes and return to private farming which had been reintroduced in the early 1960s was taking China in the wrong direction because it was dangerously 'revisionist'. While Mao had eventually conceded that the famine had come about because of the Great Leap Forward and had therefore empowered Liu, Deng and Chen Yun to take whatever steps were necessary to restore food supplies to acceptable levels, he refused to accept that the commune system itself was inherently flawed. He preferred to blame individuals, such as poorly trained cadres or lazy peasants, for failing to implement the communes properly. Mao was anxious that China was taking the 'capitalist road' and his decision to summon the 7,000-cadre conference in 1962 was designed to put a stop to any further drift in this direction, even if the outcome was not what he had planned.

Even worse ideologically was the fact that China began importing grain from the USA. As soon as the economic situation improved in China, Mao wanted to restore the 'correct' socialist approach, and purging those Communist leaders who accepted the pragmatic economic approach would be vital in order to achieve this.

A final ideological factor motivating Mao was his desire to 'blood' the younger generation in revolutionary activity. By encouraging the creation of Red Guard units in 1966 and assuring the

A strong opening paragraph that directly addresses the question and uses some selected detail to indicate the direction of the argument. No overall judgement has yet been made, but that will not matter as long as it has emerged by the end.

The first ideological reason is explained here. The comparison with Russia shows wider knowledge and is relevant. This has been recognised as evidence of a political motive, which shows how hard it is to disentangle the two.

Three more aspects of how Mao was motivated by ideological considerations are tackled here. Each is made relevant to the question and the level of support is adequate, avoiding unnecessary detail.

young that it was 'right to rebel' against authority, a new mass mobilisation campaign could be set in motion which would harness the enthusiasm of the young and in the process make them identify more closely with the new China. Lin Biao and Chen Boda had been preparing the ground for this by developing the Mao cult among the teenage generation since at least 1963, and by 1966 Mao felt the young were ready to be unleashed.

However, it is hard to separate these ideological motives from his political aim to restore his own power and sideline potential rivals before they became too popular. These political factors account for the timing of the Cultural Revolution. It began as an attack on individuals within the hierarchy of the Communist Party, before broadening into the attack on the 'four olds' in society at large by the Red Guards.

> This paragraph is useful because it explains how the argument is moving from one side of the case to the other, and shows some conceptual understanding that the two reasons cannot always be separated.

By 1963, Mao was seeking to reassert the political power he had conceded when he had installed Liu in his place as head of state in 1959, and he had moved even further into the background when Liu and Deng, the Party secretary, began the painful process of restoring the economy in the early 1960s. Not only did Mao have ideological objections to their economic policies, but he was also concerned on a political level that both were getting too popular.

The Socialist Education Movement of 1963 can be seen as Mao's first attempt to regain the political initiative. Mao launched the movement in order to reintroduce basic socialist values in the countryside and relaunch the class struggle at a local level, but its impact was limited by Liu who, as head of state, was able to use central control to prevent it becoming as radical as Mao wished. To Mao this was further evidence that Liu was dangerous, and he accused him openly of taking the 'capitalist road' at the 1964 Party Conference.

> These three paragraphs explain the development of Mao's political manoeuvring against Liu and Deng. There is some description of events, but this is made relevant and it helps to explain the stages by which Mao defeated Liu, and therefore the timing of the start of the Cultural Revolution.

By 1965, Mao felt strong enough to test the waters again by authorising the attack on Wu Han's play, although, like a guerrilla leader, he was ready to back off and distance himself if things went wrong. However, this was not necessary because the personality cult that Lin Biao had been building up through 'The Little Red Book', and the recent promotion of the Shanghai radicals to the politburo, meant that Mao now had enough support within the Party hierarchy to defeat his enemies. By launching the 1966 poster campaign in the universities over the head of Liu, and whipping up the students into a force that Liu could not stop, Mao left Liu powerless to prevent his demotion later in the year. It was clear from the positions in the background that Liu and Deng occupied on the podium at the first mass Tiananmen Square rally in August 1966 that they had fallen from grace. It was these political machinations against Liu, and to a lesser extent Deng, that provided the catalyst for the start of the Cultural Revolution – they explain the timing of its outbreak.

The events at the start of the Cultural Revolution and its timing, therefore, owed much to Mao's political calculations. In early 1966 he was manipulating events in the hope of flushing out his political rivals at a time when he felt strong enough to do this, which he had not been earlier. However, to Mao, ideological considerations were paramount and constant, whereas political motives came and went depending on circumstances. Mao's ideology dictated that a new mass mobilisation campaign was necessary every few years, and one which involved the next generation was essential in order to guarantee the long-term future of communism. Bearing this in mind it is safe to say that political motives, while definitely significant to Mao in the short term, were of secondary importance overall compared to his ideological priorities.

> A strong conclusion because the judgement is made clear, and it has been supported by the evidence presented in the rest of the answer.

Verdict

This is a strong answer because:

- it analyses relevant ideological and political considerations, using accurate and detailed support

- it shows a clear grasp of what is being asked and conceptual awareness that Mao's motives cannot be separated
- it reaches an overall judgement neatly based on the evidence, and is structured logically and coherently.

The German Democratic Republic, 1949–90

In 1949, four years after the end of the Second World War, the German Democratic Republic (GDR) was formally established. The GDR existed as a communist state for just over 40 years until it became part of the Federal Republic of Germany (FRG) in October 1990. Throughout its history, the GDR found itself on the very front line of the **Cold War**, and its capital, Berlin, often became a stark focus of the superpower rivalry between the USA and the USSR (Soviet Russia).

KEY TERM

Cold War
The period of political conflict, military tension and competition between the USSR and the USA and their allies following the end of the Second World War until the early 1990s. Tension arose due to their different ideologies and each believing the other wanted to expand their influence and territorial control.

How was the GDR established?

The GDR, along with the FRG, was created as a result of divisions between the victorious powers (the USSR, the USA, Britain and France) after the Second World War. Their failure to agree on the status of post-war Germany meant that the country was divided up. While the Western sectors were merged to form the FRG, East Germany became a socialist state supported by the USSR. It was, in effect, a one-party state led by the Marxist-Leninist Socialist Unity Party of Germany (SED). Yet the existence of the GDR could only be sustained by the construction of a wall to stop its citizens from emigrating to the West.

How did the GDR develop between 1961 and 1985?

The construction of the **Berlin Wall** in 1961 was to become the most symbolic feature of the GDR's control of its own citizens. For the GDR, the Wall was regarded as an essential defence against the West. The GDR government saw the FRG and its Western allies as expansionist powers that threatened the survival of the GDR. For the West, the Wall was a cruel construction by a government that had resorted to imprisoning its own people.

Behind the security of the Wall, the GDR was able to implement socialist policies with some success. While the GDR compared unfavourably with the much more affluent capitalist FRG, when compared with its communist counterparts in Eastern Europe, the GDR demonstrated a very successful economy and consequently higher living standards. Although the GDR was viewed by the West as an artificial puppet state of the USSR, it was able to gain some international recognition and prestige.

KEY TERM

Berlin Wall
This was built in 1961 to close the border between East and West Berlin. Berlin had been divided after the Second World War, and the USA, France and Britain controlled what became known as West Berlin. East Berlin was controlled by the GDR. Many left the GDR by crossing from East into West Berlin. This led to the GDR government closing the border between the two parts of the city. The Wall remained until 1989.

1945 – 1945 – End of the Second World War

1949 – May 1949 – The establishment of West Germany (FRG)
October 1949 – The establishment of East Germany (GDR)

1951 – 1951 – First Five-Year Plan

1961 – 1961 – The building of the Berlin Wall

1989 – October 1989 – Soviet leader Gorbachev visits East Berlin for the GDR's 40th anniversary celebrations
Honecker replaced by Krenz as General Secretary of the SED
November 1989 – The opening of the Berlin Wall

proportional representation. However, the reality of the system of government was very different in practice.

SOURCE

3 Victor Klemperer's diaries were published in 1995 and they are an account of his life in Germany from the Weimar Period until near his death in 1960. After the Second World War, Klemperer settled in the GDR. He worked as a languages lecturer and was a delegate to the *Volkskammer* as a part of one of the mass organisations – the Cultural Association.

1949, 12th October, Wednesday evening.

The German Democratic Republic. There's been nothing else on the wireless since yesterday. The presidential election, the parades, the speeches. I do not feel comfortable with it. I know how everything is fixed and how spontaneity and unanimity are prepared. I know that under the Nazis it sounded just the same and proceeded in just the same way. I know how little reality there is behind it. 20 million are not even a third of the German people and of the 20 million at least 12 are anti-Soviet. I know that internally the Democratic Republic is a lie, the SED supports and desires a Socialist Republic, it does not trust the middle-class parties, and the middle-class parties distrust it. At some point there will be a civil war... I am counted one of the Russian lackeys.

AS Level Exam-Style Question Section A

Study Source 3 before you answer this question.

How much weight do you give the evidence of Source 3 for an enquiry into the political system established in the GDR in 1949?

Explain your answer using the source, the information given about it and your own knowledge of the historical context. (12 marks)

Tip:
Think about whether Victor Klemperer is making a valid point about the nature of the political system in the GDR. Use your own knowledge to support/challenge his view. How does the origin and purpose of this source affect the weight you might give it as evidence?

The head of state

Initially, the GDR constitution included a head of state, known as president or prime minister, but with a purely ceremonial role, and the position was only ever held by Wilhelm Pieck. Like Ulbricht, Pieck had been in exile in the USSR for most of the duration of the Third Reich and returned to Germany in 1945. He played a major role in the formation of the SED and became prime minister when the GDR was set up in 1949. When he died in 1960, the position was abolished and replaced by the *Staatsrat* or Council of State, which was chaired by the SED leader.

The *Volkskammer* (People's Chamber)

In the original 1949 constitution, elections were to be held every four years. The first elections were held in 1952, but the 500 members of the *Volkskammer* – who represented the people – were not elected in the Western sense of democracy. The GDR, unlike the USSR, allowed other political parties to exist. Among the parties allowed were the Liberal Democratic Party and the Farmers' Party, and each was able to put forward candidates for elections. This gave an outward appearance of democracy, but there was no contest in elections between parties. The number of seats for each political party were predetermined by the SED before the election, so the actual outcome was already decided. Obviously, the largest number of seats were allocated to the SED to maintain its leading role. Most of the other political parties also had to accept control by the SED in what was known as the 'national bloc' of political parties. The *Volkskammer* also included representatives of the mass organisations, such as the Free German Youth (FDJ), Free German Trade Union Federation and the Democratic Women's Federation, which were all co-ordinated as a 'National Front of the GDR'.

Election results always gave the appearance that members were elected by the democratic will of the people. Turnouts in elections were very high, often over 90 percent, but this was in reality a reflection of the fact that voting was compulsory and there were fines, or even prison sentences, for those who failed to vote. The overwhelming approval that elections seemed to confer on those elected was also a product of the method used to vote. A voter simply took the ballot paper, which contained only one name, and dropped it into the ballot box. If a voter did not wish to approve the candidate, they would cross out the candidate's name, but they had to do so in a separate voting booth without any secrecy. The consequences for such an act of defiance could be severe – loss of one's job or expulsion from university, and close surveillance by the secret police. Thus, the elections did not provide a way of removing a government or even altering the balance within it. The only way of voting for an alternative was with one's feet and leaving the country, until the Berlin Wall was built in 1961.

To give the appearance that the *Volkskammer* was a body made up of a coalition of differing political organisations, the President of the *Volkskammer* was usually from a party other than the SED. The first President, Johannes Dieckmann, who was a member of the Liberal Democratic Party, served from 1949 to 1969.

The *Volkskammer* passed legislation, but this was predominantly a ratifying function, approving laws already decided by the Politburo of the SED. A sign of its relative lack of power was the fact that it met only for a few days each year.

The *Länderkammer* (States Chamber)

The *Länderkammer* represented the five historic German states (*Länder*) within the GDR. It was made up of representatives from the assemblies of the different *Länder* and operated on the same principles as the *Volkskammer*, with representatives chosen from a range of political parties on a predetermined basis and with the SED dominant. Its role was that of an upper house: it had the power to suggest new laws and veto any of the laws approved by the *Volkskammer*. In practice, it acted as another rubber-stamp for laws already decided by the Politburo and never used its power of veto.

The increasing differences in the development of the GDR and the FRG led to the five *Länder* being abolished in 1952. They were replaced with 14 *Bezirke* (districts), each of which was under the control of an SED officer. These smaller regions made it easier for central government to repress any dissent and prevent any strongholds of regional power. In 1958, the *Länderkammer*, surplus to SED requirements, was abolished.

The dominance of the SED and its General Secretary, Ulbricht

In Marxist-Leninist theory, the SED's role was to guide society through the transitional phase – when the established capitalist order would be gradually replaced by a socialist society. During this phase, the SED needed to maintain control of government and society. Therefore, certain rights – such as the freedom of speech, the right to strike and freedom of religion – were subordinate to the SED's stated aim of the building of socialism.

The structure of the SED was based on the principle that it represented the people of the GDR.

Party Congresses

Party members in local and regional branches elected representatives to Party Congresses, where issues could be raised. The lack of influence exerted by Party Congresses is reflected in the fact that there were only four during the period 1950–63. The chief function of the Congress, however, was to elect members to the Central Committee of the Party.

The Central Committee

This was a smaller body of about 80 to 130 members; the exact number varied over the years. Although it was, in theory, the main decision-making body of the SED, the Central Committee was considered by the Party to be too large to function effectively. Therefore, the Central Committee delegated decision-making to the much smaller Politburo. As a result, the Central Committee only met periodically.

The Politburo

The Politburo was the policy-making committee of the SED, and this was where most political power and decision-making lay. It was chaired by the Party's First Secretary. The Politburo was often referred to by the general population as the 'Council of Gods', a term that did not always reflect a positive view of its relationship with the general population. The principle of **democratic centralism** meant that decision-making passed down from the Politburo to carefully selected SED officials in regional areas and then continued to local levels, such as the workplace and residential blocks. This structure could allow the Politburo to appear to represent the people and it did provide a channel for views and opinions to reach the higher levels of the Party. In reality, however, it acted more as an instrument for imposing orders from the Politburo on the population.

KEY TERM

Democratic centralism
A Marxist-Leninist concept that claims democracy is achieved by the people giving central government the authority to make decisions.

The most important day-to-day work of the Central Committee was undertaken by the Politburo, a small circle of senior party officers, comprising between 15 and 25 members, along with approximately ten non-voting candidate members. The Politburo members included approximately ten Central Committee Secretaries. The country's government, formally headed by the Council of Ministers, was required only to implement the decisions of the Politburo. This meant that the Council of Ministers was under the permanent control of the Party Committees, a structure that ensured the 'leading role of the Party', a role that had been implicit in the constitution of the GDR. The chairman of the Council of Ministers and the President of the *Volkskammer* were also members of the Politburo.

Party organisations

The power and influence of the Party extended to the general population through the creation of social organisations, each under the control of party officials at both national and local level. The most important of these included the Free German Youth (FDJ), the German Gymnastics and Sports Association (DTSB) and the Democratic Women's Federation (DFD). Thus, the dominance of the SED covered virtually all aspects of life. These organisations had large memberships: 75 percent of young people joined the FDJ, and the German Gymnastics and Sports Association had 2.8 million members by 1970, out of a population of 17 million. These organisations allowed the SED to give the impression of mass participation.

The dominance of Ulbricht

Walter Ulbricht dominated politics within the GDR from 1950 to 1971.

- Ulbricht's position and power was based on the fact that he was Moscow's man. His years training in the USSR had given him a sense of the importance of loyalty to the USSR. In his early years, he relied on the support of those who had formed part of the 'Ulbricht Group' in Moscow. As the GDR was a product of Soviet foreign policy and its deterioration in relations with the West, Ulbricht knew that his position depended on him carrying out the wishes of the USSR. His slavish devotion to the Soviet Union bordered on the obsessive, his favourite slogan being 'To learn from the Soviet Union is to learn victory'.

- The basis of his power over the SED also lay with the positions he held. He was First Secretary of the Party, giving him control over the Central Committee and the power to set agendas for meetings. The position also gave him the role of Chairman of the Politburo.

- To secure his position, Ulbricht used the SED's internal disputes of the early 1950s as opportunities to suppress those with differing views, and mass purges took place in 1951 and between 1956 and 1958. By the end of the 1950s, Ulbricht's position had been clearly secured, with a younger generation of loyal SED members and more party political control of the legal system, the police and armed forces, and the development of the Stasi.

- His immense personal power increased further with the building of the Berlin Wall, which gave his position even more security.

- A cult of personality was developed, which encouraged the adoration of Ulbricht and his achievements (see Source 4). This was a hard task; he had little charisma. Seen as inflexible and unlikeable, even by his close colleagues, Ulbricht was, nonetheless, intelligent and shrewd. He was a politician who knew how to work the party apparatus to his advantage.

Ulbricht's position within the Party was secure, but not all East Germans bought into the image of Ulbricht as a great leader. In 1950, Ulbricht was pelted with tomatoes by a football crowd in Dresden. Ulbricht had been guest of honour at the final match of the football season between Dresden-Friedrichstadt (a privately run club) and Zwickau (a club of a workers' co-operative). To ensure a politically correct result in front of the Party leader, the referee declared that Zwickau had won 5-1, a result that bore no resemblance to the actual number of goals scored. The crowd took out their anger on Ulbricht; the Dresden football team voted with their feet and left for West Germany.

It was not until the late 1960s that the Party started to question Ulbricht as leader. His position was to become gradually eroded due to a combination of his own fading health and the actions of Honecker, Secretary for the Economy, who increasingly began to undermine Ulbricht's role.

SOURCE
4

Members of the FDJ, the youth organisation of the SED, carrying a placard of Ulbricht during a parade in East Berlin in 1954.

SOURCE
5

Heinz Lippmann, a Free German Youth officer, describes a Politburo meeting in the early 1950s.

At the start of the meeting, Ulbricht would ask: 'Does anyone have any objections to the agenda?' Most of the time there were none. Then Ulbricht would read the first item, e.g. 'spring planting,' recommend some changes in the proposal, which would be recorded, and then ask, 'Are there other suggestions?' Since no one besides the Politburo member whose department was directly concerned with the question had read the proposal, there was usually no discussion, and a decision would be made that agreed with Ulbricht's original opinion.

ACTIVITY
KNOWLEDGE

The GDR as a democracy

1 In what way does the name 'German Democratic Republic' give a distorted impression of the system of government in East Germany?

2 Look at Sources 4 and 5. How useful are these sources as evidence of the ways in which the SED exercised control?

Conclusion

To all outward appearances, the constitution of the GDR displayed the features of a democracy: it had established a range of representative bodies that played a role in the drafting, ratifying and implementation of laws. It proclaimed itself as the state of the German workers and peasants. Yet the reality was that power rested in the hands of the SED and, within the Party, this power was concentrated in the hands of the Politburo. The result is that many historians have viewed the GDR as a dictatorship of the SED. As the master of the Party apparatus, Walter Ulbricht was able to exert a firm hold over the direction of policy, but he was in many ways a puppet of his masters in Moscow. The policies introduced to develop the economy of East Germany were to illustrate this situation.

HOW SUCCESSFUL WAS THE DEVELOPMENT OF THE GDR'S ECONOMY IN THE YEARS 1949–61?

The GDR faced serious obstacles to its aim of developing a socialist economy. It suffered lasting damage as a result of the Second World War. Berlin lay in ruins by the end of the war. Dresden, one of East Germany's largest and most beautiful cities before the war, had been devastated by British and American bombing in February 1945. Its ancient city centre was laid to waste. Other cities, such as Leipzig and Magdeburg, were also heavily damaged. The impact of this damage was to severely reduce the prospects of economic growth in the Eastern zone of Germany due to the fact that it contained so few industrial areas. This contrasted with West Germany, which contained the Rhineland and the Saar coalfield, both large and important centres of industry. Both the Russians and the Americans had seized many of the best scientists in Germany after the war, such as Werner

Border-crossers

The situation was also more difficult for the GDR authorities to control because approximately 50,000 so-called 'border-crossers' lived in the GDR, but worked in West Berlin. From the mid-1950s onwards, the GDR increasingly used various measures to discourage individuals from being border-crossers by implementing controls on how they could exchange wages paid in West German currency, and by increasingly labelling them as politically unreliable due to their frequent exposure to capitalist West Berlin.

From the mid-1950s onwards, increasing numbers of both Stasi officers and police officers were employed to identify individuals trying to emigrate, as well as checking mail for those that were posting ahead their treasured possessions. As well as creating a relatively easy way for individuals to escape from the GDR, the existence of West Berlin was a threat as a centre from which Western intelligence operations operated.

Emigration from the GDR threatened to decrease the available workforce by as much as ten percent over the course of the Seven-Year Plan (1959–65). This was clearly unsustainable in economic terms, but it also had political consequences. It allowed the FRG to undermine the GDR's credibility and assert the failings of socialism. The FRG continued to refer to those who had left East Germany as 'refugees' rather than as 'migrants'. Once they arrived in the FRG, in order to receive higher levels of financial and housing assistance from their new state, it was in the former East Germans' best interests to convince the authorities that they had been persecuted.

SOURCE

11
The statistics below show the numbers emigrating from the GDR to the FRG from the establishment of the FRG and GDR in 1949 until the building of the Berlin Wall. Taken from N. Bushnell and A. Leonard, *Germany Divided and Reunited 1945–91* (2009).

Year	Number of emigrants from the GDR to the FRG
1949	125,000
1950	198,000
1951	166,000
1952	182,000
1953	331,000
1954	184,000
1955	253,000
1956	279,000
1957	262,000
1958	204,000
1959	144,000
1960	199,000
1961	155,000 (to the building of the Berlin Wall in August)

SOURCE
12
A speech by Ulbricht at a meeting of Berlin SED members on 21 May 1957. The speech was published in *Neues Deutschland* (the official SED newspaper) on 23 May.

West Berliners know that West Berlin lies within the GDR. The ties of the agents of imperialism and NATO propaganda extend into West Berlin, but NATO's military power will never extend that far. The West Berlin situation has sharpened since West Germany became part of NATO and West Berlin a centre for the operations of NATO agents against the GDR as well as a radar base. Everyone understands that West Berlin's population may some day have to pay very dearly.

EXTRACT

1 A historian, David Childs, writing in 1983, describes life in the GDR during the early 1960s.

Each stalled summit, each new rumour, each new bellicose speech by a SED leader, each new pin-prick against West Berlin increased the flow, so did job opportunities in the West, and shortages of all kinds in the East. No tomatoes for a Sunday salad, no hinges to fix that faulty cupboard door, no inner tubes for the bike, no cosmetics for self-confidence, no hire purchase furniture, no flat for the married daughter and no likelihood of a family holiday. For many people in Halle, Merseburg or Dessau [cities in the GDR], towns like Hanover, Marburg or Düsseldorf [cities in the FRG] had become romantic places and there were no language problems either. There were other complaints too, even among the great majority who had no land, no firm and no shop to lose, were not very political and were not active church members. They got fed up with the rules and regulations, with having to sign petitions and attend meetings concerning issues about which they were at best indifferent. They were fed up with the 'voluntary' financial contributions to solidarity funds for the Congo, Egypt, Algeria and Vietnam. Rumours about possible closure of the open 'frontier' between East and West Berlin convinced waverers they had better get out while the going was good.

ACTIVITY
KNOWLEDGE CHECK

Emigration from the GDR

1 What factors existed in relation to the following?

   a) To encourage emigration from the GDR.

   b) To discourage emigration from the GDR.

2 Look at Source 12 and Extract 1.

   a) In what ways does Source 12 differ from Extract 1 in its explanations for migration from the GDR?

   b) How would you explain these differences?

Reasons for the crisis of 1960–61

A second Berlin Crisis began in 1958. It started in November, when Khrushchev demanded the withdrawal, within six months, of the three Western powers' troops from their sectors in Berlin. Khrushchev argued that this would then allow for Berlin to become a demilitarised free city state (but with its status still guaranteed by the four powers). In reality, the continued existence of such a free city state would always be dependent on the goodwill of the GDR and the USSR. Rather than accept the ultimatum, the USA offered to negotiate, which led to Khrushchev visiting the USA in September 1959. However, President Eisenhower and Khrushchev were unable to resolve any of their differences over West Berlin, with the Western powers continuing to remain in the city with guaranteed legal rights of access. A follow-up meeting was planned to be held in Paris in May 1960.

The planned Paris summit was abruptly cancelled by Khrushchev due to a rapid deterioration in superpower relations following the U-2 crisis in May 1960, when a US spy plane flying in Russian airspace was shot down by a Soviet missile. Worsening international relations increased the sense that the borders between East and West Berlin could soon be closed permanently, and during 1960 alone, nearly 200,000 East Germans left the GDR, usually through Berlin. In the summer of 1961, Khrushchev met the new US President Kennedy and threatened war unless the Berlin question was finally settled. Kennedy responded with a public statement, where he guaranteed the continued status of West Berlin, but he was also careful to make it clear that he had no intention of challenging the USSR's influence in the GDR, including East Berlin.

SOURCE 13

A senior member of the USSR's army, Marshal Vassili Chuikov, speaking about Berlin in June 1961. Recounted in R. M. Slusser, *The Berlin Crisis of 1961* (1973).

The historic truth is that during the assault on Berlin [in 1945] there was not a single American, British or French armed soldier around it, except for the prisoners of war, whom we freed. Therefore the claims of the United States, British and French ruling circles to some kind of special rights in Berlin are entirely unfounded. They did not take it. They came there to fulfil the conditions of surrender, and on the basis of the fulfilment of these conditions, the occupation of Berlin should long since have ended.

SOURCE 14

Kennedy's public statement on Berlin in June 1961.

West Berlin has now become as never before the great testing place of Western courage and will. I hear it said that West Berlin is militarily untenable. Any dangerous spot is tenable if brave men will make it so. We do not want to fight but we have fought before. We cannot and will not permit the Communists to drive us out of Berlin, either gradually or by force. For the fulfilment of our pledge to that city is essential to the morale and security of West Germany, to the unity of western Europe, and to the faith of the entire world... We will at all times be ready to talk, if talk will help. But we must be ready to resist with force, if force is used upon us. We seek peace but we shall not surrender.

ACTIVITY
KNOWLEDGE CHECK

The Berlin Crisis, 1960–61

1 What words would you use to describe the tone of Sources 13 and 14?

2 Select words and phrases from each source to illustrate their tone.

3 Use your own knowledge of the context of these sources to explain the tone adopted.

The building of the Berlin Wall and its importance

On 15 June, Ulbricht made a surprise public announcement that 'No one intends to build a wall!' Yet, after a series of intense and secret meetings with the leaders of the Warsaw Pact, and with Khrushchev's support, it was decided that the only solution to solve emigration from the GDR, as well as to alleviate security concerns, was to seal the border between East and West Berlin.

Up to the early 1960s, the USSR had consistently refused suggestions from the SED to completely close the border between East and West Berlin. There were fears that such action would be so provocative that it could lead the West to impose trade restrictions with the GDR or even escalate into outright military confrontation. Further, the USSR argued that the technical difficulties in sealing the border were insurmountable. Instead, the USSR had tried to persuade Ulbricht to pursue more moderate policies, in the hope that this would deter East Germans from emigrating by persuading them of the benefits of life in the GDR.

By 1961, however, the GDR was genuinely facing a crisis. At a meeting of the Eastern bloc states in Moscow on 3–5 August 1961, the decision was taken to close East Berlin's border with West Berlin. The intense secrecy surrounding the preparations meant that not all of Ulbricht's senior ministers were informed. In the early morning of 13 August, what was code-named Operation Rose was efficiently and swiftly carried out. Only East German troops were used and, by six o'clock in the morning the eastern sector of the city was completely blocked off from West Berlin and telephone lines between the two parts of the city were cut. East Germans were told that the measures were for protection from the imperial aims of the West and that the GDR was promoting conditions for international peace.

Initially, partly due to the pressure of time, but also Khrushchev's fear of military confrontation, Khrushchev urged for the sealed border to be constructed gradually. The 'Wall' was made from barbed wire and concrete slabs. When no retaliation from the West followed, a more permanent concrete wall was gradually erected, which was almost complete by the end of the year. Eventually, the Wall ran 45 km along the border of the Soviet sector of Berlin and a similar wall wound around the 160 km of West Berlin and the surrounding territory of the GDR.

Economic developments in the GDR, 1970–85

1 What factors promoted economic growth in the GDR during this period?

2 What factors hindered economic growth?

3 'The economy of the GDR was unable to match the success of that of the FRG, but was nonetheless successful during this period.' How far do you agree with this statement?

Conclusion

The period 1961–85 can be split into two distinct parts: the Ulbricht-inspired experiment of the NES and ESS, with their slight diffusion of control and experimentation with profit making, and the Honecker-led Unity of Social and Economic Policy, which, after 1971, restored central planning and nationalised private businesses. However, there were similarities between them.

- Both economic phases advocated full political control by the SED. Any economic concessions within the NES would not be mirrored with political concessions. The contract between worker and state of Honecker's 'consumer socialism' may have tried to improve the living standards of the population, but the cost was still repressive control.

- Both were dependent on Soviet agreement and co-operation for success. Ulbricht fell foul of Brezhnev's stricter application of ideology than Khrushchev, whom he replaced in 1964. Honecker worked with the Soviets until the USSR's own economic problems started to impinge on the GDR.

- Despite the best of intentions, both failed to tackle the poor supply and quality of consumer products, unless you had the special privilege to use *Intershops*.

The result was a GDR economy that was in many ways superior to other Eastern bloc countries. The GDR had the unique advantage that it could trade with both the USSR and the FRG, giving it access to Western credit and investment that other socialist states did not have. However, it would seem that the economic systems of East and West were not always compatible, and by 1985, over two decades of economic management by the state had not created a strong enough foundation to support an increasingly technological and international economy.

AS Level Exam-Style Question Section B

How accurate is it to say that the GDR experienced a period of economic stability from 1961 to 1972? (20 marks)

Tip

You will need to weigh up evidence of stability against evidence of instability in the economy. Make sure you make a reasoned judgement supported by precise evidence.

HOW SUCCESSFUL WAS HONECKER IN DEVELOPING A DISTINCT IDENTITY FOR THE GDR DURING THE YEARS 1971–85?

Ulbricht had promoted the view that there was a single German nation divided into two states. He held the belief that these two states would one day be united under socialism. When Ulbricht was forced to resign as leader of the SED in 1971, this view changed. The new leader, Erich Honecker, recognised the reality of the division of Germany that had become entrenched when the Berlin Wall was erected in 1961. Any hope of future reunification seemed remote, and Honecker adopted an approach that he felt would be more likely to preserve the continuation of socialism in a German state, distinct from the bourgeois state in the West. A range of measures was put in force that attempted to develop a separate identity for the GDR, and to instil in its population a sense of pride in its achievements.

Honecker and the development of a GDR identity

By the early 1970s, Ulbricht had lost favour with the Soviet Union and his own colleagues in the Politburo. His stubbornness in continuing to follow policies that were increasingly at odds with Soviet foreign policy was one of many reasons for his fall from favour. In May 1971, Honecker visited Ulbricht at home, accompanied by senior GDR guards armed with machine guns, who surrounded the building. Honecker entered Ulbricht's home and, after more than an hour, gained Ulbricht's agreement to resign.

Honecker had been responsible for implementing the decision to build the Wall in 1961, and he was fully aware of the pressures that had resulted in large numbers of the GDR's population migrating to the West. The Wall was an effective way of stemming the flow of migrants, but it had done little to enhance the reputation of the regime abroad, or indeed at home. A more positive approach was also needed: one that would convince the population of the GDR that they lived in a country of which they could be proud.

Following Honecker's takeover as leader of the GDR, a number of measures were taken to stress the differences between the FRG and the GDR. The aim was to provide a clear demarcation between the two states. This became a deliberate policy to give the GDR a more confident sense of its own unique identity. SED propaganda portrayed the FRG as becoming Americanised, and also claimed that the GDR did not have responsibility for the crimes of the Nazi government. Exports from East Germany were no longer labelled 'Made in Germany', but instead said 'Made in the GDR'. Mass media and sport became two methods of cultivating a sense of national identity in the East German people.

Mass media

The media was strictly controlled by the SED and had a clear role in the campaign towards the building of a communist state. The GDR and the USSR were both promoted, and media coverage of the West would often include comments on the historical inevitability of the downfall of capitalism. The media was put to use to reinforce the evils of capitalism and the superiority of socialism.

Newspapers

The main national newspaper was the SED's *Neues Deutschland*, which had a large circulation, but others were published by the National bloc political parties, and regional newspapers were also permitted. All newspapers were given instructions by the government on what to write. Honecker had daily meetings with the editor of *Neues Deutschland* to approve the front page. There was only one news agency that disseminated information on international events to all newspapers. Newspapers were also funded from government money, so there was no competition for income from circulation or advertising. Before 1961, although it was easy for foreign newspapers to be brought into East Berlin, it was illegal to display or read Western newspapers anywhere in the GDR. After the construction of the Berlin Wall, many Western visitors had newspapers taken from them when entering the GDR. The only Western newspapers allowed to enter the country or to be put on sale there were those published by Western communist parties. There were also strict controls on printing machines and photocopiers, to prevent the distribution of any publications that were subversive to the SED. These measures were largely, if not completely, successful.

All newspapers had the same underlying messages. SED leaders were adulated, while widespread social problems in the FRG (such as homelessness, unemployment and drug addiction) and anniversaries (such as the USSR liberating Germany from Nazism, the establishment of the GDR and the formation of the SED) were promoted.

The Party directly controlled 70 percent of all publications in the GDR; most of the rest were papers and magazines produced by the mass organisations, such as the Free German Youth (FDJ) and trade unions, and tended to either be non-political or follow the Party line. The only publications that were not controlled by the SED were those from Church organisations, but these were expected to write solely on religious matters and be strictly non-controversial.

Radio

Radios had been widespread in Germany since the 1920s, and a range of stations existed at the time of the creation of the GDR in 1949. By the 1970s, there were several radio stations broadcasting in the GDR: Radio DDR 1 was established in August 1953, and Radio DDR 2 followed in 1958. In addition, the station *Berliner Rundfunk* catered for the capital. In 1964, a youth music station, DT 64, was added. These stations broadcast a mix of music and spoken word, sports reporting being particularly popular. By 1985, there were 6.6 million licensed radios in the country, or 39.9 for every 100 people. Yet, what the population was listening to on their radios was a matter of concern to the regime. Western radio stations were broadcast across most of the GDR and were often more popular than GDR output. The demand for Western music was high among the young, and this tended to weaken the hold that the GDR stations had on this group of the population. The government attempted to jam foreign signals, but this was outlawed by international agreement and risked the West jamming East German radio stations in retaliation.

Television

By the 1970s, televisions were widely available in East German homes, and the state took particular care to ensure that the population of the GDR received access to information that glorified socialism. This was a particular concern because most homes in the GDR could pick up Western stations broadcast from West Berlin. Television was controlled by *Fernsehen der DDR* (DDR-FS), and the state-run company had two stations by 1969. Colour programming also began in this year. Care was taken to ensure news programmes were not broadcast at the same time as those on FRG stations, as most people would have preferred to watch West German news. Popular entertainment was scheduled at the same time as West German news broadcasts, to discourage viewers switching their aerials to the West.

The output of the GDR television stations was heavily political and often not very subtle. Karl Eduard Von Schnitzler was the regime's leading propagandist. His weekly programme *Der Schwarze Kanal* (*The Black Channel*) bombarded viewers with uncompromisingly hostile views of the West; the FRG was referred to as 'the Land of Wolves', and the West German Chancellor Konrad Adenauer as 'Hitler's Heir'. Many East Germans claimed not to watch it, but most did, aghast at the content and its delivery. Von Schnitzler was one of the most despised men in the GDR. By the mid-1970s, Honecker recognised that a more subtle approach was likely to be more effective, but Von Schnitzler, while often out of favour (he had been dismissed from his role as a political director of GDR television in 1958), always resurfaced in another role as a television discussion host.

It would be unfair to see East German television output as little more than turgid propaganda. Many of its programmes were popular. The East German version of the children's programme *The Sand Man* was adored by generations of East Germans, and was a cultural icon of the GDR that was to last longer than the country that produced it. East Germans may have been very sceptical of the claims of their own television news broadcasts, but this did not mean that they believed the news transmitted by West German channels.

Impact

The SED regime saw language as a key element in developing ***Abgrenzung* (demarcation)** from West Germany, and the media was instrumental in this process. By the 1970s, the impact of the

KEY TERM

Abgrenzung (demarcation)
The policy of developing clear differences between the GDR and the FRG, actively pursued by Honecker.

media, alongside education, had produced distinct differences in the use of language. East Germans did their shopping in a *Kaufhalle* (buying hall), never in a *Supermarkt* (the term used in the FRG). The word 'secretary' was not used in the East to describe administrators, except Party officials. The GDR preferred to give many office workers the title 'skilled worker for writing technology'. The capital city of the GDR was never referred to as East Berlin, because it drew attention to the fact that the city was divided. Road signs simply declared 'Berlin, capital of the GDR'. The term 'West Berlin' was run together as Westberlin to give the impression it was another city altogether.

There was a tendency to Sovietise the language used in East Germany, with terms such as *Kollectiv* (collective) and *brigade* (group of workers) commonly used. This trend was enhanced by the use of Russian as the foreign language studied in schools. These trends led to the emergence of different and distinct cultural developments in East Germany.

Most people would purchase a copy of *Neues Deutschland* to give an outward appearance of conformity. They would watch GDR television programmes and listen to GDR radio broadcasts, but, uniquely among other Eastern bloc states, this was supplemented by access to television and radio programmes produced in the West. This significantly undermined the SED's propaganda about current affairs, as well as making East Germans fully aware of the much higher living standards and personal freedom in the FRG. Viewing and listening to West German programmes was officially illegal, but it was impossible to control as it was so widespread. In 1974, the SED finally admitted to fighting a losing battle. Western stations were to be discouraged, but tolerated.

SOURCE
4
From O. Fritz, *The Iron Curtain Kid* (2009). Oliver Fritz lived in the GDR from his birth in 1967 until reunification in 1990.

Every year in the DDR [GDR], there were two big demonstrations – the first on May Day, the international Fighting and Celebration Day of the Working People, and the second on 7 October, the National Holiday, to celebrate the inauguration of the DDR in 1949.

On both days the party and state leadership occupied two hastily erected stands in the heart of East Berlin, in the early years at Marx-Engels Platz (a huge square) and later at the Karl-Marx-Allee, our capital's most prestigious boulevard...

The televised events on 1 May and 7 October always followed the same pattern: Berliners would walk past the stands, accompanied by music and chanted slogans from loudspeakers ('A hip, hip, hooray to our party and leadership!') The media in return would label these processions as 'powerful illustrations of the bond between the people and the party and state leadership'. These demonstrations took place virtually in every town and village up and down the country, though the military parade was exclusive to the capital...

Yet what all demonstrations had in common was that most participants aimed for one thing: saving most of the day by finishing the march as quickly as possible.

ACTIVITY
KNOWLEDGE CHECK

Mass participation
Look at Source 4. How valuable is this source as evidence of support for the GDR government?

The importance of sport, especially Olympic successes and women's sports

The SED actively promoted the value of sport for several reasons. As well as improving the population's well-being, the benefits of sport on individuals' health was regarded as a means to boost productivity in the workplace. It could also perform a key role in developing pride in the state.

Sport as a mass participation activity

As sporting organisations were controlled by the SED and were not overtly political, they became an effective method of bringing large numbers of the population under the influence of the regime. By 1982, 3.3 million East Germans belonged to a sports club. Football, fishing and gymnastics were the most popular. These sporting clubs were part of the German Gymnastics and Sports Association (DTSB), an umbrella organisation directed by the SED. In 1980, there were over 28,000 sporting festivals in the GDR, ranging from the children's *Spartakaiden* to those where factory teams, villages and clubs competed against each other. These festivals attracted a high participation rate, as did walking, rambling and chess. Surveys conducted by the DTSB in the mid-1980s are revealing about participants' attitudes to these activities. When asked why they participated in sports, only 14 percent gave the officially appropriate answer; 80 percent responded 'because it was fun'. Poor investment in sports facilities, especially swimming pools that were often closed for repairs, sometimes dampened enthusiasm. Nonetheless, sport did provide a valuable tool for bringing a large part of the population under the influence of the regime.

SOURCE

5
Regina Gläsel, born in 1952, reminisces in 2014 about sport in the GDR. She lived in Reinsdorf, a small village near Wittenberg in the GDR. She was an active member of the local handball club from the age of ten. She played in the second-highest league in the GDR and won medals as a member of the GDR's youth team.

Sport in the GDR was very, very important and we had the motto 'Everyone in every place'. At school sports lessons were two hours long and three times a week, as well as extra-curricular sports which were run by volunteers. A huge emphasis was put on competitions which were conducted in all sports at school, district, state and country level. At the sports centres the best were trained and supported and there was a continuous scouting for those that were talented. This meant that it was always possible to have sufficient top athletes in all sports for European and World Championships right up to the Olympics. Everyone could participate regardless of cost as all sport provision was financed by the state and was not influenced by profit. For adults sports days were held at work.

As a result a spirit of unity and self-confidence was strengthened and present.

These disputes were also more often a reflection of the wider context of the increase in Cold War tensions at the start of the 1980s. As the USSR and the USA became increasingly polarised and belligerent towards each other, the secondary nations had to echo this feeling. The GDR was still dependent on the USSR as the dominant Eastern superpower, so restrictions on travel were implemented. However, these were restrictions rather than outright bans. The GDR always hoped that the policy would facilitate its economic progression and modernisation, while the FRG never shifted from the basic principles of *Ostpolitik*. For the GDR, any economic gains would be nullified by its failure to control the social consequences and economic reliance on the FRG that *Ostpolitik* entailed. This eventually helped to tear the East German people, though not the leadership, from its allegiance to the USSR.

EXTEND YOUR KNOWLEDGE

The role of *Ostpolitik* and the removal of Ulbricht

Traditionally, *Ostpolitik* has been seen as the primary cause in the downfall of Ulbricht as leader of the SED in 1971. It was his opposition to the policy, as well as the wider trend of détente, that caused his dismissal and subsequent replacement by Honecker. However, this view has been challenged since the fall of the GDR.

Evidence indicates that Ulbricht was open to the FRG's economic aid, while Honecker was less accepting than previously suspected. It seems that the vital difference between the two leaders was a willingness to be led by Brezhnev and the USSR. The aftermath of the crushing of the Prague Spring in 1968 made it clear to all that the USSR was the centre of power in the region, and Brezhnev saw Ulbricht as too independent.

THINKING HISTORICALLY   Cause and consequence (6b)

Attitudes and actions

Individuals can only make choices based on their context. Prevalent attitudes combine with individual experience and natural temperament to frame the individual's perception of what is going on around them. Nobody can know the future or see into the minds of others.

Context	Action
• West German governments did not want to give the GDR any credibility. • The Berlin Wall had caused outrage and anger against the GDR in West Germany. • In the late 1960s, détente had developed between the USA and the USSR, encouraging co-operation across the Iron Curtain. • Willy Brandt was mayor of West Berlin when the Berlin Wall was built. • Brandt became leader of the left-wing SPD Party in 1964. • Brandt became the first SPD leader to be elected chancellor of the FRG in 1969.	• On becoming chancellor of the FRG, Brandt pursued a policy of *Ostpolitik*. He was able to improve travel arrangements between East and West Germany, allowing many people to visit relatives for the first time since the Berlin Wall was erected. Brandt hoped that the GDR government would adopt more liberal policies if he started negotiations with its leaders. The GDR gained many advantages from *Ostpolitik*, reducing the diplomatic isolation it had suffered after 1961 and gaining financial help from the FRG, but it did not adopt more liberal policies.

Answer the following questions individually and discuss your answers in a group.

1 Why might Brandt have believed that most Germans, both in the East and West, would support *Ostpolitik*?

2 Why might Brandt have believed that the GDR would become more liberal if the FRG started to negotiate?

3 What other information would have been useful to him to help him decide on his course of action?

4 How reasonable was Brandt's course of action, given what he understood about the situation at the time?

5 How far should the historian try to understand the context of the beliefs and values of people in the past when explaining why individuals make choices in history?

The debate surrounding the GDR and Ostpolitik

1 In what ways did the GDR benefit from *Ostpolitik*?

2 In what ways did *Ostpolitik* undermine the GDR?

3 To what extent do you agree with the view that *Ostpolitik* brought more benefits than disadvantages to the GDR?

HOW SUCCESSFUL WAS THE GDR IN IMPROVING ITS INTERNATIONAL PRESTIGE IN THE YEARS 1961–85?

During the 1970s, the GDR achieved full international recognition by joining the United Nations. The two Germanys recognised each other in the 1972 Basic Treaty, and the GDR had gained formal diplomatic recognition from 123 countries by 1978. The treaties agreed between the FRG, GDR and the USSR led to far greater international recognition of the GDR and allowed both German states to be admitted as members of the United Nations in 1973. It helped the SED leadership legitimise its rule, even if its self-perception of the GDR's worth could be questioned. An East German saying of the time asks, 'Which three great nations in the world begin with "U"?' The answer is: 'USA, USSR and Our GDR (*Unsere DDR*).' This pertains to the fact that the SED not only referred to itself as 'our GDR', but also exaggerated its world status.

International recognition of the GDR

Although the Berlin Wall gave SED leaders a sense of reasonable security, there was also a desire in the SED to end the GDR's international isolation. In 1961, the GDR only had diplomatic relations with the other Eastern bloc states and some developing countries, such as North Korea and North Vietnam. The FRG's Hallstein Doctrine severely restricted international recognition of the GDR, and made it even more dependent on its relations with the USSR and the other Eastern bloc states. This influence would ensure that many countries did not formally recognise the GDR for the first two decades of its existence.

Both German states wanted to build themselves a reputation based on international relations and global standing. The West Germans wanted the international community to see them as the only lawful representative of the German nation. To gain acceptance of the GDR as a legitimate state, East Germany was keen to have diplomatic relations that were not aligned to the Warsaw Pact or NATO. Threats by the FRG to withhold aid if Third World countries recognised the GDR became complicated in the Middle East during the Arab-Israeli conflict in the 1960s. When West Germany recognised the state of Israel, it opened the door for East Germany to develop relations with some of the opposing Arab states. Subsequently, in 1969, a number of Arab states recognised the GDR.

A change in attitude by the FRG about how to deal with the GDR, demonstrated by the *Ostpolitik* policy, opened the door for a thaw in international relations. Therefore, the Basic Treaty of 1972 between the two Germanys meant that the GDR was formally recognised by the FRG. The two states pledged to respect one another's sovereignty. This paved the way for East Germany to join the United Nations as its 133rd member in September 1973, as the Western powers in the UN Security Council agreed not to veto the GDR's membership. The impact of membership was immediate. The GDR would now be involved in other international agreements. Honecker, seated between Chancellor Schmidt and US President Gerald Ford, signed the **Helsinki Accords** in 1975. While both Honecker and Brezhnev totally ignored the human rights aspects of the accords, involvement boosted the GDR's international standing. Honecker concluded that the conference showed that the GDR was the socialist heart of Europe. It is ironic that the reporting of the full text of the Helsinki Accords in the SED newspaper *Neues Deutschland* resulted in it selling out for the first time in its publication. This illustrates the dual nature of being on the international stage. What occurs at the international level, for good or bad, has an impact on domestic affairs that often cannot be anticipated.

Though the prestige of the GDR joining the international club undoubtedly helped the SED justify the independence of East Germany as a separate entity to West Germany, it also forced the GDR

KEY TERM

Helsinki Accords (1975)
This was a series of accords agreed to by 35 European states, as well as the USSR and the USA. The agreements were split into three 'Baskets'. Basket One saw all European borders as 'inviolable' (they could not be altered by force). Basket Two focused on trade and technology links. Basket Three emphasised human rights and freedom of movement. At the time, it was seen as the ongoing success of détente, but, in fact, it was its peak and it had a rather superficial impact.

The Accords are sometimes referred to as the Helsinki Final Act.

to interact with other nations. The trouble for a nation at the heart of Europe was that it was connected to all of them, making diplomacy a careful balancing act. It meant contact with Western states while trying to limit any cultural and political penetration. It meant maintaining relations with an increasingly tense Eastern bloc. Finally, it meant being subservient to the USSR while trying to increase its own sovereignty.

State visits

The first official state visit by Ulbricht was to Egypt in 1965. It marked the end of the GDR's political isolation. Agreements were announced regarding economic and technical co-operation, scientific-technical relations, culture and trade. It was also agreed that an Egyptian delegation would visit the GDR in the future. This helped to provide international recognition of the GDR.

The period of détente allowed greater diplomatic relations between the two Germanys. In March 1970, Brandt made the first visit by an FRG chancellor to the GDR (see Extracts 1–3). This first visit had much more symbolic value than any decisions actually being made. The visit was reciprocated by Willi Stoph, the prime minister of the GDR, to Kassel in the FRG in May that year. The GDR government was not pleased that the enthusiastic welcome of East Germans towards Brandt was not repeated by the West Germans towards Stoph.

In December 1981, there was also a visit by FRG Chancellor Schmidt to the GDR, but on this occasion, the East German crowds were carefully chosen and controlled by the SED and the Stasi, to ensure the crowd were loyal citizens. However, the visit was successful in that it showed that, in the international climate of Cold War tension, the two Germanys were still intent on maintaining a relationship based more on *Ostpolitik* than mistrust. Honecker was invited to the FRG on this occasion. However, the Soviet leadership imposed enough pressure for this to be postponed until 1987.

It was the official state visits to countries that were neither COMECON nor socialist that really gave both the GDR and Honecker, as its leader, international prestige and recognition as a permanent country. In 1980, Honecker visited his first Western state, Austria, and then his first NATO country, Italy, in 1985. Honecker also visited Belgium, Spain, Sweden and France, while the leaders of Greece, Austria and Denmark visited the GDR. However, there were limits to the impact these visits had on the international status of the GDR. Despite his wishes, Honecker never received an invitation to visit the UK or the USA. Indeed, the American-manned crossing point at Checkpoint Charlie in Berlin was in service for nearly 30 years, but it remained as a small wooden building, little more than a shed. It was a subtle statement that such a simple construction was all that was needed for a temporary state of affairs. In 1983, the new West German chancellor, Helmut Kohl, repeated the invitation for Honecker to visit, but the Soviet authorities in the USSR made it clear that the visit was not to go ahead.

The increase in state visits reflected the growing international recognition of the GDR that emerged after the 1972 Basic Treaty. However, by their very nature, the visits also helped to open up the GDR to outside influences. The contact may help to portray the image of the GDR as independent, but it also encouraged the East German public to have a more positive attitude to foreign states, who were no longer viewed as the absolute enemy they once were. When Honecker finally visited West Germany in 1987, the Stasi reported that young people saw the visit as proof of the obsolescence of the Berlin Wall and the redundancy of anti-FRG propaganda.

EXTRACT

An analysis of the meeting between Willy Brandt and Willi Stoph by historians N. Bushnell and A. Leonard in *Germany Divided and Reunited 1945–91* (2009).

In March 1970 Willy Brandt met Willi Stoph (leader of the GDR's Council of Ministers) in Erfurt in the GDR. This was the first ever meeting between senior government figures of the FRG and GDR and demonstrated that measures to develop better mutual relations were being taken very seriously by both Germanys. The attitude of the East German public was evident in the enthusiastic public welcome which Brandt received. Brandt was greeted with large crowds of excited East German citizens lining the streets with banners displaying a big 'Y' to show it was Willy Brandt rather than Willi Stoph that they were cheering for.

The changing status and role of women

There were two main principles that formed the basis for the SED's policies towards women:

- First, there was a need to reverse the GDR's demographics of an ageing and declining population, which was partly, but not sufficiently, solved with the building of the Berlin Wall.

- Second, there was the ideological need to work towards achieving greater gender equality both in the workplace and in the home.

Both of these principles encouraged a drive to raise the status of women and change their role from the traditional housewife into a more economically productive citizen.

The Family Code of 1966 stated that in order to ensure the development of socialist personalities and to promote female employment, men and women should share equally in childcare and domestic work. The Code emphasised women's equality in marriage and family. It was expected that a husband and wife would have an arrangement, which allowed both to develop their abilities for themselves and for the benefit of society. Therefore, it provided for a woman's right to control her own life. This independence for women was partly a product of the distorted demography of the GDR. The Second World War had created a higher proportion of women to men, while emigration to the FRG during the 1950s was disproportionately made up of younger men.

Although the SED's policies towards women, which were intended to increase the birth rate, proved to be successful, the extent to which gender equality was achieved in the home and workplace is debatable.

The Eighth SED Congress of 1971 introduced a range of new social policies aimed at improving the working and living conditions of women. Abortion was legalised in 1972 and contraceptives became available free of charge. Welfare reforms were used to try to counteract the falling birth rate. Incentives for mothers included the extension of maternity leave from 18 to 26 weeks. All mothers received a lump sum of DM1,000 when their baby was born. Working hours were limited to 40 a week for mothers and they were not required to do shift work or overtime. Help was also given with housework, with mothers receiving one day off work every month to carry out domestic duties. This help was also provided to single fathers. Crèches and nursery schools were expanded, and by 1974, 60 percent of infants up to the age of three were placed in such facilities. This figure exceeded much of the Western world at the time. These measures proved popular with women, but in some respects they preserved traditional roles rather than reduced them – the support was for mothers rather than women. The traditional attitude towards 'men's' and 'women's' work was remarkably persistent in the GDR.

By the late 1980s, the GDR had one of the highest proportions of female employment in the world (around 90 percent, compared to 50 percent in the FRG). Their role in the economic well-being of the GDR had been taken seriously by the government. Social policy, especially increased access for women to further and higher education, had made important strides towards gender equality and reducing the dependence of women on men.

Nonetheless, the status of women was not always equal to that of men. Women made up a much higher proportion of the workforce in lower-paid and unskilled jobs. Further, while women made up half of all teachers and doctors by the mid-1980s, the majority of higher-level positions were held by men. Women were very under-represented in senior politics: the only female minister in the GDR's history was Margot Honecker, and her role as Minister of Education did not give her a place in the Politburo.

EXTEND YOUR KNOWLEDGE

Sexuality in the GDR

The GDR was genuinely progressive regarding sexuality. The emphasis placed on increasing the economic independence of women resulted in women demanding more in the bedroom. By the 1970s, it was common for women to want a sexually fulfilling relationship, and many were prepared to end a relationship where this need was not being met. The state's social policy made singlehood, even single motherhood, possible and acceptable. This contrasted with the portrayal of women as sexual objects, as was common in the West. As one East German woman in her late 40s put it, when asked about attitudes to sex after reunification, 'East-women have more fun, everybody knows that.'

Attitudes to homosexuality were also progressive in some respects. Homosexuality was made legal in the Criminal Code of 1957 and struck out of the Criminal Code altogether in 1968. Although frowned upon by the Party, lesbians and gay men were allowed to socialise in public places with considerable freedom and toleration. By the early 1980s, the Ministry of Health was raising concerns about the spread of AIDS and the impact this could have on homosexual men in the GDR.

ACTIVITY
KNOWLEDGE CHECK

The role and status of women in the GDR

How far did the role and status of women in the GDR change in the 1970s and 1980s?

The development of an extensive social welfare programme

The government viewed good health as essential for high productivity, and as a result it devoted considerable resources to its promotion. Health-care systems were provided on a collective basis, according to need, with a series of polyclinics based in every district. The polyclinics offered a range of general health care and some specialist treatment through teams of doctors and nurses. In 1971, a choice of doctor within the polyclinic was allowed, a response to patients' demands.

Much of the health care was based on preventative medicine and early diagnosis. Welfare measures that eased the working load of mothers also helped to improve the general health of the female population. For the elderly and disabled, care homes were provided by the state, but many preferred to live in the family home.

The increasing demands of the population for improvements in welfare provision led to a series of measures being announced at the Ninth Party Congress in May 1976. The SED was aware that welfare provision was one method of keeping social stability, minimising the attraction of the West and providing good publicity for the GDR in the international arena. It duly introduced increases in the minimum wage, a 20 percent rise in pensions and, for working mothers, increased holiday entitlement.

Results

- In the 1960s and 1970s, the GDR was able to bring about real improvements in the health of its population. Life expectancy increased to levels comparable with the West. Pre- and antenatal care was another area where success was tangible. As early as 1959, the number of mothers dying in childbirth was lower than occurred in the FRG.

- Social welfare provision aimed at supporting mothers, and therefore encouraging the birth rate to rise, was successful. Mothers with children under the age of 18 were entitled to shorter working hours and had more days of paid holiday. In 1985, the East German birth rate was 13.7 per thousand, higher than the 9.6 per thousand of the FRG.

- In terms of quantity, welfare provision in the GDR was good. In 1970, there were just under 160 doctors per hundred thousand people, rising to 242 in 1989. The number of hospital beds in 1977 was at a level comparable with that of the FRG. However, quantity was no guarantee of quality. Even the most basic medical equipment was often in short supply. In the early 1970s, hospitals were complaining of a lack of rubber gloves and syringes.

- By the end of the 1970s, economic resources for social provision were increasingly under pressure. This was partly a result of the worsening economic situation in the GDR, but it was also due to an increasingly aged population, coupled with the spiralling costs of new technology. Government statements and promises had resulted in higher expectations, and that put pressure on the health-care system.

- Care of the economically unproductive was far less impressive than that directed at mothers and workers, especially care of the elderly and the disabled. They were often placed in care homes where staff may have had good intentions, but they were given very little training and physical resources were poor. However, mothers of severely disabled children were allowed extra days off work to help provide care in their own home.

- Limited economic resources led to a system of prioritisation whereby the best facilities, often at university hospitals, were reserved for top Party officials and specialised workers who were seen as vital to the economy. The Party leadership were treated at the Berlin-Buch hospital in relatively comfortable conditions, with the most up-to-date technology the GDR could afford.

The development of social welfare in the GDR was to echo the general theme of good intentions undermined by economic shortcomings. The records of the Ministry of Health reveal that Ludwig Mecklinger, Honecker's Minister for Health, was forceful in presenting the case for extending welfare provision on humanitarian grounds, as well as political ones, but he was

thwarted by the influence of Mittag at the Ministry for the Economy. The promotion of good health could also be limited by the social attitudes of many East Germans, who were heavy eaters and drinkers.

ACTIVITY
KNOWLEDGE CHECK

Social policy

1 What criteria would you use to judge the success of the social and welfare policies of the GDR?

2 How successful were the social and welfare policies of the GDR in bringing about social change by 1985?

3 What were the main obstacles to their success?

ACTIVITY
WRITING

Degrees of change: words as precision tools

The following are words used to describe different degrees of change:

Transformation; fundamental; superficial; ephemeral; partial; revolution; underlying; deep-seated; central; insignificant; temporary; façade; upheaval; inconsequential.

1 Give definitions of these terms. You may need to use a dictionary to check their exact meaning.

2 Rank these words on a scale from those denoting a very large change to those that describe no change.

3 Which words would best describe the degree of change that occurred in the GDR between 1961 and 1985 for the following aspects of social policy?

a) Housing provision

b) Education

c) The role of women

d) Social welfare provision.

A Level Exam-Style Question Section B

How effective were the social welfare programmes of the GDR in meeting the needs of its population between 1949 and 1985? (20 marks)

Tip

This question requires you to define the needs of the population of the GDR and then assess whether the social welfare programmes of the government met them. Make sure you come to a reasoned judgement about the degree to which these needs were successfully met.

DID A COMBINATION OF REPRESSION AND SUPPORT KEEP THE SED IN CONTROL?

The most obvious and visible form of state repression and control of its own population was the Berlin Wall, and during its existence it became increasingly difficult to attempt escape. During the 1970s and early 1980s, modifications were made by creating a second wall on the GDR side. The area between this second wall and the original wall became known as the 'death strip' and included watchtowers, mines and guard dogs. The Wall and the inner-German border were guarded by GDR soldiers and border troops, who received honours and extra pay and buildings or roads named in their honour if they killed a GDR citizen attempting to cross into West Berlin or the FRG.

Various escape attempts made from East to West Berlin, or from the GDR to the FRG, included hot-air balloons, driving at high speed through a checkpoint, hiding in suitcases and digging tunnels. It is estimated that there were approximately 5,000 successful escape attempts from the GDR to the FRG between August 1961 and the opening of the Wall in November 1989. However, during the Wall's existence, nearly 200 people were shot at the border, and by the mid-1970s almost 5,000 had been held in GDR prisons, with sentences from two to eight years for attempting flight from the republic.

The Ministry of State Security (the Stasi): its methods and activities

The Stasi and the SED

The State Security Service was set up in 1950 to defend the GDR against any acts of sabotage, from within East Germany as well as by agents working for the capitalist West. It saw itself as both the shield to protect the GDR and the sword to attack, but colloquially it was known as 'The Firm' and was given authority directly from the Politburo to protect the GDR's socialist achievements and the border.

At its beginning, the Stasi employed approximately 1,000 full-time staff, and within three years this rose to around 4,000. After the 1953 uprising, the leader of the Stasi, Wilhelm Zaisser, was removed and replaced by Erich Mielke. Mielke remained in charge until the collapse of the GDR in 1990, and it was under his guidance that the Stasi grew in scale and influence. By the late 1980s, the organisation had more than 90,000 full-time employees, as well as using an estimated 175,000 **IMs (Informal Members)**. The particularly rapid increase in the Stasi's size in the 1970s was a direct response to counteract what many in the SED saw as the negative effects of *Ostpolitik,* such as the increased exposure of GDR citizens to visitors from the FRG and West Berlin. Under Honecker, Mielke became a member of the Politburo, the Minister for the Stasi.

The range of the Stasi's activities

The Stasi's work was designed to create a climate of fear among the general population and deal with any undermining of the SED.

The Stasi had direct authority to open mail, bug homes, access bank statements, view medical records and use psychological torture. Cameras and recording equipment were hidden in ties, briefcases and cigarette boxes. The Stasi worked at border crossings, passport offices, hotels and airports, as well as in factories, universities, the armed forces, hospitals, schools and the Church.

In the 1970s, the Stasi had to refine its methods. As part of the *Abegrenzung* policy, to counter Western influence, its role was to root out the enemies of socialism in all forms of social life. The Stasi even operated at least one brothel in an effort to gather useful information, especially from Western visitors. However, as the GDR became more accepted on the world stage, the Stasi had to reign in its more violent methods of control. Individuals and opposition groups were targeted with a series of subtle attacks to destroy their reputation. Telephones were bugged (over 1,000 phones a day were bugged just in the city of Leipzig); false rumours were spread; burglaries took place; and the post was investigated (in Dresden, around five percent of all post was opened and read by the Stasi every day). This barrage of shady tactics would break down the opposition over time and was therefore known as 'operational decomposition'.

Other functions of the Stasi included collating 'mood reports' for the SED to ascertain public opinion. This was then used to help determine government policy or areas to focus on for propaganda, especially at critical points such as the building of the Berlin Wall or the uprising in Czechoslovakia. The Stasi had a department that worked in foreign countries, especially in the FRG, to obtain secret information. At certain times the Stasi also liaised with terrorist groups around the world, such as the **Irish Republican Army (IRA)**, the **Palestinian Liberation Organization (PLO)** and the left-wing **Red Army Faction** in the FRG. This would involve bringing members of these terrorist groups into the GDR for arming, training and financial support, as well as sending agents out as military advisers. Yet, while welcoming this support from the Stasi, none of these organisations depended on it.

KEY TERMS

IM (Informal Member)

A person recruited to work as an informer for the Stasi for short periods of time, usually to target a specific individual. It is estimated that, by the 1980s, almost 175,000 IMs were being used to inform on family members, friends and colleagues.

Irish Republican Army (IRA)

An Irish nationalist group that carried out a campaign of terrorist acts against British rule in Northern Ireland during the 1970s and 1980s.

Palestinian Liberation Organization (PLO)

A group that waged a terrorist campaign against the state of Israel.

Red Army Faction

A left-wing terrorist group that operated within the FRG. Also known as the Baader-Meinhof Gang, after its leaders Andreas Baader and Ulrike Meinhof. The group was particularly active in the 1970s and was responsible for at least 34 deaths in the FRG. It continued to exist until 1998.

Conclusion

Despite the early crises over the discrimination against the *Junge Gemeinden* and then the atheistic *Jugendweihe* ceremony, the Church had managed to successfully navigate through dangerous waters to arrive at a situation where Church and state could exist and even work together. The 1978 accord harmonised relations at a national level and there were areas, both internationally and domestically, where both strove for the same goal. However, tensions remained. The imposition of military training in schools caused resentment in the Church, and even helped to spark the first peace groups that began to question state policy. The self-immolation of Pastor Brüsewitz was repeated in September 1978 by Pastor Rolf Günther. Yet these were small and spontaneous local cases. Overall, the Church was loyal, unsurprising considering the extent of Stasi influence. It was a genuine achievement for the Church to survive in the GDR, a state based on the ideology of Marxism-Leninism, and with dwindling numbers of the faithful.

ACTIVITY
KNOWLEDGE CHECK

The SED and religion

To what extent did the Protestant Church offer effective opposition to the East German government between 1949 and 1985?

HOW FAR DID WESTERN INFLUENCES HAVE AN IMPACT ON LIFE IN THE GDR?

The Berlin Wall may have prevented the mass exodus of East Germans to the West, but it did not stop Western influences travelling in the other direction. After 1961, the spread of these influences into the GDR increased due to the gradual lifting of travel restrictions between East and West that developed under *Ostpolitik*. Even though the movement of people remained severely restricted, ideas and consumer goods were more able to cross the border. Despite searches by border guards, grandparents were able to bring back souvenirs from the West, and, despite the interception of post and parcels from the West, Western consumer goods often made it to families in the East. The role of Western radio and television, beamed into the GDR, did much to make the population of the GDR aware of the latest music and fashion trends, as well as giving them a different version of the news. The impact of these influences was mixed. It is tempting to see them as encouraging people to flee the GDR for a more materialistic life in the West, where standards of living and personal freedoms were greater. This was certainly the fear of many in the government. However, by the late 1970s, Honecker recognised that turning a blind eye to Western influences could act as a useful safety valve for a population that was often dissatisfied with the failure of their own government to meet their needs.

THINKING HISTORICALLY   Cause and consequence (5b)

Causation relativity

Historical events usually have many causes. Some are crucial, while some are less important. For some historical questions, it is important to understand exactly what role certain factors played in causing historical change.

Significant factors in the establishment of a dialogue between the Protestant Church and the state from 1975:

Ostpolitik developed in the 1970s.	The Protestant Church in the GDR retained links with that in the FRG after 1949 and received financial donations from Western counterparts in hard currency.
The Helsinki Accords on human rights were signed.	The Protestant Church had a long history of submitting to political authorities going back to the 16th century.
The increasing use of Stasi infiltration and surveillance methods in the 1970s.	Honecker wanted to use the Church to promote socialism.
From the 1960s, the Protestant Church provided a considerable amount of social care by running hospitals, orphanages and homes for the disabled and elderly.	From the 1950s, membership of the Protestant Church declined.

Answer the following questions on your own.

The timing of the establishment of a dialogue between the Protestant Church and the state:

1 How important was *Ostpolitik* in explaining the timing of the dialogue?

2 In what ways did the Helsinki Accords change the state of affairs caused by *Ostpolitik*? How far did this speed up the establishment of a dialogue between the Protestant Church and the state?

3 How might Honecker have delayed the kind of reform contained in the dialogue? What might have been the consequences of this?

The nature of the establishment of a dialogue between the Protestant Church and the state:

4 How far had the creation of the GDR in 1949 affected the attitudes of the people who were involved in establishing the dialogue?

5 What role did the above factors play in the way that the dialogue developed and the agreements it made?

6 Would the nature of the dialogue have been the same if the membership of the Protestant Church had not been declining?

7 What roles did each of the above causal factors play in determining the nature and timing of the dialogue between Church and state?

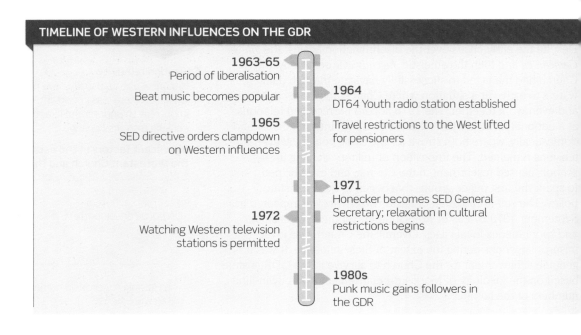

TIMELINE OF WESTERN INFLUENCES ON THE GDR

1963–65
Period of liberalisation

Beat music becomes popular

1964
DT64 Youth radio station established

Travel restrictions to the West lifted for pensioners

1965
SED directive orders clampdown on Western influences

1971
Honecker becomes SED General Secretary; relaxation in cultural restrictions begins

1972
Watching Western television stations is permitted

1980s
Punk music gains followers in the GDR

The impact of *Ostpolitik* on travel between the two German states

Willy Brandt, the architect of *Ostpolitik*, had begun the process of pushing to reduce travel restrictions while he was Mayor of West Berlin in the 1960s. Since 1964, East German pensioners had been allowed to visit West Berlin, and the West Germans were allowed East for up to 30 days a year. When Brandt was elected chancellor of the FRG in 1969, the policy of *Ostpolitik* was expanded at the national level. This continued for the next 20 years, despite changes in the FRG leadership.

SOURCE

10

Oliver Fritz is describing the typical trips his father, a furniture installer from East Berlin, would undertake to West Germany in the early 1980s. Taken from his book, *The Iron Curtain Kid* (2009).

Normally, six to ten colleagues from the East worked together in the West, alongside local employees. Mostly the work involved kitting out hotels with furniture, but there were other jobs too. For example, revamping the offices of a West German newspaper or fitting a millionaire's house with wardrobes and cabinets. The owner seemed to have close dealings with the DDR [GDR], as nearly everything within the house came from the East. Even the fence was of communist origin, made of East German railways sleepers. It was easy to see why this guy was a millionaire – with summer temperatures hovering around the 30-degree mark, Dad and his colleagues were not offered any water, let alone a cup of tea or coffee, in the week they worked there...

Not everyone who Dad met in the West was so stingy. Some hotel owners did not charge the workers for meals, others gave them free access to their carpools. One morning, while staying and working in a hotel at the West German seaside, Dad and his colleagues found a small DDR flag standing on their breakfast table – it was 7 October, East Germany's National Holiday. For the evening, hotel staff had organised a skittles competition: the Federal Republic of Germany against the German Democratic Republic. The DDR came out victorious and the prize – bottles of champagne, wine and beer – was shared with the other side.

ACTIVITY
KNOWLEDGE CHECK

Travel to the FRG

1 How valuable is Source 10 as evidence of differences between East and West Germans during the early 1980s?

2 What might explain these differences?

3 Why do you think Oliver Fritz's father did not take the opportunity to stay in the West?

East to West travel

For East German citizens, gaining the right permits and passports to travel to the FRG was not easy. For diplomatic meetings and sports competitors it was possible, but there were harsh restrictions on what was allowed. They were monitored by Stasi agents, and therefore their impact back in the East was limited. Other, potentially problematic, citizens with access to state information were completely banned, as they were labelled 'secret-carriers'. These included SED officials, army officers and scientists. While emergency access for a single individual could be granted, the most common and important in terms of their influence were workers permitted to travel to the FRG for business.

The workers needed to be carefully vetted by the Stasi and were always over 26 and married. The family left behind would therefore give them the incentive to return. If these conditions were met, then the worker was given *Reisekader* (travel cadre) status, allowing them to travel to the West. Typically, these were skilled workers whom the FRG could employ at significantly less cost than their West German equivalents (see Source 10).

These work trips provided opportunities to gain Western currency and goods to bring back to the East. The large variety of clothes and foodstuffs were eagerly consumed in the East – for many, this was their only access to new flavours like kiwi fruit, pineapple and bananas. These workers could make several trips a year, of up to six weeks at a time, and were not accompanied by a guard or member of the security forces. However, they were expected to write a *Reisebericht* (travel report) for the security forces upon their return, to explain every detail of their trip and, in particular, any West German military personnel seen. Most workers filled these out with positive and generic phrases to complete this duty as quickly as possible.

The impact of these trips was twofold. First, there were the consumer products and currency that the state may have felt helped to keep the East German population content. The right to travel, which needed an unblemished and loyal career, was a privilege that most people desperately wanted and would strive for. The goods were not confiscated upon their return and no restrictions were placed on the workers while in the West. This suggests that the state saw more benefits than harm in the exposure to capitalist market forces. Ironically, some of the best-quality goods available in the FRG were made in the GDR, but only for export.

Also, there was a deeper and, potentially for the regime, more dangerous psychological outcome. Contact between the two states was a constant reminder that Germany, and especially Berlin, was a divided entity. East Berlin maps portrayed West Berlin as a blank space, with maybe just a few roads and rivers. The Wall marked the start of this desert, even though the bustling modern city could be clearly seen from windows of the East's *Plattenbau* tower blocks. Many East Germans were surprised when they travelled between East and West and discovered just how similar, just how German, the West was. It was clear that *Ostpolitik* for the FRG was achieving its long-term goals, in reminding the East that it was part of a divided Germany, not an independent country. As travel restrictions were eased in the mid-1980s, this realisation grew.

West to East travel

For West Germans visiting the East, the impact was less significant. Goods were brought in, but security checks were much tighter, and throughout the 1970s and early 1980s, the SED introduced higher currency exchange qualifications, which reduced the numbers travelling East. These usually followed a particular rise in international tension, such as NATO's announcement of the deployment of nuclear missiles in the FRG in 1983, which led to a steep rise in the amount of money to be exchanged. When dealing with Western businesses in meetings in the East, goods were frequently handed over as a show of goodwill, but anything other than basic stationery had to be given to management, to discourage corruption. Once passed on, these client gifts seldom reappeared.

It was the East Germans travelling to the West and then returning home that helped to show the opportunities available. But for many, particularly the young or individuals that the state did not trust, the only way to experience the West was by accessing Western media.

The influence of television, films and popular music

Western influences came in many forms, but popular music, television and films were the main way in which East Germans found out about life in the West. The Berlin Wall did nothing to stop Western

severe economic problems of its own. With the USSR's refusal to lend to the GDR as a last resort, and the failure of the GDR to maintain export surpluses to pay debts, the economy was approaching terminal decline.

High spending on health and welfare

Although personal incomes and overall standards of living in the GDR compared unfavourably to those in the FRG, in many ways the population had a greater level of security, due to the very high levels of government spending on health and social welfare. Expenditure on subsidised housing, education, health and welfare rose from DM72.9 billion in 1980 to DM112.3 billion in 1985.

Health was an important issue for the GDR. A healthy workforce encouraged productivity, while a leading health-care system gained the GDR not just a humanitarian sense of well-being, but international prestige as well. Some analysts have suggested that a strong welfare system had clear social and political consequences in maintaining a certain public satisfaction with the state, and therefore prevented opposition within the GDR from reaching significant levels of mass protest against SED rule.

By the 1980s, many European health-care systems were experiencing the strains of an ageing population, expensive new technologies and heightened expectations, but East Germany had additional costs because of specific problems. Heavy industry had contaminated its cities, and the resulting environmental damage affected its inhabitants. Air pollution was the worst in Europe, and this caused respiratory problems such as chronic bronchitis. Some towns, such as Bitterfeld, were so polluted by power stations, chemical works and coal mines, that if United Nations criteria had been applied they would have been declared unfit for human habitation. The process of industrialisation had been implemented with scant regard for the health of its workers, while unsafe machinery and working practices caused numerous accidents. This had put further strain on the health-care system. It was a system that had been favourably compared with the West in the 1970s, but it increasingly fell behind during the 1980s.

The health-care system itself remained serviceable, but the inadequate funding and wider economic problems began a spiral into decline. The ill-health of the people reflected the failing economy, the shortfalls of which led to a lack of investment in health and safety, which increased the burden on an ailing health service.

EXTEND YOUR KNOWLEDGE

Under the influence
By 1987, it was estimated that one in eight East Germans suffered from some form of alcoholism. Clearly this would be an extra economic burden on the health-care system, but it also had an economic effect on East Germany's productivity. There was a culture, especially among adult working-class males, of *Sauferei* (constant drinking) in the workplace, usually revolving around the mixing of beer and cheap spirits.

Trade unions, whose leaders were not free from alcohol themselves, confirmed the inflammatory role of alcohol in factory disputes and unofficial strikes. Indeed, some strikes were held over the quality and quantity of the beer available at work!

The poor quality of consumer and other goods

The focus on heavy industry established a trend for the neglect of consumer goods. This neglect had an impact on the availability and quality of consumer goods for the remainder of the existence of the GDR. Attempts had been made to halt this trend, most notably in the 1970s, when Honecker ordered factories that were producing for the industrial sector to ensure five percent of their output was made up of consumer goods. The result was a strange combination of products, such as a steel mill producing microwave ovens, or brown coal-fired power plants making ironing boards. This led to the production of poor-quality goods and subsequent consumer discontent.

Some of the shortfall in goods was made up by the private sector, which grew slightly in 1985 for the first time in many years. Though these private craftsmen had a small impact on the overall economy (just 2.8 percent of net national product), they were important in certain areas. This included the manufacture of spare parts for cars, refrigerators, washing machines and televisions, all of which had become more readily available during the 1980s.

East Germany's population had little difficulty obtaining most essential goods, such as meat, butter, potatoes, bread and basic items of clothing. However, they often had to spend a considerable amount of time shopping for them. People regularly had to hunt for what they required, and often purchased items after queuing for long periods, even if those items were not what they needed. This was because they did not know when the item might become available again. One common example was clothing, with limited numbers of sizes available in the shops. A person might go in to buy shoes, but walk out with a tie, as they could not get what they wanted, but decided to leave with something that would possibly be of use later. There was also a widespread culture of family members, friends and neighbours informally exchanging goods with one another.

Just as bartering became a more common way to complete a small transaction, the unease about the economic ability of the country to meet the needs of its people was reflected in the growth of the second economy. These more illegal activities involved various tips or bribes to get the desired item or service, particularly a product in short supply. These became known as *Bückware*, or duck goods, as they were found below the counter. The economic impact of the 'second economy' may be hard to measure and largely anecdotal, but it did highlight the deficiencies in the East German service sector. Goods had long been scarce and many people had large savings. With cash in hand, the temptation to pay extra to guarantee a sought-after product must have been easy to yield to.

SOURCE 2

Oliver Fritz reminiscing about his childhood and forming the right contacts to get the right products. From *The Iron Curtain Kid* (2009).

Having the right connections in East Germany meant that you could nearly get everything – provided you could afford to bribe people or repay their favours with other sought-after goods. Anyone else had to rely on family members or friends being in charge of distributing services or goods. Knowing the right people was called 'Vitamin B' – B standing for *Beziehungen*, which means connections, so in English it could have been 'Vitamin C'. One popular saying was: Socialism without connections is like capitalism without money. That sums it up nicely.

ACTIVITY
KNOWLEDGE CHECK

Economic problems in the late 1980s

1 How does Source 2 reflect the growing economic problems in the GDR?

2 How would you describe the tone of this source? What words and phrases would you use as evidence to illustrate this tone?

While essential items could be obtained, that was not always the case for high-quality or less essential items. Fruit and vegetables were more difficult to obtain. Even high-quality goods produced in the GDR, such as cameras, were difficult to obtain within the GDR, as they were produced primarily for export. Although goods were more available than in the neighbouring Eastern bloc states, East Germans had to live with inferior-quality products compared to Western standards. This was a fact of which the population of the GDR was acutely conscious. Access to West German television stations along the borders offered glimpses of Western capitalist lifestyles, including music, cinema and fashion. On one occasion in June 1987, some of the music speakers at a rock festival in West Berlin's Reichstag building were turned towards the East, to allow over 4,000 young East Germans to hear, if not see, the likes of David Bowie and Genesis. The transference of Western culture allowed the sharp contrast in living standards to become apparent, thereby raising the expectations of the potential of a consumer society, and making the failure of socialism to provide improved living standards all too obvious.

A well-known joke of the time illustrates the frustration of living within an economy that often failed to deliver. A customer orders a Trabant car and the salesman tells him to come back to pick it up in nine years' time. The customer immediately asks, 'Shall I come back in the morning or in the evening?' Stunned, the salesman replies, 'You're joking, aren't you?' 'No, not at all,' the customer says. 'It's just that I need to know whether the plumber can come at 3pm or not.' To the East German people it was clear that joke would not work in the West.

Economic relations with West Germany

It was evident that the economic focus of the GDR throughout the 1980s shifted towards the West. By 1989, non-socialist countries made up a majority of both the GDR's exports and imports. The

economic relationship between the GDR and the FRG had grown through the 1970s, though it had been predominantly one-way traffic, as the GDR borrowed heavily to finance increasing imports of consumer goods, as well as having to cover very expensive welfare costs.

By 1989, 20 percent of all GDR trade was with West Germany, with whom the GDR had special trade relationships that avoided tariffs and quotas, while providing interest-free credit. Huge charges were made for transit across GDR territory to West Berlin, and West Germany had also bought the freedom of around 34,000 **dissidents**, usually individuals and families who had been caught trying to escape to the West. This had first started in 1963, with a cash payment for the so-called 'enemies of socialism', but it had grown throughout the period, and payment was whatever product was in short supply, ranging from food to diamonds. It is estimated that, through this scheme, West Germany paid up to DM3 billion to the ailing GDR economy.

KEY TERM

Dissident
A person who actively challenged the authority of the SED and was punished by the state, usually by imprisonment.

The economic consequences of inter-German co-operation prolonged the existence of the GDR, as the FRG offered life support, albeit of a limited extent, by managing the levels of debt. However, it also raised the political assumption that perhaps the FRG was not as dangerous as the previous 40 years of ideological propaganda had suggested. This feeling was fostered further after Honecker's visit to West Germany in 1987.

SOURCE 3

An East German report conducted by the local branch of the SED from Frankfurt-an-der-Oder in October 1987, reflecting on Honecker's visit. From M. Fulbrook, *Anatomy of a Dictatorship* (1995).

The fact cannot be overlooked that among a section of the population of all ages and social classes, there are heightened expectations above all in relation to travel restrictions. This is particularly the case among youngsters, religiously inclined citizens, members of the medical profession and the cultural intelligentsia, as well as tradespeople, artisans, and craftsmen. Such expectations are more or less disassociated from the real situation concerning relations with the FRG and its position with regard to basic questions of the sovereignty and independence of the GDR. Evidence of this is the continuing rise in the number of applications in the third quarter of 1987 for a permanent change of residence to the FRG or Berlin (west), in which connection many individuals express the expectation that it would now be easier to move across to the FRG.

ACTIVITY
KNOWLEDGE CHECK

The impact of improved links with the FRG

1 What does Source 3 suggest was the impact of Honecker's visit to West Germany?

2 The report was produced by local SED officials. How much value can a historian attach to a report such as this?

In conclusion, the GDR, unlike other countries in the Eastern bloc, was able to survive in relative prosperity (though its living standards were roughly half those of its Western counterparts). It could be argued that this enabled the regime to maintain its legitimacy. However, the problems were mounting, and in late 1989, the SED requested a new billion Deutschmark loan from the FRG (though the subsequent political collapse meant the West lost interest in favour of reunification plans). Hard currency debts, falling standards of living, a lack of investment and a labour shortage gave the impression of an economic system grinding to a halt. As the limited prosperity ebbed away, so did the regime's claim to legitimacy. Its unique economic relationship with both the USSR and West Germany may have postponed the call for reform, but it would not prevent it indefinitely. However, the direction that this call would arrive from came as a surprise.

ACTIVITY
KNOWLEDGE CHECK

The economy of the GDR by the late 1980s

1 Make a list of the economic problems facing the GDR in the late 1980s.

2 Rank these problems in order of their seriousness. Justify your decision.

A Level Exam-Style Question Section B

To what extent did economic weaknesses seriously undermine the existence of the GDR after 1985? (20 marks)

Tip
This question requires you to explain the impact of economic weaknesses, so do not just list them. Make sure you assess the seriousness of the roles of the economic weaknesses in undermining the continued existence of the GDR.

HOW SIGNIFICANT WAS GORBACHEV'S REFUSAL TO CONTINUE TO SUPPORT THE GDR?

From the early 1980s onwards, a series of reform movements gradually began to develop in many Eastern bloc states. The initial impetus for reform within communist states began in Poland with the **Solidarity** movement, which then led to increasing dissent in Czechoslovakia. Growing popular demands for political reforms, such as genuine multi-party elections, freedom of speech and the freedom to travel, however, gathered significant impetus when Gorbachev became leader of the USSR in 1985. By the late 1980s, these movements were starting to demand far more radical change than had even been envisaged by Gorbachev.

KEY TERM

Solidarity
The name of a federation of trade unions that emerged in Poland from 1980 onwards. It reached a total membership of nearly ten million workers. It was not controlled by the ruling Communist Party in Poland and became a broad movement that promoted political and social reforms.

The impact of perestroika and glasnost on the GDR's government and people

Gorbachev wanted a radically new direction for the USSR, based on two main ideas - **perestroika** and **glasnost**. For the domestic reforms that Gorbachev envisaged to have any chance of success, it was essential that the USSR's ailing economy improved. The Cold War was a financial drain on the USSR, and, increasingly, Soviet leaders regarded support for the Eastern bloc as an economic burden. By the late 1980s, it was clear that any advantages to the USSR of maintaining a military presence in communist European states were clearly outweighed by the costs. This realisation led to Gorbachev announcing the abandoning of the Brezhnev Doctrine. This radical change in Soviet foreign policy had a profound effect on the GDR government. The SED could no longer count on the USSR's support to intervene if there was any domestic unrest.

KEY TERMS

Perestroika and glasnost
The key concepts underpinning Gorbachev's reform programme for the USSR. Perestroika (restructuring) aimed to bring about radical economic changes, such as allowing private enterprise. Glasnost (openness) was to bring about democratic changes such as freedom of speech, free elections and a system of government that would include the direct participation of non-communist political parties.

The SED government also became very concerned at sudden developments in relations between the USSR and the FRG. During the late 1980s, a series of formal state visits took place between the FRG and the Soviet Union, which included FRG Chancellor Kohl making a formal state visit to Moscow in 1988, and Gorbachev visiting the FRG in 1989.

EXTEND YOUR KNOWLEDGE

Helmut Kohl (1930–present)
He was chancellor of the FRG from 1982 to 1990, and then of the reunited Germany from 1990 to 1998. During the rapid series of events in 1989, he seemed at first determined to slow down the pace of change and prevent large-scale emigration from the GDR to the FRG. However, by November 1989, he promised widespread prosperity for East Germany and used the GDR's March 1990 election results to push for the rapid reunification of the GDR and the FRG.

The impact of Gorbachev's desire for reform left the SED leadership with a conundrum. In essence, the GDR was created as a direct result of Cold War hostility between the superpowers. As an artificial country, it had been more reliant on Soviet support that other communist regimes. Therefore, to undertake a fundamental political restructure of the GDR's system of government would mean departing from communist ideological principles. Such changes would mean that the GDR would not be distinct from the FRG and would, in many ways, take away any justification for its separate existence. On the other hand, failure to reform risked the rise of significant domestic opposition to SED rule.

EXTEND YOUR KNOWLEDGE

Day of Fate: (9 November)

This day has proven critical in many separate years of Germany's history:

1848: The Liberal revolutionary Robert Blum was executed for his part in the 1848 Revolution

1918: The end of the German monarchy in the November Revolution

1923: Hitler's attempted seizure of power in Munich

1938: The destruction of synagogues and Jewish property during *Kristallnacht*

1989: The SED government opened the Berlin Wall

Following the reunification of Germany, 9 November was considered for a new national holiday. However, this was seen as inappropriate, especially due to the associated events of 1923 and 1938. Therefore, the date of the formal reunification of Germany on 3 October 1990 was used instead.

SOURCE

Brigitte Tismer reminiscing in 2014 about when she was 13 years old and living in Dresden, at the time of the opening of the Berlin Wall.

I cannot remember exactly what I thought or did on the evening the Berlin Wall opened. I do remember my parents watching the news almost in disbelief. Almost overnight the supermarket shelves filled with Mars Bars, Milka chocolate and the *Hamburger Morgenpost* [the name of a daily newspaper from Hamburg, a city in West Germany]. Things I only knew from Intershops or Christmas parcels from family friends in the FRG.

A few weeks after the 9th November, our teacher ordered us to open our planners and she told us to cross out Saturdays. No more school on Saturdays! Next, she told us that the subject of *Staatsbürgerkunde* (citizenship) will be changed. We will not be following the set syllabus anymore, but we will discussing current affairs instead and it will not be graded. I was very relieved to hear that because I was failing that course (having had a 5*).

[*Grades went from 1 to 5 (A–F equivalent)]

ACTIVITY
KNOWLEDGE CHECK

The immediate impact of the opening of the Berlin Wall

1 What does Source 8 reveal about the immediate impact of the opening of the Berlin Wall?

2 Do you think the evidence of a schoolchild would be of particular value to the historian?

Conclusion

The events of 1989 show the complexity of external, national and local issues that can combine to create momentous events, such as the opening of the Berlin Wall. Hungary, Czechoslovakia and Poland were undergoing their own revolutionary dramas. Their new-found openness gave the route for some East Germans to make it into the West. Ironically, the Soviet Union played its most vital part by doing nothing. This left the SED on its own, with a population that was unwilling to obey and, finally, unafraid to rebel. The SED destroyed itself in a futile effort to sustain its role in power. On 9 November 1989, it was the peaceful bravery of East Berliners, and East German citizens overall, prepared to stare down the border troops and the SED, that brought about change. It was an expression of people power that brought East and West to each other. Together they hugged, kissed and danced on top of the concrete slabs of the Wall, like they were upon the tombstones of a now extinct world.

However, the opening of the Berlin Wall introduced the next logical question. If the two German peoples could meet as one, then why could they not be as one?

THINKING HISTORICALLY   Interpretations (5c)

Good questions/bad questions

Below are approaches attributed to three individuals who wrote about the opening of the Berlin Wall.

Anne McElvoy	Maxim Leo	John Lewis Gaddis
She was a journalist, working as the East Berlin correspondent for *The Times* newspaper. She reported on the events of 1989 from East Berlin and her reports were used by *The Times* to inform its readership in Britain.	He was born in 1970 and was living in East Berlin in 1989. In 1997, he became an editor of the *Berliner Zeitung*, one of Berlin's leading daily newspapers. In 2009, he wrote *Red Love*, an account of the impact of the GDR and its collapse on his family. His mother had been a journalist in the GDR, but she quit her job due to the restrictions placed on her work by the government.	He is one of the leading American historians of the Cold War. He is a leading member of the Society for Historians of American Foreign Relations and he has been researching international history since 1968. His books on the Cold War include *We Now Know*, published in 1997, which looked at the role of Berlin and other factors in the rise and fall of the Cold War.

Work in groups.

1 Devise three criteria of what makes a good historical question.

2 Consider what you know about the fall of the Berlin Wall in November 1989.

   a) Each write a historical question based on the fall.

   b) Put these in rank order, with the best question first, based on your criteria.

3 Using a piece of A3 paper, write the names of the three writers so that they form a large triangle.

   a) Write your questions from 2a) on the piece of paper so that their positions reflect how likely the writers are to be interested by that question. For example, a question about the role of Günter Schabowski in the fall of the Berlin Wall would interest McElvoy and Gaddis, but not Leo, and so would be somewhere between McElvoy and Gaddis, but nowhere near Leo.

   b) Add some further questions. Try to think of questions that only one of the three would be interested in.

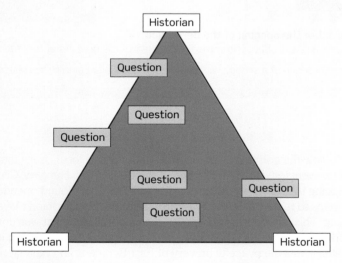

4 Take it in turns to try to answer the questions you have created in the style of one of the writers. See if the other members of the group can guess which writer it is in each case.

Answer the following questions individually, using the examples created by the above activity:

5 Does one method of constructing history lead to better reasoning than the others? Explain your answer.

6 Explain why all commentators who deploy rigorous methodology are, to an extent, useful sources for the study of the past.

ACTIVITY
KNOWLEDGE CHECK

1989

1 In what ways was 1989 a turning point in the history of the GDR?

2 How likely was the end of the GDR as a separate country by the end of 1989?

WHY WAS THE REUNIFICATION OF THE GDR AND THE FRG SO RAPID?

The opening of the Berlin Wall did not necessarily mean the end of the GDR as a country, or even the end of SED political domination. However, as physical, economic and social access to the West increased, the SED failed to act decisively. Weakened by internal divisions and the inability to respond effectively, the SED quickly withered away. The policy for an independent and democratic GDR favoured by the opposition groups was swept aside by the groundswell of public opinion. The call for reunification gained momentum, and it proved to be the West German chancellor, Helmut Kohl, who was flexible enough to react quickly and try to steer the process. Even then, the people's desperation for a single country following the FRG model took everyone by surprise. The 1990 March elections in the GDR revealed an overwhelming mandate for rapid reunification. Therefore, Kohl, with the blessing of the wartime Allies (albeit sometimes reluctantly), was able to speed up the reunification programme from a projected decade to under a single year. On 3 October 1990, Germany became a single country with shared currency and borders, though values would take longer to unite.

The collapse of the SED government in 1989 and the elections of March 1990

In the rest of November 1989, more than five million East Germans visited West Berlin. The vast majority returned to the GDR, but by the end of the year, nearly one million had decided to remain in the West. Despite the best efforts of Krenz, the opening of the Berlin Wall did nothing to restore the people's faith in the GDR or trust in the SED. Indeed, it was in the immediate months following 9 November that the SED fell apart, from the bottom up.

At the local level, officials felt that the Party mechanics were failing to function. Revelations of corruption at the highest levels became public knowledge, such as the relative splendour of the SED leaders' guarded forest community, and their exclusive access to Western goods through the Intershops. This hypocrisy affected the grass-roots members: feeling ideologically lost, their will to hold onto power slipped away. The opening of the Wall and the rapid rotation of leaders in the Politburo had destroyed the illusion of stability and permanence. This psychological blow crippled the Party's self-belief throughout the regional offices. Without this support, the leadership in Berlin was merely hanging on, desperate to survive, but just delaying the end.

Krenz's government tried to stem emigration from the GDR with the promise of further reforms. Proposals included free all-party elections, a media free from government control, and the liberalisation of controls on the economy. As well as government ministers being divided on whether such measures were far too radical, there was also a division forming within the Party as to whether a reformed GDR state should continue to exist as a German nation separate from that of the FRG, or whether the two German states should be reunited.

On 1 December, the *Volkskammer* amended the GDR constitution to end the SED's leading role, and two days later, Krenz, resigned to the reality that it was now impossible to gain popular support for an SED-led government, stepped down after only 44 days as General Secretary. Immediately, the **Round Table** was convened to facilitate talks between the traditional bloc parties who were no longer subservient to the SED, and the new oppositional groups such as Democracy Now and New Forum. The Round Table was an organisation designed to promote internal GDR reform such as national elections, a new constitution and the dissolution of the Stasi (renamed, if not remodelled, as the Office for National Security). It is important to note that the oppositional groups that had helped to bring the revolution about still wanted a GDR identity. They believed there was a 'third way' in which a democratic and neutral GDR could exist alongside the FRG. It was not just a case of a communist GDR or a reunified Germany. However, the hopes of these groups were dashed, as popular opinion overwhelmed them as well, and East Germany moved towards rapid reunification with the FRG.

KEY TERM

Round Table
This organisation was based on a Polish model from April 1989 and was started by the group Democracy Now. It was a forum in which representatives from the old bloc parties (such as trade unions and the women's league) came together with representatives from the new opposition groups (that had evolved from the autonomous groups of the late 1980s). Of the 33 voting members, 17 were from the new opposition groups. Echoing this new democracy, many local Round Tables were set up in cities across the GDR. Their final meeting took place in March 1990.

The last action of the SED was the promotion of Hans Modrow as leader, who now fronted a relaunched Party called the Socialist Unity Party of Germany-Party of Democratic Socialism, or SED-PDS (the SED was not dropped until February, in readiness for the national elections). Modrow had a reputation as a reformist and was apparently Gorbachev's preferred choice of leader. The new government had its political structure redesigned to remove the Politburo and Central Committee in favour of the Council of Ministers, which quickly included members of the opposition groups as the Round Table was incorporated into it. Modrow, as the new prime minister, announced free elections and economic reforms that reduced, though did not end, socialist-style central planning (see Source 9). But the continued promises were not enough to persuade the people to stay.

Paper 2: AS Level sample answers with comments

Section A

Part B requires you to:

- interrogate the source
- draw reasoned inferences
- deploy your own knowledge to interpret the material in its context
- make judgements about the value (weight) of the source in terms of making judgements.

Study Source 10 (Chapter 1, page 300) before you answer this question.

How much weight do you give the evidence of Source 10 for an enquiry into the reasons for the uprising of June 1953? (12 marks)

Average student answer

The source is useful because it gives a view of the reasons for the uprising of June 1953. It calls the uprising 'a fascist provocation' and states that the uprising was organised by the enemy from 'across the sector border'. It outlines how the West encouraged the workers in the GDR to 'lay down their tools' and how Western agents 'mislead them with inflammatory slogans'. The result was that the workers in the GDR demonstrated against the government. The source suggests that the uprising was not an uprising of the people but an organised series of actions by the West that was designed to bring down the government of the GDR. This view is presented by the East German Politburo, the main decision-making body in the GDR, and clearly has weight as evidence of how the regime saw the uprising.

The uprising was a serious threat to the government of the GDR and was mainly caused by the actions of the government. The workers were unhappy because, in June 1953, the government had announced the need for industrial productivity to increase by ten percent while workers' wages would remain unchanged. The uprising began when 300 builders working on a construction project to develop East Berlin's 'Stalinallee' went on strike, demanding the lowering of the ten percent increase in productivity. Other builders joined the protests, and strikes and demonstrations spread across the whole of the GDR, partly due to East Germans listening to the news on West Berlin radio stations. The demands of the protestors became increasingly political, with calls for an end to the SED and a genuine choice of political parties at elections. The source gives us the perspective of the government in relation to these events.

Overall, this source carries some weight as evidence of the reasons for the uprising because it gives the historian a clear view of how the government of the GDR viewed it. This interpretation offered by the government was, however, propaganda and ignores the fact that it was the government's own actions that had played a large part in causing the uprising to take place. The source is, therefore, trying to discredit the West by blaming them for stirring up the unrest rather than the SED taking responsibility itself.

> This is a weak introduction because it is not sharply focused on the weight of the evidence. The answer tends to summarise the content of the source. It would be better to draw inferences from the evidence about how the Politburo wished to present the uprising to its population. The last point is better, but needs developing and illustrating, for example, why was the label 'fascist' used?

> This section has good own knowledge about the uprising, but it is not used to put the source within its historical context. It would be better to use this context to highlight what is ignored by the source and to consider the reasons for this.

> A thoughtful conclusion that contains a judgement focused on the weight of the evidence. It would be better if these points were developed and supported within the answer.

Verdict

This is an average answer because:

- there is some interrogation of the source, but it contains descriptive passages without relevant inferences
- there is some background information, but this is not securely linked to the focus of the question

- there is an overall judgement, but it lacks substance.

Use the feedback on this answer to rewrite it, making as many improvements as you can.

Paper 2: AS Level sample answer with comments

Section A

Part A requires you to:

- identify key points in the source and explain them
- deploy your own knowledge of the context in which events took place
- make appropriate comments about the author/origin/purpose of the source.

Study Source 5 (Chapter 4, page 368) before you answer this question.

Why is Source 5 valuable to the historian for an enquiry about the reasons for growing dissatisfaction within the GDR in 1989? (8 marks)

Strong student answer

Source 5 is of value to the historian enquiring about the growing dissatisfaction in the GDR because it outlines the main reasons for negative attitudes to the state, as compiled by a government agency that collected a vast amount of information on which to base its findings. The source draws attention to the point that many in the population were dissatisfied despite recognising that there were advantages to the socialist system. By advantages the source is referring to social provision, such as childcare and support for women, especially in the workplace. The education and health systems of the GDR were generally effective, but it often lacked the resources of their West German equivalents. By 1989, the contrast with the West had become a particular issue for many East Germans. Source 5 mentions that many people had come to the conclusion that improved living standards were 'only attainable in the FRG or West Berlin'. This attitude had grown as East Germans became more aware of life in the West through exposure to Western television and radio.

The source is valuable because it provides good evidence that the population was making links between the problems they faced and the political system, as the source states 'doubt and disbelief exist as to… the correctness of party and government'. The key point is made that growing dissatisfaction was, by 1989, becoming more critical of the SED party and moving towards thoughts of reforming, and even dismantling, the socialist system. Thus, we can infer that the reasons for dissatisfaction were political as well as economic. These thoughts had been promoted by Gorbachev, the Soviet leader, and his ideas of perestroika and glasnost.

The conclusions drawn by Source 5 are given considerable value because they were made by the GDR's Ministry of State Security or Stasi. This organisation, controlled by the SED, used an extensive system of surveillance involving over 90,000 full-time informers. The Stasi was incredibly well informed and therefore its conclusions were based on a lot of evidence. The fact that this report was compiled in September 1989, one month before the celebrations of the 40th anniversary of the GDR and with Hungary about to open its borders to the West, probably reflects growing anxiety on the part of the East German government, suggesting that dissatisfaction was growing to the point where large numbers of GDR citizens not only wished to leave their country, but were about to do so.

To conclude, Source 5 is valuable because it highlights the complexity of reasons for the growing dissatisfaction in the GDR. The fact that the source is provided by the Stasi makes it valuable as evidence based on a vast range of information that also indicates the regime was well aware of this dissatisfaction.

> These sections are effective because they use own knowledge to explain points made from the source. There is a focus on the value of the evidence.

> The nature and origin of the source are used well to consider the value of the source and it is focused on the specific question.

> A sharply focused conclusion with a clear judgement.

Verdict

This is a strong answer because:

- it selects key points from the source relevant to the specific question

- the value of the source is discussed and related to the focus of the enquiry
- it deploys appropriate own knowledge accurately and effectively in combination with the source.

Paper 2: AS Level sample answer with comments

Section A

Part B requires you to:

- interrogate the source
- draw reasoned inferences

- deploy your own knowledge to interpret the material in its context
- make judgement about the value (weight) of the source in terms of making judgements.

Study Source 10 (Chapter 1, page 300) before you answer this question.

How much weight do you give the evidence of Source 10 for an enquiry into the reasons for the uprising of June 1953? (12 marks)

Strong student answer

The source would carry limited weight and value for any enquiry into the reasons for the rising of June 1953. As a statement by the Politburo, the top decision-making body of the Party, the source gives the historian the perspective of the SED government relating to the causes of the rising and how it wished the rising to be portrayed to its own population. It does not, however, give us a full picture of the reasons for the rising.

> This answer starts with a relevant assertion that can be argued through the answer.

The source illustrates how the government of the GDR blamed 'fascist provocation' from the enemy 'across the sector border'. This is a reference to agents from the West who were supposedly acting to stir up trouble against the GDR. To label these agents as 'fascist' was a useful method of discrediting the West because it recalled the struggle against the Nazis. Other techniques are used to discredit the West in the source, such as calling the rising 'organised' and listing its targets as 'food warehouses, school dormitories, clubhouses and shops' – targets that would disrupt the lives of the workers themselves. These accusations are of limited value as historical evidence. It is true that there were Western agents, intent on stirring up trouble, who were operating in the GDR at this time, but this detracts from the evidence of participants in the protest that the uprising was a spontaneous reaction to the government's directive to increase industrial productivity by ten percent, without raising wages. These demands, coming on top of the hardships endured by the workers due to the impact of the Second World War, were the last straw for many. In this sense the government had provoked the uprising, not fascist agents. This source highlights how the Politburo tried to deflect attention from their own responsibility for the rising by trying to discredit the West. In contrast, the GDR is described in positive terms as a guardian of 'unity and peace'. When this purpose of the statement is considered, the weight of the source as evidence becomes more limited.

> A focused and well-balanced discussion of the weight we can attach to the evidence by reference to the purpose of the source. Own knowledge is used to consider the reliability of the source's content.

Although the source ignores the economic causes of the rising, it does acknowledge that the protests turned into 'a demonstration against the government'. Where the source is correct is in highlighting this political dimension. The protestors' chants also took on an increasingly overt political tone. The targets of the protestors included prisons, police stations, offices and courthouses, symbols of SED power. This allows us to question the reliability of the statement in the source about attacks on social targets, such as schools and food warehouses.

> This section is effective because it uses own knowledge to confirm and challenge the source.

Overall, the weight of this source as evidence of the true reasons for the rising is decidedly limited as it ignores the economic decisions made by the GDR government that provoked the protests. The angle taken by the Politburo statement is one that seeks to hide the responsibility of the SED for the workers' unrest, an embarrassment for a government that was supposed to represent the interests of the workers.

> This is an effective conclusion because the judgement is based on sound reasoning.

Verdict

This is a strong answer because:

- it has a sharp focus on the issues relevant to the question
- it makes effective use of own knowledge to confirm and challenge the content of the source

- it makes an overall judgement about the value of the source that is reasoned and supported.

who were probably influenced by what they heard their parents say in their homes. As such, it gives the historian a valuable insight into the views of the general population, which differ from those of government officials. The fact that one of Anne's friends 'shouts' her criticisms of the government suggests a level of anger had built up against the way the GDR government was ruling. This was a reflection of the controls imposed by the government on people's lives that had produced mass emigration from the GDR. It was the sheer level of this migration to the West that had to be stopped if the GDR was not to face economic collapse.

Source 15 makes reference to the issue of migration to West Germany, but instead of blaming the actions of the GDR government for this, it blames it on 'deception, bribery, and blackmail' used by the West. There is some truth in this statement. The FRG had introduced a series of measures to encourage East Germans to flee from communism. East Germans who emigrated to the FRG were automatically entitled to FRG citizenship and received generous financial and housing assistance. Western agents had even been known to enter East Berlin to recruit skilled workers. Once they arrived in the FRG, many GDR citizens who had emigrated claimed they were victims of a repressive regime because it was in their best interests to convince the authorities that they had been persecuted in order to receive higher levels of financial and housing assistance from their new state. Whatever the real causes of migration the consequences were to prove devastating for the GDR. Despite emigration from the GDR to the FRG being illegal from 1952 onwards and classified as 'flight from the Republic', 2.5 million East Germans emigrated to the FRG between the formation of the GDR in 1949 and the building of the Berlin Wall 12 years later. This meant that the population of the GDR actually decreased from 18.5 million in 1949 to just over 17 million in 1961. Furthermore, those that emigrated were mostly young, skilled and educated – the very people the GDR was most dependent on for its economic development. This was clearly unsustainable in economic terms, but it also had political consequences. It allowed the FRG to undermine the GDR's credibility and assert the failings of socialism. The FRG continued to refer to those that had left East Germany as 'refugees' rather than as 'migrants'. For this reason the statement made in Source 16 that the GDR was 'busy saving its own skin' was certainly valid.

> This section uses detailed own knowledge of the causes of mass migration to explain the references in the sources. The perspective of Source 15 is assessed by considering how far it can be supported and challenged.

A full picture of the reasons behind the building of the Wall must take into account the role played by the USSR. Source 15 states that 'the Soviet government fully understands and supports the actions of the Government of the German Democratic Republic', but the reality was more complicated than this. Khrushchev, the Soviet leader, had consistently refused suggestions from the SED to completely close the border between East and West Berlin. There were fears that such action would be so provocative that it could lead the West into imposing trade restrictions with the GDR or even escalating into outright military confrontation. Khrushchev wanted to use the status of Berlin as a tool in negotiations with the West. By 1961 this tactic had failed and, as the situation in East Germany reached crisis point, Khrushchev gave permission for the Wall to be erected. At a meeting of the Eastern bloc states in Moscow on 3–5 August 1961, the leaders of the Warsaw Pact, with Khrushchev's support, decided that the only solution to solve emigration from the GDR was to seal the border between East and West Berlin.

> This section considers the role of the Soviet Union, especially that of Khrushchev. The reference in Source 15 is discussed and explained by reference to detailed own knowledge.

In conclusion, Sources 15 and 16 provide useful evidence that reflects on the reasons for the building of the Berlin Wall. They both highlight the fact that the GDR was under enormous pressure to ensure its survival. While the official line that mass emigration from the GDR was a product of Western provocation is presented by Source 15, Source 16 highlights that this needs to be put into the context of the actions of a 'lousy dictatorship'. There were sections of the GDR's population that were unconvinced by the official explanation and the historian also needs to be wary of accepting this perspective. Ultimately, the decision to build the Wall could only be taken with Soviet approval, a further sign of the weakness of the GDR.

> This conclusion is effective because it makes a relevant judgement that sees how the two sources can be used in combination.

Verdict

This is a strong answer because:

- it makes inferences from the key features of the sources and relates them to the issue

- it uses a sound range of own knowledge to discuss the points raised by the sources
- it assesses the origin and purpose of the sources to consider their validity as evidence.

Paper 2: A Level sample answer with comments

Section B

These questions assess your understanding of the period in some depth. They will ask you about the content you learned about in the four key themes, but may not ask about more than one theme. For these questions remember to:

- give an analytical, not a descriptive, response
- support your points with evidence
- cover the whole time period specified in the question
- come to a substantiated judgement.

To what extent was Honecker successful in his attempts to improve the international prestige of the GDR? (20 marks)

Average student answer

On its creation in 1949 the German Democratic Republic was considered to be a temporary state that would, at some time in the future, reunite with West Germany. The tensions of the Cold War had resulted in the division of Germany and, to the Western powers, the GDR was an artificial state that only existed because of Soviet support. Many politicians in West Germany, especially those on the political right, refused to acknowledge the authority of the East German state. It was against this background that the government of the GDR struggled to gain international prestige.

In order to improve the international prestige of the GDR Honecker took advantage of the opportunities presented by Willy Brandt's policy of Ostpolitik to establish a more meaningful relationship with West Germany. Brandt decided to abandon the Hallstein Doctrine whereby West Germany had refused to acknowledge the existence of East Germany as a separate state. The groundwork for agreement was laid by a series of visits between the leaders of the two German states. In March 1970, Brandt made the first visit by an FRG chancellor to the GDR to Erfurt and a return visit was made by Willi Stoph, the prime minister of the GDR to Kassel in the FRG in May the same year.

Honecker's response to Ostpolitik led to a number of agreements between the FRG and the GDR. The 1971 Four-Power Treaty allowed West Berliners to visit East Berlin and secured Soviet acceptance of this provision. In effect, this made another situation such as the Berlin Blockade impossible and significantly reduced the potential threat of conflict over Berlin. This was followed by the Basic Treaty of 1972 that saw the FRG and GDR both acknowledge the existence of both German states and agree to settle disputes without threatening or using force. The fact that the FRG was willing to acknowledge the GDR was an important step forward for the international position of the GDR. Most Western governments followed the lead of the FRG in their diplomatic relations with East Germany and, therefore, getting the West German government to establish diplomatic relations was important. One sign of improvement was the admission of both German states to the United Nations in 1973 as full members. As a member of the United Nations, Honecker signed the Helsinki Agreement on Human Rights of 1975 – one of 35 countries to do so.

This is a weak introduction because, although it highlights the context within which the GDR had an issue with its international prestige, it does not address whether Honecker was successful in improving this situation. It would be better to start with an assertion that deals directly with the focus of the question.

This section is weak because it does not focus on whether these actions were successful or not. It would be improved by linking phrases, such as 'this led to' or 'as a result', that allow discussion of the extent of improvement in international prestige.

This section is better because it starts to mention the ways in which the agreements improved the international prestige of the GDR. It would be even better if the answer explored the impact of these agreements in more depth, for example, assessing the limits to these agreements.

Diplomacy was, however, only one tool by which the GDR could improve its international prestige. Sport became increasingly important as a means by which East Germany could show the supposed superiority of socialism over capitalism, as well as a means to help reduce the GDR's diplomatic isolation. In the 1964 Tokyo Olympic Games, the FRG and GDR were represented as one all-German team, a process which involved a level of co-operation. Thereafter, each German state entered separate teams in the Olympics and other sporting competitions. The GDR's performance was frequently impressive, especially given its size relative to that of West Germany. In the 1968 Olympic Games, for example, the GDR gained nine gold medals compared to five for West Germany. At the 1980 Moscow Olympics East Germany took 11 of the 13 gold medals available in women's swimming. In athletics the world record for the women's 400 metres was set in 1985 by Marita Koch who ran it in 47.60 seconds. These were achievements that made the rest of the world take notice of the GDR.

> This section has good detail and there is some focus on success. It would, again, be better with a more in-depth exploration of the degree of success. The question asks 'to what extent' and this should be assessed, for example: East German sporting achievements were often accompanied by international scepticism and accusations of drug-taking.

Honecker did not only take measures to improve the international prestige of the GDR in the West, he also attempted to improve its status in the Eastern bloc. In 1950, the GDR became a member of COMECON and its economy was tied into the economies of the socialist states. One of the roles performed by COMECON was to organise a degree of centralised planning that encouraged specialisation within the socialist countries. East Germany's role in producing large amounts of manufactured goods reflected the fact that it possessed a sophisticated industrial economy relative to the rest of the Eastern bloc. The GDR supplied the USSR and other COMECON members with vital technology in areas such as chemicals, microelectronics and electrical engineering at well below world market prices. The standard of living of East Germans may have been below that of West Germany, but it was the envy of the rest of the socialist bloc. In fact, the differences were sometimes the cause of tension between the GDR and its socialist neighbours. Exchange controls had to be set up in the 1980s between Poland and Germany as resentment grew from Germans at Poles who crossed into the GDR to buy goods that were unavailable in Poland. A similar measure had to be introduced in Czechoslovakia to prevent Germans buying goods there. Governments of the socialist countries were sometimes influenced more by nationalist sentiments than socialist solidarity. Resentment of the GDR's position within the Eastern bloc was also problematic due to lingering memories of German brutality during the Second World War. This was a particular issue for Poland and Hungary. Declarations of friendship between the governments of the socialist bloc were often little more than propaganda. Changes to the GDR's constitution made in 1968, and again in 1974, declared the GDR to be forever and irrevocably allied with the USSR. A friendship treaty the following year with the USSR bound the GDR even closer.

> This is a better paragraph on the prestige of the GDR within the Eastern bloc. It mentions successes and limitations to the prestige of the GDR. The point about international friendship being propaganda could be explored further.

Overall, therefore, Honecker was able to raise the international prestige of the GDR by a range of methods. He made good use of the opportunities offered by Brandt's policy of Ostpolitik to secure diplomatic concessions for the GDR. Sport and trade were other areas where the status and prestige of the GDR was raised. The Trabant car might have been a joke in the West, but for many citizens in the socialist bloc, it was a much sought-after consumer good.

> The conclusion is brief and consists largely of repetition of points made in the body of the answer. It would be better to try to develop the overall reasoning in support of the judgement.

Verdict

This is an average answer because:

- it tends to describe the actions of Honecker's government rather than explain and analyse their impact
- it needs greater supporting material
- there is an attempt to reach a judgement, but it is limited in its sophistication and depth.

Use the feedback on this answer to rewrite it, making as many improvements as you can.

Paper 2: A Level sample answer with comments

Section B

These questions assess your understanding of the period in some depth. They will ask you about the content you learned about in the four key themes, but may not ask about more than one theme. For these questions remember to:

- give an analytical, not a descriptive, response
- support your points with evidence
- cover the whole time period specified in the question
- come to a substantiated judgement.

To what extent was Honecker successful in his attempts to improve the international prestige of the GDR? (20 marks)

Strong student answer

On its formation in 1949 East Germany (the GDR) was seen as a temporary state, with German reunification anticipated at some time in the future. The very existence of the GDR was considered fragile, a view reinforced by the building of the Berlin Wall in 1961 to stop the citizens of East Germany fleeing their own country. The Berlin Wall was highly detrimental to the international prestige of the GDR, especially in the West where it was viewed as a cruel and inhumane division erected by a state that could only survive by imprisoning its own population. It was in this context that Honecker, as leader of East Germany, was keen to improve the international prestige of the GDR. Under his leadership relations were developed with both the capitalist and socialist powers, but it was the relationship with West Germany that really mattered in the eyes of the East German government. By the 1980s, Honecker had successfully established diplomatic relations with West Germany, but the international prestige of the GDR was still limited. In 1987, Honecker met the West German chancellor, Helmut Kohl. It was a highly significant meeting of two supposedly equal leaders, but the photographs of the occasion seemed to symbolise the relative prestige of the two states: Kohl at 6 feet 4 inches towered over the much smaller figure of Honecker.

The key to improving the international status of the GDR was West Germany's abandonment of the Hallstein Doctrine. The Doctrine had effectively prevented not just West Germany refusing to establish diplomatic relations with East Germany, but also West Germany's allies from doing the same. This deliberate snub to the GDR could only be overcome by a change in the approach of the West German government. Honecker was able to take advantage of the opportunities presented by Willy Brandt's policy of Ostpolitik between 1969 and 1974. Brandt decided to abandon the Hallstein Doctrine in order to provide a dialogue with the GDR to remove travel restrictions and establish trade links between the two states. The fact that in doing so the West German government was acknowledging the authority of the government of the GDR was a success for Honecker. The impression was given that both governments recognised that the existence of East Germany was likely to be more permanent than previously anticipated. As a result of this rapprochement, the 1971 Four-Power Treaty was signed. It allowed West Berliners to visit East Berlin and secured Soviet acceptance of this provision. This treaty was followed by the Basic Treaty in 1972, which saw the FRG and GDR acknowledge the existence of both German states and agree to settle disputes without threatening or using force. This marked a further improvement in the international standing of the GDR as it opened up the possibility of an ongoing dialogue with the West over points of tension, such as travel restrictions and human rights. This change also had a significant impact on diplomatic relations with other Western powers. Formal diplomatic recognition of the GDR rose from 38 countries in 1972 to 123 by 1978. A further symbol of the growing prestige of the GDR was its admission into the United Nations in 1973. As a consequence of membership, East Germany signed

This is a strong start to the answer. The answer is placed within the context of the creation of the GDR and the reasons why international status was an issue for Honecker. A relevant assertion is made that can be argued throughout the answer.

The answer is effective because there is a strong focus on the question. It considers the degree of success of measures to improve international prestige. The points made are supported with some good information.